Sacred Place

THEMES IN RELIGIOUS STUDIES SERIES

Series Editors: Jean Holm, with John Bowker

Other titles

Worship
Making Moral Decisions
Myth and History
Attitudes to Nature
Sacred Writings
Women in Religion
Picturing God
Human Nature and Destiny
Rites of Passage

Sacred Place

Edited by

Jean Holm

with John Bowker

PINTER

Pinter
A Cassell Imprint
Wellington House, 125 Strand, London WC2R 0BB

First published in 1994

Reprinted 1997, 1998

British Library Cataloguing in Publication Data

A CIP catalogue record for this book is available from the British Library

ISBN 1 85567 104 2 (hb)
ISBN 1 85567 105 0 (pb)

Library of Congress Cataloging in Publication Data

Sacred place / edited by Jean Holm, with John Bowker.
p. cm. – (Themes in religious studies series)
Includes bibliographical references and index.
ISBN 1-85567-104-2 (hb). – ISBN 1-85567-105-0 (pb).
1. Sacred space. 2. Religions. I. Holm, Jean, 1922– .
II. Bowker, John Westerdale. III. Series.
BL580.S2297 1994
291.3′5–dc20 94-13745
CIP

Typeset by Mayhew Typesetting, Rhayader, Powys
Printed and bound in Great Britain by Biddles Ltd, Guildford and King's Lynn

Contents

Series Preface

The person who knows only one religion does not know any religion. This rather startling claim was made in 1873, by Friedrich Max Müller, in his book, *Introduction to the Science of Religion.* He was applying to religion a saying of the poet Goethe: 'He who knows one language, knows none.'

In many ways this series illustrates Max Müller's claim. The diversity among the religious traditions represented in each of the volumes shows how mistaken are those people who assume that the pattern of belief and practice in their own religion is reflected equally in other religions. It is, of course, possible to do a cross-cultural study of the ways in which religions tackle particular issues, such as those which form the titles of the ten books in this series, but it soon becomes obvious that something which is central in one religion may be much less important in another. To take just three examples: the contrast between Islam's and Sikhism's attitudes to pilgrimage, in *Sacred Place*; the whole spectrum of positions on the authority of scriptures illustrated in *Sacred Writings*; and the problem which the titles, *Picturing God* and *Worship*, created for the contributor on Buddhism.

The series offers an introduction to the ways in which the themes are approached within eight religious traditions. Some of the themes relate particularly to the faith and practice of individuals and religious communities (*Picturing God, Worship, Rites of Passage, Sacred Writings, Myth and History, Sacred Place*); others have much wider implications, for society in general as well as for the religious communities themselves (*Attitudes to Nature, Making Moral Decisions, Human Nature and Destiny, Women in Religion*). This distinction, however, is not clear-cut. For instance, the 'sacred places' of Ayodhya and Jerusalem have figured in situations of national and international conflict, and some countries have passed laws regulating, or even banning, religious worship.

Stereotypes of the beliefs and practices of religions are so widespread that a real effort, of both study and imagination, is needed in order to discover what a religion looks – and feels – like to its adherents. We have to bracket out, temporarily, our own beliefs and presuppositions, and 'listen in' to a religion's account of what *it* regards as significant. This is not a straightforward task, and readers of the books in this series will encounter a number of the issues that characterise the study of religions, and that have to be taken into account in any serious attempt to get behind a factual description of a religion to an understanding of the real meaning of the words and actions for its adherents.

First, the problem of language. Islam's insistence that the Arabic of the Qur'ān cannot be 'translated' reflects the impossibility of finding in another language an exact equivalent of many of the most important terms in a religion. The very word, Islam, means something much more positive to a Muslim than is suggested in English by 'submission'. Similarly, it can be misleading to use 'incarnation' for *avatāra* in Hinduism, or 'suffering' for *dukkha* in Buddhism, or 'law' for Torah in Judaism, or 'gods' for *kami* in Shinto, or 'heaven' for *T'ien* in Taoism, or 'name' for *Nām* in Sikhism.

Next, the problem of defining – drawing a line round – a religion. Religions do not exist in a vacuum; they are influenced by the social and cultural context in which they are set. This can affect what they strenuously reject as well as what they may absorb into their pattern of belief and practice. And such influence is continuous, from a religion's origins (even though we may have no records from that period), through significant historical developments (which sometimes lead to the rise of new movements or sects), to its contemporary situation, especially when a religion is transplanted into a different region. For example, anyone who has studied Hinduism in India will be quite unprepared for the form of Hinduism they will meet in the island of Bali.

Even speaking of a 'religion' may be problematic. The term, 'Hinduism', for example, was invented by western scholars, and would not be recognised or understood by most 'Hindus'. A different example is provided by the religious situation in Japan, and the consequent debate among scholars as to whether they should speak of Japanese 'religion' or Japanese 'religions'.

Finally, it can be misleading to encounter only one aspect of a religion's teaching. The themes in this series are part of a whole interrelated network of beliefs and practices within each religious tradition, and need to be seen in this wider context. The reading lists at the end of each chapter point readers to general studies of the religions as well as to books which are helpful for further reading on the themes themselves.

Jean Holm
November 1993

List of Contributors

Jean Holm (EDITOR) was formerly Principal Lecturer in Religious Studies at Homerton College, Cambridge, teaching mainly Judaism and Hinduism. Her interests include relationships between religions; the relationship of culture to religion; and the way in which children are nurtured within a different cultural context. Her publications include *Teaching Religion in School* (Oxford University Press, 1975), *The Study of Religions* (Sheldon, 1977), *Growing up in Judaism* (Longman, 1990), *Growing up in Christianity*, with Romie Ridley (Longman, 1990) and *A Keyguide to Sources of Information on World Religions* (Mansell, 1991). She has edited three previous series: *Issues in Religious Studies*, with Peter Baelz (Sheldon), *Anselm Books*, with Peter Baelz (Lutterworth) and *Growing up in a Religion* (Longman).

John Bowker (EDITOR) was Professor of Religious Studies in Lancaster University before returning to Cambridge to become Dean and Fellow of Trinity College. He is at present Professor of Divinity at Gresham College in London, and Adjunct Professor at the University of Pennsylvania and at the State University of North Carolina. He is particularly interested in anthropological and sociological approaches to the study of religions. He has done a number of programmes for the BBC, including the *Worlds of Faith* series, and series on Islam and Hinduism for the World Service. He is the author of many books in the field of Religious Studies, including *The Meanings of Death* (Cambridge University Press, 1991), which was awarded the biennial Harper Collins religious book prize in 1993, in the academic section.

Douglas Davies is Professor of Religious Studies in the Department of Theology at the University of Nottingham, where he specialises in teaching the social anthropology of religion. He trained both in theology and social anthropology and his research continues to relate to both disciplines. His interest in theoretical and historical aspects of religious studies is represented in a major study of the sociology of knowledge and religion, published as *Meaning and Salvation in Religious Studies* (Brill, 1984), and in a historical volume, *Frank Byron Jevons 1858–1936, An Evolutionary Realist* (Edwin Mellen Press, 1991). Professor Davies is also very much concerned with practical aspects of religious behaviour and is a leading British scholar of Mormonism and, in addition to various articles, is author of *Mormon Spirituality* (Nottingham and Utah University Press, 1987). He was joint Director of the Rural Church Project, involving one of the largest sociological studies of religion in Britain published as *Church and Religion in Rural Britain* (with C. Watkins and M. Winter, T. & T. Clark, 1991). As Director of the Cremation Research Project he is conducting basic work on Cremation in Britain and Europe and has already produced some results in *Cremation Today and Tomorrow* (Grove Books, 1990).

Martin Boord holds a post at the DPC Academy in rural west Sikkim, India, prior to which he taught MA students at SOAS, University of London. With help from the Stein-Arnold Exploration Fund administered by the British Academy, he is currently engaged in research into the sacred history and geography of Sikkim, 'the hidden valley of abundant rice', from local oral and Tibetan literary sources. His particular interest is in the Northern Treasures (*Byang-gter*) revelationary tantric teachings of the Old School (*rNying-ma-pa*) of Tibetan Buddhism. Among his major published works are *Mandala Meaning and Method* (Kailash Editions, 1994), in which the Vajrayāna rites of the Buddhist *maṇḍala* are thoroughly explored, and a study of the wrathful buddhist deity *Vajrakila* (Institute of Buddhist Studies, 1993). Sometimes resident in India, Rev. Dr Boord utilises Sanskrit, Tibetan and traditional oral sources for his work and a number of his translations have been published by the Chhimed Rigzin Society, Kalimpong.

Anuradha Roma Choudhury is a Librarian working with the South Glamorgan County Library Service and is responsible for its Asian language section. She is also a part-time tutor with the Department of Continuing Education of the University of Wales, Cardiff. She studied Sanskrit Literature at the University of Calcutta, India, and taught in schools for a number of years. She holds Gita-bharati diploma in Indian music from Calcutta and is an accomplished singer. She lectures extensively on topics related to Indian music, customs, family life and Hinduism. She is the author of a book on Indian music called *Bilati-gan-bhanga Rabindra-sangeet* (Influence of British music on Rabindranath Tagore's songs) written in Bengali and published in Calcutta, 1987. She is also one of the contributors to *The Essential Teachings of Hinduism* (ed. Kerry Brown, Rider, 1988). She is actively involved with multi-cultural arts and inter-faith groups.

Clinton Bennett is a Lecturer in Study of Religions at Westminster College, Oxford, and a Baptist Minister. His research interests include Islamic theology and philosophy, historical and contemporary encounter between Muslims and non-Muslims, Islam and anthropology, and religious beliefs as agents of social transformation. Dr Bennett, who edits *Discernment: An Ecumenical Journal of Inter-Religious Encounter*, is the author of *Victorian Images of Islam* (1992), has travelled and worked in the Muslim world, and was a member of the World Council of Churches' (WCC) working party that produced *Issues in Christian–Muslim Relations: Ecumenical Considerations* (1991). He currently serves on the WCC's 'Consultation on the Church and the Jewish People'.

Seth Kunin is a Lecturer in the Department of Theology at Nottingham University. He trained for the Rabbinate at the Leo Baeck College in London and has served several congregations in Cambridge and Nottingham. Rabbi Kunin has analysed Jewish mythology and culture from a structuralist perspective. His PhD thesis, 'A Structuralist Analysis of Hebrew Mythology', will be published as a book later this year.

Beryl Dhanjal is a Lecturer at Ealing Tertiary College. She works on the programme for teaching ESOL (English to Speakers of Other Languages) and has special responsibility for developing community links, working mainly with people from the new commonwealth and with refugees. She studied Panjābi at the School of Oriental and African Studies, University of London. She has lectured at St Mary's

College, Strawberry Hill, and the West London Institute of Higher Education, and has worked in adult education. She has written and translated many books, and particularly enjoys writing books for children and young people – she has written bi-lingual English/ Panjābi books for children.

Xinzhong Yao is Lecturer in Chinese religion and ethics at the University of Wales, Lampeter. His research interests include philosophy, ethics and religion; he is currently focusing on comparative philosophy and comparative religion. Dr Yao is author of *On Moral Activity* (People's University Press, Beijing, 1990), *Ethics and Social Problems* (City Economic Press, Beijing, 1989), co-author of *Comparative Studies on Human Nature* (Tienjin People's Press, Tienjin, 1988), co-editor of *Applying Ethics* (Jilin People's Press, Changchun, 1994), and main translator of Charles L. Stevenson's *Ethics and Language* (Social Sciences of China Press, Beijing, 1991). He is also Deputy Director of the Institute of Ethics, People's University of China, Beijing.

Ian Reader is Senior Lecturer in the Department of Japanese Studies at the University of Stirling, Scotland. He has spent several years in Japan travelling, teaching at Japanese universities and researching into contemporary Japanese religion. His major research interest is in the study of pilgrimage, and he is currently working on a volume on pilgrimage in Japan. Dr Reader is author of *Religion in Contemporary Japan* (Macmillan, 1991), and editor (with Tony Walter) of *Pilgrimage in Popular Culture* (Macmillan, 1992). He has also published numerous articles in journals and collected editions on Buddhism, Japanese religion, pilgrimage and Japanese popular culture, and is a member of the Editorial Advisory Board of the *Japanese Journal of Religious Studies*.

Introduction: Raising the Issues

Douglas Davies

Among the most visible aspects of religions are those sacred places either built as ritual arenas or else selected from nature through association with the history and myths of a religion. This seems to be true, as the chapters on Hinduism, Islam and Sikhism make clear, even when a religion wishes all life-contexts to be sacred. This becomes quite apparent when a sacred place is a small domestic shrine, as in Hindu households, or a single crucifix in a Roman Catholic family home.

The different names given to sacred places are among the best-known features of world religions and demonstrate the fact that sacred places are fundamental elements of religion. Most people know that Hindus and Buddhists have temples, that Sikhs meet at gurdwaras, Jews at synagogues, Christians at churches, and Muslims at mosques. But simply listing places of worship easily overlooks the fact that they are not the only, and sometimes are not even the primary, sacred places for a religion. To sketch the fuller picture, these regular locations of meeting and worship need to be set within a framework of sites of special historical significance, especially those where some crucial revelation was obtained by a religion's founder.

Makkah, for example, is a historically significant sacred place for Muslims, while the mosques where they worship day by day have a different level of significance despite the obvious link that all worship takes place facing Makkah. Similar double-levels of significance occur throughout the following chapters as primacy of place is accorded to centres of special religious interest. Often they are grounded in the myth or mythical history of a religion, as with the Himalayan Mountains or River Ganges at Banaras for Hindus. So too with Bodhgaya as the site where the Buddha gained enlightenment. The city of Jerusalem provides one of the most complex examples, serving as a sacred place for Jews, Christians, and Muslims, as discussed in their respective chapters.

The ritual of local sacred places is closely linked to the key sacred places or events of a tradition like Makkah, Banaras or Jerusalem. At Jerusalem, for example, very many Christian traditions have established their own place of worship, not only those from the numerous Eastern Orthodox and Roman Catholic traditions, but also from Lutherans, Anglicans, and even the Mormon Church of Jesus Christ of Latter-day Saints. The faithful engage in a kind of participation with the past as part of worship itself, an imaginative involvement also reflected in the religious art and architecture of sacred places. The eternal dimension of deity or ultimate reality unites both the devotees' local site and the key locations of their religion. If we define a symbol as something participating in what it represents, we can see how local sacred places draw power from their association with the central site. The chapter on Judaism gives a very clear example of how both Jewish synagogues and homes represent and, in some sense, replace the destroyed Jerusalem Temple in the life of faith of ordinary Jews. That chapter also provides an excellent example of an anthropological analysis of sacred space.

Another example of a link between a contemporary ritual event and a key moment in the history of a religion is reflected in the chapter on Christianity. When the eucharist is celebrated at thousands of Christian altars there is an underlying link both with the events of the Last Supper celebrated by Christ and also with his death by crucifixion. Both Catholic and Protestant theologies agree that the faithful are somehow linked with that night in which Jesus was betrayed and the day on which he was killed. Where they disagree is on the mode of participating in those past events. In a rather similar way thousands of representations of Hindu deities in temples across India and the world symbolically express and share in the one deity depicted in the statues.

This is not to say that religions are always happy with the consequences of possessing sacred places. In fact there is a very real tension present in many religious traditions, deploring the fact that devotees may place more emphasis on the physical place than upon its spiritual significance. A clear Sikh example comes in the writings of Guru Nanak. In his own day he decried the use of pilgrimages to sacred places, arguing that genuine pilgrimage was a kind of internal journey, a matter of the heart. A very similar picture already existed in Buddhism where the Buddha deplored pilgrimage as a worthless activity. In terms of religious studies one of the advantages of central sacred sites of pilgrimage is that they lead to a mixing of the many cultural diversities among devotees, as the chapter on Buddhism suggests.

Each religion's theology adds a distinctive dimension to its overall approach to sacred places. The chapter on Buddhism, like that on Islam, argues that all things are potentially sacred, but goes on to say that they require a suitably sacred mind to appear in their true character. The construction of *maṇḍala*s, representing key religious ideas, and temples, which also mirror those concepts, shows the close interconnection of religious ideas and practices. The Buddhist tradition of, for example, building *stūpa*s over sites where the cremated remains of the Buddha were located, represents the general religious tendency of sacralising historical sites. The importance of history to a religion is very obvious in the case of the Sikh commitment to the Golden Temple at Amritsar. This building reflects the lives and work of several of Sikhism's early Gurūs, and also marks, in an especially concrete fashion, the existence of this particular way of devotion to God as separate from that of Hinduism or Islam, other historical religions of the Panjab in Northwest India.

The chapter on Chinese religions reflects an ancient tradition, one found in many cultures, by which a people sees its land as the centre of the world and, in this case, as intrinsically sacred. This chapter also introduces the important distinction between sites whose sacredness derived from some natural quality, and those whose sacredness was created directly by human association. In other words, there are some sites whose very nature impresses itself upon people, while others have a status impressed upon them following some special event. This sense of power of a place is well expressed in the chapter on Hinduism as it begins with a focus on the Himalayan Mountains, mythologically representing some Hindu deities, and symbolically reflected in the architecture of Hindu temples whose pinnacles are viewed as mountain peaks. This feature of the intrinsic power of places such as mountains, caves or rivers can be understood in terms of a disclosure or revelation, a hierophany – a showing forth of the holy – as Mircea Eliade called such moments (1968: 124). A most complex and symbolically intricate example comes from the Chinese imperial ritual and sacrifices associated both with the worship of heaven and of the ancestors, a complexity linked with the position of the stars.

In a similar way the chapter on Japanese religions shows how the very land of Japan was deemed sacred in such a way as could engender very deep-seated motivation of a nationalistic kind, especially during war. Similarly, the idea of Israel as a promised land given by God belongs not only to a longstanding biblical tradition, but is vitally important in the politics of the middle east at the close of the twentieth century.

Sacred places are not only ancient places, as various claims to modern visions of the Virgin Mary in Roman Catholicism show. In the quite different tradition of Mormonism, for example, the nineteenth century witnessed the rise of the State of Utah and of Salt Lake City as a kind of focal point of this new religion, while, in a negative direction, the twentieth century has seen the decline of Tibet as the world centre of Tibetan Buddhism under the political control of China. Instead of associating this form of Buddhism with the country of Tibet, it is, under present circumstances, more easily focused on the person of the Dalai Lama himself. This is an interesting example of how an individual can help define and constitute the sacred element of a religion.

At the other end of the spectrum from particular individuals we find natural phenomena. If we follow the distinction between natural and social sacred places, we find mountains and rivers as classic examples of the former. Mountains, as potential bridges between heaven and earth, have long impressed human beings with a sense of awe and power. The chapter on Judaism furnishes an interesting example of how the mountain, as a sacred feature, influences the architecture of synagogues.

Another feature of sacred sites involves political issues and other aspects of competition for power among religious groups, as is clearly discussed for religions in China. Similar competition for sacred sites continues in Jerusalem, not only between Jews, Christians and Muslims, but also within various Christian churches themselves.

The essence of sacred places

It is not surprising that many sacred places share the fact of stressing links with their founder or other important figure in the history of their religion. The historian of religion, Mircea Eliade, has pointed out the more intriguing fact that many sacred places in different religions are, for example, said to represent the centre of the universe. Such sacred places are 'meeting points between heaven and earth', 'a point of junction between earth, heaven and hell, the navel of the earth, a meeting place for the three cosmic regions' (1958: 375). Eliade went on to show how the architecture and symbolism of many sacred buildings – temples, churches and mosques – echo something of the central sacred space of a religion.

The chapter on Islam gives a good description of the *Ka'bah* at Makkah, exploring its significance through Eliade's general perspective and showing how tradition depicts it as the very centre of significant world history, marking the place where human life began. It also shows how other places, Madinah and the Dome of the Rock in Jerusalem, came to share in Makkah's sacredness.

The religions discussed in this book, as in the whole series, reflect two aspects of religion, one local and the other universal, and we have already discussed how these dimensions are related to each other. Both dimensions also involve the identity of religious believers in relation to sacred places. Some religions like Hinduism, Sikhism, Judaism and the Chinese and Japanese traditions, represented in successive chapters, are what might be called ethnic religions. They belong to the very cultural framework of a society and of the identity of its individual members. For them, sacred places are also fundamental aspects of the people and their lives. But, as the chapter on Hinduism makes very clear, the prime sites may be natural features, as in mountains, rivers and woodlands, while temples are, ultimately, of lesser significance. Even so, great care may be taken with temples and, in the case of Hinduism, we see how a concern over measuring the proper dimensions of temples was linked to the realm of mathematics.

Christianity and Islam also link universal and local aspects of religion in those societies where these faiths have existed for many hundreds of years. In this sense, for example, Ireland has been a Christian country for nearly two thousand years, and in such countries Christianity and Islam do convey a fundamental sense of identity for those born into the religion. The longer a religion exists in a particular geographical area, the more likely it is to validate and create new sacred places in the new territory. In Catholic Christianity, for example, the growth of new sacred places has often been associated with belief in appearances of the Virgin Mary to one or more faithful believers. Lourdes, Fatima, and Knock represent only three European locations which have become sacred centres of pilgrimage.

But Christianity and Islam are also profoundly missionary movements, despite quite different means of spreading their faith. Throughout the eighteenth and nineteenth centuries Christianity expanded in much of Africa as Islam has done more recently. Periods of missionary expansion are of interest in the study of religion because during the period of growth and establishment of a religion, local sacred places, belonging to earlier and indigenous religious traditions, can be either swept away by missionaries and zealous converts, or else be thrown into an inferior position under the dominance of a sacred place located well beyond local experience. The lands and days of Jesus or Muhammad come to occupy centre stage for people who had, until recently, never heard of Jerusalem or Makkah. The new sacred places which supersede local 'pagan' temples are validated and endued with power by the historical links they have with the central sites of the history or mythical history of the religions concerned.

Although this division between ethnic and missionary religions is important, it should not be too firmly emphasised. Throughout the later nineteenth century and especially in the twentieth century, many movements derived from the older ethnic religions have, themselves, become missionary-minded. Several Eastern Hindu and Buddhist groups have become popular in the West; the Hare Krishna movement from Hinduism and several traditions of Yoga are good examples. These movements show just how exportable religions can be and how sacred places can be constituted not simply by awesome natural sites, or by ancient revelation, but also by a group of people. The case of Japanese religions offers a clear example of the power of natural places, just as Islam does of a historical site, and Charismatic Christianity the sacredness felt to derive from the experience of believers worshipping together. A similar idea underlies the fact that, for example, even small groups of Muslims or Jews can constitute a mosque or synagogue for the purpose of prayer.

This, finally, raises the distinction between immanence and transcendence as two dimensions of the sacred underlying many of the religious traditions represented in this book. Religious teachers regularly stress the vital need of sincerity of intention in believers in encountering the transcendent mystery of their faith, rather than any grossly materialistic adherence to a physical place for its own sake.

FURTHER READING

Eliade, M. (1958) *Patterns in Comparative Religion*, London, Sheed and Ward.

—— (1968) *Myths, Dreams and Mysteries*, New York, Fontana.

1. Buddhism

Martin Boord

Origins

Life, it is said, may be defined in terms of movement or growth. In India of the sixth century BCE, the era of the Buddha, spiritual growth was popularly precipitated by the act of *pravrajya*, 'going forth' from home in order to enter the religious life as a monk or wandering ascetic. The term is employed in Buddhist scriptures (e.g., *Dhammapada* x.i.89) in reference to one who has abandoned the mundane world in search of the transcendent, 'the deathless' state beyond the vicissitudes of a painful series of rebirths in *saṃsāra*, and among the earliest representations of the Buddha are those in which his presence is indicated merely by a pair of footprints. The sacred space occupied by his holy person, it was felt, could not be encompassed by any pictorial device, however sublime the symbol or skilled the artist, for the Buddha was called *Tathāgata*, 'He by whom the state of "thusness" has been reached'.

To Buddhists of the early period, naturally, the site of supreme sacredness, towards which the home-renouncing wanderer should head forthwith, was that place where the Buddha himself was to be found. There the mendicant could expect a welcome with the words '*Ehi bhikṣu*', 'Come, monk!' and thus find himself ordained within the Buddhist community.

Although the Buddha was surrounded throughout his teaching career by a large gathering of the fourfold assembly consisting of monks, nuns, laymen and laywomen, he at all times stressed the supremacy of the *Dharma* over the presence of his person. These two aspects came to be recognised as two 'bodies' (*kāya*) of the Buddha; the *Dharmakāya* consisting of his scriptural tradition to be honoured, recited and studied by the monastic community; and the *rūpakāya* or 'body of form' which merely served as the temporary vehicle for the transmission and explication of eternal verities inherent in the former. The superior body of the Buddha was the *Dharmakāya* and any monk who perceived that was said to have seen the real Buddha. 'What good to you is this body of filth?', the Buddha is said to have asked. 'He who sees the *Dharma* sees me' (*Samyutta-nikāya* III.120). Indeed, his first sixty followers, each one of whom had gained supreme insight into the meaning of his teachings upon first hearing, were dismissed from the Buddha's presence and instructed to spread themselves out in all directions of the world in order to preach 'the good law' (*saddharma*) for the benefit of others. Sacredness was understood to be a quality of truth, a quality fundamental to the teachings, not a quality of time or place, teacher or retinue. Any pilgrimage undertaken by a wanderer in search of the Buddha in the outer world, therefore, could never be more than a prelude to the higher spiritual journey along the paths of meditation in search of the *buddha*-nature within. The act of renouncing home and family at the outset of the spiritual quest was viewed as a means of generating merit that would be helpful once the essential, inner, exploration had begun. The popular Hindu tradition of pilgrimage to sacred sites, as much in evidence at the time of the Buddha as it is today, was rejected by the Teacher who perceived merely 'heedless pilgrims scattering widely the dust of their passions'.

To Buddhists of all periods, all places are potentially 'sacred' or, at least, to be treated with some respect. The sun, moon, planets and stars are each considered the homes of deities or spirits and this earth is abundant with them. Throughout the world there are to be found sacred rivers, lakes, rocks, mountains, trees and the rest, even the least of which are the abodes of life. Buddhists readily adopted the prevailing Indian notion of deities charged with the guardianship of the ten directions (the four cardinal and intermediate directions and above and below), and the four Great Kings who rule the north, south, east and west are said, even in the earliest texts, to have presented the Buddha with offerings. Indeed, the very earth itself is sacred. Personified as a golden goddess, it was she who witnessed the Buddha's defeat of Māra on the eve of his final enlightenment and each plot of earth, no matter how small, is considered to have its ruling *nāga* king with responsibility for the welfare of those who inhabit his domain, right down to the tiniest worm or insect. Monks have traditionally been forbidden to till the soil for fear of harming the creatures who dwell there and, should disturbing the earth prove unavoidable for the construction of a *vihāra*, for example, prayers should be offered for the sake of the ground's original inhabitants.

Later Buddhist architectural texts go into great detail concerning the appeasement or subjugation of the earth-dwelling *nāga* whose domain is required for human use. Marking out the desired plot of land in the form of a square aligned to the cardinal directions, astrologers then determine the position of the chthonic serpent who is thought to dwell beneath its surface. This natural 'owner of the site' is said to revolve slowly in his underground home so as to face each of the four sides in turn during the annual cycle of four seasons, and the four corners of the square, therefore, are thought to be the locations of the serpent's head at the beginning of a season. Calculating that the serpent's head travels with a regular motion along the western side of the square during the three months of spring, the northern side during the summer and so on, it is a simple matter for the architects and priests to determine the layout beneath the ground of the *nāga* on any given day of the year. Having done so, they dig into the earth at the spot calculated to correspond to 'the armpit' of the serpent and bury precious offerings there in payment for the ground in order to secure his goodwill and the future protection and welfare of the site.

Even more elaborate rites may involve summoning the four Great Kings: Dhṛtarāṣṭra, ruler of the east; Virūḍhaka, ruler of the south; Virūpākṣa, ruler of the west; and Vaisravaṇa, ruler of the north. They may then be requested to consecrate and bless the site as sacred and to guard over it while religious works are being performed there. The ten direction protectors also, consisting of the vedic deities, Brahmā, Indra, Yama and the rest, are often invited by Buddhists and their beneficent influence sought for the protection of the site. A more wrathful method of later times involves the demarcation of the site by sharp wooden pegs (*kīla*) which are driven into the four corners and along the boundary of the sacred area with curses to destroy all demons and their malignant power.

Despite the development of such elaborate rites focused upon the external world, however, the superiority of internal sacred space was never forgotten. Although the Buddha taught that the earth and its inhabitants were to be honoured at all times by his followers, whose personal demeanour he required to remain humble, he also announced:

> Verily I declare to you my friend, that within this very body, mortal as it is and only an armspan in height but conscious and endowed with mind, is the world and the waxing thereof and the waning thereof and the way that leads to the passing away thereof.
>
> (*Aṅguttara-nikāya* II)

The notion put forward here of the Buddha's body being equivalent to the whole world, remained of fundamental importance throughout all subsequent developments of Buddhist religious ideology. Soon the Buddha is reported to have declared:

> All lands are in my body and so are the Buddhas living there. Watch my pores and I will show you the Buddha's realm.
>
> (*Avataṁsaka-sūtra* IV)

The external world and the human body are, of course, each considered to be composed of the four great elements (*mahābhūta*) known to ancient science: earth, water, fire and air. Early Buddhist *Abhidharma* texts describe the manner in which the world comes into being as a direct manifestation of the *karma* of those sentient beings who are destined to become its inhabitants, and in the later elaborations of this theme it is said that the element of earth arises as a result of their stupidity. It is due to the oppressive weight of choking ignorance and the heavy bonds of karmic formations that this element assumes its characteristics of mass and solidity. Water is said to arise as the result of a constant flow of desire, a defilement within which so many are drowned. Hatred and anger are responsible for the fire which burns away all goodness and the free movement of air reflects the all-pervading nature of jealousy. The *rūpakāya* or body of a *buddha*, on the other hand, arises from no such causes. His appearance in the world is for the sake of others, for the mental defilements considered necessary for rebirth in *saṃsāra* have all been entirely eliminated from his own mind-stream during the course of the three incalculable aeons of his training. In order to manifest in a form compatible with those humans around him who are to be trained, however, the Buddha generates the solidity of earth from the unshakeable firmness of his *samādhi*, and the tears of his great compassion flow forth as water. His enthusiasm for the path of *dharma* and his devotion to the highest good glow with the warmth of fire and his utterances of truth, his skilful acts and his prayers and muttered *mantra* give rise to the element of air. Unlike others, the body of a *buddha* also possesses the subtle element of space derived from his enlightened qualities of wisdom and bliss.

The *maṇḍala*

According to this theory, therefore, the manifestation of a *buddha* in the human realm conforms to a set of norms quite unlike the laws of physics, chemistry and biology by which humankind is governed. Although the body of a *buddha* is perceived by those around him to consist of flesh and blood, it is understood by the wise to be, in reality, an illusory play of enlightened compassion made only of light. Any appearance to the contrary derives merely from the viewer's own lack of capacity to see things in their true nature. At one time, for example, the disciple Sariputra demanded to know why his master, the Buddha, was forced to dwell in this world of ours with its rocky paths, steep cliffs and sharp thorns when other *buddhas* were known to reside in paradise. It was explained to him then that all such impurities were merely the reflections of those impurities still lurking within his own mind and the Buddha, touching the earth with his toe, caused the entire universe to appear more splendid than any heaven. 'My *kṣetra*, Sariputra, is always as pure as this', he said (*Vimalakīrtinirdeśa-sūtra* I.16–17).

In the view of the later Vajrayāna school, the equation of mind and space is axiomatic. Sacred or holy space, then, cannot exist in independence of sacred or holy mind. Upon the *maṇḍala* map of this sacred space the central area is generally marked in blue, designating the central wisdom of the *buddha*-mind which perceives the deep, space-like nature of all phenomena as boundless in potential and uncreated in fact. This wisdom of openness, free of all mental propositions is referred to as the pristine cognition of the utterly pure expanse of reality (*suviśuddhadharmadhātujñāna*) and is one of five such pristine cognitions that designate the territory of sacred space or mind. To the east is an area marked in white which corresponds to the 'mirror-like' pristine cognition (*ādarśajñāna*), the enlightened capacity to perceive simultaneously all phenomena without distortion or prejudice, just as a good mirror will faithfully reflect all the objects set before it without accepting some and rejecting others. To the south, the map is marked in yellow colour, indicative of the pristine cognition of sameness (*samatājñāna*) which recognises the equality of all phenomena in their being unoriginated and lacking a self. With regard to all sentient beings, this wisdom is cognisant of the fact that all beings are the same in their desire for happiness and the avoidance of suffering, and thus the southern quarter of the map marks also the impartial quality of enlightened compassion. The western quarter of the map is red. Here is located the pristine cognition of discernment (*pratyavekṣaṇajñāna*) which recognises the particular value and function of each individual aspect of phenomena down to the smallest detail. It knows the individual destinies of beings as well as how to discriminate between what is appropriate and what is inappropriate in the light of given circumstances and the law of cause and effect. All of this is united into a single, co-operative wisdom in the northern quarter where the pristine cognition of establishing the deeds to be done (*kṛtyānuṣṭhānajñāna*) is marked on the map in green. It is by means of this knowledge that the *buddha*s achieve all that is to be accomplished with regard to their aspiration for the welfare of all beings.

To that extent, then, the *maṇḍala* functions as a map of the sacred mind. Let us now examine the manner in which it charts the relationships of phenomena in the physical world. The nature of humans, according to the early Buddhist texts, is made up of five 'aggregates' (*skandha*) which are itemised as form (*rūpa*), feeling (*vedanā*), perception (*saṃjñā*), impulse (*saṃskāra*) and consciousness (*vijñāna*). As the king of the five, consciousness is placed in the centre of the *maṇḍala* with form and the rest in the four directions beginning with the east. There they become known as the five *Buddha*s, supreme among the *maṇḍala* gods and progenitors of the five families of *maṇḍala* deities. The sense faculties of the body then take their place within the scheme as male deities while the objects of the senses in the four directions of the surrounding world are viewed as their female consorts. The inner and outer elements are positioned on the map with water in the east, earth in the south, fire in the west and air in the north. Ruling them all is the subtle central element of space. In their esoteric form these are regarded as the consorts of the five *Buddhas*, and by a gradual multiplication of correspondences the *maṇḍala* increases in significance until it can truly be said to function as a map for the entire universe of sacred space.

Perceived as operating in the ordinary external world, then, the *Buddhas* are said to perform their particular functions in accordance with the *maṇḍala* plan. Thus, acts of pacification such as healing the sick, calming those who are disturbed and bringing reconciliation to embittered rivals, are said to be carried out in the eastern quarter of the *maṇḍala* within a circular area, white in colour. Acts of encouragement that bring about an increase of desirable qualities are said to be performed in the south within a square area of yellow colour. Acts of control that seek to harmonise chaotic energies and establish compassionate wisdom as the dominant force take place in the west within a bow-shaped (semi-circular) area of red ground. Acts of wrath, in which totally negative forces are destroyed, are carried out in the north within a black triangular space, and these four acts in the four directions of the *maṇḍala* are all performed in accordance with a general understanding of the *maṇḍala* as a map of the sacred space of buddhahood.

Building *stūpas*

In his final injunctions to the *saṅgha*, delivered just before the time of his death and recorded in the *Mahāparinirvāṇa-sūtra*, the Buddha stressed once more the importance of the *Dharma* as a refuge and guide in their lives. Instructing his monks to work out their own salvation with diligence, he told them to place no faith in transitory phenomena such as the body of the Teacher, but to revere instead the doctrines he had taught. The monks were 'not to hinder themselves by honouring the remains of the *Tathāgata*'. The cremation of the body and monumental interment of relics were matters to be left entirely in the hands of interested lay parties who would subsequently worship them in a fitting manner. The layfolk, it was said, would honour the funereal monument (*stūpa*) with garlands of flowers, wreaths of incense and all the traditional Indian paraphernalia of worship. They would maintain the upkeep of the shrine's superstructure and rejoice and be glad in its presence.

Whereas, then, the *stūpa* of the Buddha was to be regarded as a suitable focus for the venerations of layfolk, it was not deemed fitting as a topic of interest for the ordained *saṅgha* whose minds should remain attuned to higher things.

Following the decease of the Buddha in Kusinagara, ten *stūpa*s were constructed in the neighbouring areas in order to house and honour his mortal remains. Relics from the cremation had been gathered together and distributed among the Mallas of Kusinagara, King Ajatasatru of Magadha, the Licchavis of Vaisali, the Śākyas of Kapilavastu, the Bulakas of Calakalpa, the Krauḍyas of Ramagrama, the Brahmans of Visnudvipa and the Mallas of Papa. Drona, the priest who had presided over the cremation, kept the urn which had enclosed the relics and the late-arriving Mauryas of Pipphalivana claimed the ashes. It is also said that the countless gods of the Trāyastrimśa heaven descended to earth at that time and each one claimed a single hair of the Blessed One's body over which was subsequently constructed a *stūpa* in heaven. The ten original *stūpa*s of the Ganges heartland are said to have been opened up, more than one hundred years after they were built, by the emperor Asoka, who divided their contents among many hundreds of *stūpa*s which he caused to be constructed throughout his realm. Other monuments were built to house the Buddha's robe and bowl, clippings of his hair, his footprints and his shadow (that is, they were built on sites rendered sacred by his presence).

More than simply commemorating the master, however, by assuming possession of the relics, the emperor Asoka aligned their spiritual power with his own political authority and thereby 'legitimated' his right to rule. Tales are told of miraculous phenomena being observed in connection with these sacred traces of the Buddha, and it became an article of popular faith that their supernatural force would assist the pious king who protected them to govern his subjects with wisdom and justice.

In Sri Lanka, Buddhist kings have traditionally honoured and protected the relic of the Buddha's tooth in the belief that the security and well-being of the kingdom were dependent in no small measure upon the security and well-being of the tooth. An annual public holiday is observed in that country, during which thousands of laypeople make the pilgrimage to the temple of the tooth and witness the splendid procession of the caparisoned relic on the back of a royal elephant. Such a celebration serves primarily to unite the

Sinhalese in a feeling of national pride, confirming their belief in themselves as inheritors and custodians of the Buddha's law. The atmosphere throughout that particular pilgrimage stands in marked contrast to the atmosphere of reverential devotion evident at Bodhgaya, where Buddhists of every nationality lose their separate identities in common worship of an 'other-worldly' spirituality.

The cult of the *stūpa* was carried with Buddhism throughout the lands of eastern Asia, and when corporeal relics were no longer to be found, *stūpa*s were built to enclose the Buddha's image or symbol. In the *Saddharmapuṇḍarīka-sūtra* it is explained that a magnificent and lofty great *stūpa*, consisting of jewels, should be erected to mark the site where the *sūtra* has either been 'declared or explained or recited or copied out', and that relics of the *Tathāgata* are not required to be placed within it because the entire mass of relics is already gathered there in unison. Similarly,

> That spot of earth where this *sūtra* is revealed; that spot of earth will be worthy of worship by the whole world with its gods, men and *asura*s, that spot of earth will be worthy of respectful salutation, worthy of being honoured by circumambulation. Like a shrine will be that spot of earth.
>
> (*Vajracchedikā* v.5)

In the ancient Burmese (Myanmarese) city of Pagan alone were constructed more than two thousand monuments and temples inspired by *stūpa* prototypes and the vast number of *stūpa*s in existence today throughout the Buddhist world can only be guessed at.

Down through the centuries, not only has the architectural form of these monuments undergone considerable change, but their symbolic significance also. *Stūpa*s no longer proclaim in simple terms merely 'The Buddha was here'; they are now understood to embody his message encoded in their structure. This change in emphasis seems to have come about, in part at least, due to the close proximity of the *saṅgha* to the ever-increasing number of monuments that were built within the actual precincts of the monasteries so that the *saṅgha* were forced into sharing responsibility for their guardianship with the layfolk. More importantly, however, due to the lack of corporeal relics, *stūpa*s ceased to function as repositories of the *rūpakāya* and became instead repositories of the *Dharmakāya*. The various *Vinaya* of all but the earliest monastic orders therefore contain minor texts that treat extensively the symbolic form and mode of worship of these most characteristic of Buddhist monuments. Although the documents of the separate schools conflict in the specifics of their various interpretations, all agree the monument to consist of a terraced base, dome, upper enclosure (*harmikā*), axial pole and superimposed parasol or series of honourific discs which, by an enumeration of their parts, stand typically for the thirty-seven aspects of enlightenment (*bodhipakṣyadharma*).

The first step of the terraced base, then, would generally be interpreted as representing the four applications of mindfulness (*smṛtyupasthāna*): mindfulness with regard to the body, feelings, mind and all phenomena. The second terrace would be said to stand for the four right endeavours (*samyakprahāṇa*): endeavours with regard to those moral defilements not yet born which must remain unproduced, those depravities already arisen which must be destroyed, unacquired virtues which must be generated and those virtues already acquired which must be increased. The four corners of the third terrace then indicate: a strong desire to succeed, enthusiastic perseverance on the path, thought and investigative penetration, which are the four bases of psychic (miracle) power (*ṛddhipāda*). The five faculties (*indriya*) of faith, enthusiasm, mindfulness, meditative absorption and insight, and their corresponding five strengths (*bala*), would be represented by the uppermost levels of the base beneath the dome, while the dome itself would be said to represent the seven limbs of enlightenment (*bodhyaṅga*). These consist of mindfulness, phenomenological analysis, enthusiasm, joy, confidence, profound concentration and equanimity. Finally the *harmikā* would stand for the noble eight-fold path of right view, right aspiration, right speech, right activity, right livelihood, right effort, right mindfulness and right meditation. The pole and parasols that served to honour the structure were then taken to indicate various levels of spiritual attainment on the basis of that thirty-seven stepped path.

The *stūpa* is also understood by some to be a representation of the entire cosmos. Thus the square base stands for the world of desire (*kāmaloka*), the dome for the world of form (*rūpaloka*), while its spire and finial point the way to the uppermost world of formlessness (*ārūpyaloka*).

Pilgrimage and the cult of traces

Despite, however, the Buddha's scornful condemnation of pilgrimage as meaningless ritual – 'If the waters of the Ganges could truly wash away sin then all fishes would go straight to heaven' – countless Buddhist pilgrims were to be found in all periods of Buddhist history flocking to the sacred sites in order to worship the *stūpa*s constructed there. The emperor Asoka had his own *dharmayātra* or 'Journey for Truth' to Bodhgaya, the pre-eminent site of pilgrimage where the Buddha attained enlightenment, recorded in stone – engraved on rock edict number eight. *Stūpa*s and shrines were constructed at every major locality connected with the Buddha's life: Lumbini Garden near Kapilavastu where he was born, Bodhgaya (regarded by Buddhists as 'the centre of the world' and known as the indestructible or *vajra* seat of enlightenment), the Deer Park at Sarnath where he first turned the wheel of the Law, the various places where miracles were performed and important discourses delivered, and at Kusinagara and surrounding districts upon his final demise. Indeed, the biography of the Buddha as a peripatetic teacher is intimately related to topographical detail, a fact of no little interest to pilgrims.

The popularity of pilgrimage and 'the cult of traces' led to the growth in ancient India of tourism as an industry. It has been suggested, in fact, that local narratives concerning the various episodes of the Buddha's biography were collected and embellished to such an extent by tourist guides anxious to entertain and inform the pilgrims that they became the actual basis upon which the biographies themselves later came to be written. In the detailed reports of their travels kept by some of the pilgrims from China, we may read of monks and monasteries, *stūpa*s, shrines, temples and images and, in particular, of the local legends associated with innumerable sacred sites. Fa-hsien, for example, left his home in Chang-an in 399 CE in search of *dharma*, traversing the whole of Central Asia and North India before embarking by ship for Sri Lanka and Java. By the time of his return to China in 412 CE he had documented an enormous cult of relics spread all the way across the Buddhist world, and similar reports were made by others of his countrymen in the centuries that followed. The small published guidebooks to local sites that these pilgrims collected could be strung together so as to form a complete history of Buddhism, revealing the religion as one fundamentally based upon its notion of sacred topology.

It should be noted here that the use of the word 'history' by Buddhists encompasses a broader range of meanings than generally assigned to the term in the West. Thus the sacred sites eagerly identified by the pious (promoted, no doubt, by their zealous guides) included all features of the landscape that could conceivably be associated with any Buddhist legend at all. Not only, then, did this sacred topology feature the birthplaces of saints and the sites of their demonstrations of miracles and so on, not only were the caves and forest hermitages once inhabited by great luminaries pointed out, but the sites of exploits of the *bodhisattva* during his previous births, as recorded in the books of the *Jātaka*, and the miraculous deeds of gods and *nāga* from beyond the human realm were also identified in large numbers upon the ground.

By drawing together large numbers of pilgrims from all over the Buddhist world, the more important sites have long served as cultural melting-pots within which the divergent views and customs of the many Buddhist sects could continuously interact with one another to their mutual enrichment. A harmonising 'cultural norm' for Buddhism has thus been maintained under their influence. The smaller, more localised sites, however, may have tended to bond culturally the few who frequented them in the customs of a particular shrine and thus have given rise to disparate local traditions.

The relevance of sacred sites as an essential ingredient of Buddhism travelled with it wherever it spread. *Stūpa*s believed to contain relics of the Buddha are to be found all over Asia, such as those at Doi Suthep near Chiang Mai in Thailand and That Luang in Vientiane, Laos. The Shwe Dagon *stūpa* in Rangoon is said to house the staff of Kāśyapa and the robe of Kanakamuni, two *buddha*s of the past, as well as eight hairs of Sakyamuni, the *buddha* of the present. Within a reliquary in the Daḷadā Māligāwa, Kandy, Sri Lanka, is to be found one of several of the Buddha's teeth, and the faithful of that land tell apocryphal tales of the Buddha having visited their island on three occasions, finally leaving the imprint of his foot upon the rocks of Mount Sumanakūṭa (Śrīpada) in the south. He is similarly said to have visited the western coast of India, Myanmar (Burma), Northwest India, Kashmir, Central Asia and elsewhere so that the cult of traces grew up in all of those places, and in every country in the Buddhist world the institution of pilgrimage as a viable mode of worship or accumulation of merit was established.

There are sixteen especially sacred sites of pilgrimage in Sri Lanka and twelve in Thailand associated with the twelve-year calendrical cycle. Four sacred mountains in China are deemed to have associations with great *bodhisattva*s of the Mahāyāna pantheon: Mount Wu-t'ai with Mañjusrī, Mount O-mei with Samantabhadra, Mount P'u-t'o with Avalokiteśvara and Mount Chiu-'hua with Kṣitigarbha. Similar traditions are instituted in Tibet where a large number of ritual circuits of holy sites are known. There are thirty-three holy places in the western provinces of Japan considered sacred to Avalokiteśvara, and another eighty-eight temples in Shikoku associated with Kobo Daishi (Kukai), the ninth-century patriarch of the Shingon sect who was born in that district. Visiting these places in turn, as prescribed by tradition, generally involves the pilgrim in an arduous ritual journey of several hundred miles (almost seven hundred and fifty miles in the case of the Shikoku circuit). Pilgrims in Japan used to wear wide, flat hats made of reed to protect them from the sun and the custom arose of writing *Doko-ninin* ('two on the trip') on these hats to signify that the traveller was accompanied along the way by the Buddha.

The activity of pilgrimage is generally considered by Buddhists to be productive of great merit through the arduous disciplines of body, speech and mind involved and, furthermore, the significance and worth of the pilgrimage are much enhanced if the traveller at every station on his journey has the opportunity to receive religious instruction and ritual empowerments. Auspicious timing thus constitutes a critical feature of the journey for it is important that the devotee arrives at each sacred site just at the time of year when its particular value is being celebrated. The result of this is that large numbers of pilgrims inevitably gather together at certain sacred sites at particular times, bringing wealth and foreign news from all directions to a central place of exchange and this is of enormous importance to local economies. An important aspect of the tradition, then, is that every local festival is as much market day as religious and social event but, however much trading and bartering are engaged in *en route*, it is generally true to say that pilgrimage among the Buddhists remains a genuine act of religious piety.

An entire literary genre seems to have been devoted to sacred sites since Asoka first engraved upon rock a record of his own pilgrimage to Bodhgaya. Local pamphlets devoted to the particular legends of their area have for centuries been a traditional feature of the major sites and these provincial materials in turn have regularly been taken and incorporated into long guidebooks covering the entire circuit route in terms of the history and significance of all that may be encountered along the way. In their treatment of such things as *stūpa*s, temples and images, these guides often prove to be valuable historical documents, while in their treatment of sacred springs, lakes, rocks, caves, mountains, trees and the rest they may also record an enormous wealth of folklore. 'Pilgrims' guides' have also been produced to such mythical sites as Śambhala, the kingdom in Central Asia within which the teachings of Kālacakra are supposed to have been preserved; Sukhāvati, the Western Paradise of the Buddha Amitābha; the continents of Uttarakuru and so on around Mount Meru as well as various heavens and hells that constitute features of early Buddhist cosmology.

Twenty-four sacred sites of the *tantra*s

With the rise in India of the tantric school of Buddhism (Vajrayāna), a series of twenty-four or thirty-two sacred places of pilgrimage were defined on the basis of the fundamental myth concerning the *buddha*s' overthrow of the demonic Rudra (Maheśvara) and his hordes. In a former age, it is said, all beings were gods possessed of bodies of light and they lived in bliss. Eventually, however, due to their craving for sensation, beings began to materialise in physical form and dwell upon the earth, eating solid food. The first areas to become inhabited by these *deva* from the sky were the seats (*pīṭha*) of Pullīramalaya, Jālandhara, Oḍḍiyāna and Arbuda. Then the nearby seats (*upapīṭha*) of Godāvarī, Rāmeśvara, Devīkoṭa and Mālava were occupied by the *gandharva* and so those eight places became known as *Khecarī* '(inhabited by) those who move in the sky'.

After that, the fields (*kṣetra*) of Kāmarūpa and Oḍra were adopted as the homes of *yakṣa* while the nearby fields (*upakṣetra*) of Triśakuni and Kośala became the abodes of their servants. Fierce *rākṣasa* moved into the areas (*chandoha*) of Kaliṅga and Lampāka and their servants came to dwell in the *upacchandoha* of Kāñcī and the Himālaya. Because these eight places were occupied by beings from the earth they became known collectively as *Bhūcarī*, 'roaming the earth'.

Then the subterranean *nāga* took control of the meeting places (*melāpaka*) Pretapurī and Gṛhadevatā while the nearby meeting places (*upamelāpaka*) of Saurāṣṭra and Suvarṇadvīpa became overrun with their servants. Finally, the *asura* emerged from the dark depths of Mount Meru and occupied the charnel grounds (*śmaśāna*) of Pātaliputra and Sindhu, their servants inhabiting the nearby charnel grounds (*upaśmaśāna*) of Maru and Kulatā. These eight places subsequently became known as *Pātālavāsinī*, '(occupied by those who) dwell beneath the ground'.

Then there arose in the world the proud spirit Maheśvara whose misuse of sacred teachings had caused him to become very powerful and dangerous. Soon he had taken complete control of the twenty-four places and all the gods and demons who dwell therein became his subjects. Instructing them in the ways of vicious depravity, this evil ruler encouraged his followers to prey upon human beings for food and thus throughout the world it was a time of great fear. Malicious demons were to be encountered roaming abroad both day and night. In their hands they carried sharp tridents (*khaṭvāṅga*) and other weapons, and upon their bodies they wore human and animal skins for clothing. Adorning themselves with the shining bones of their victims, these demons wore tiaras of skulls upon their heads while around their necks hung garlands of severed heads dripping with blood. Whenever they were thirsty they would satiate themselves on human blood and at night they would cohabit with one another's wives.

Witnessing this dreadful situation upon the earth and deeply moved by the plight of suffering humanity, the *buddha*s assembled together on the peak of Mount Meru and elected from among their ranks the *bodhisattva* Vajrapāṇi to subdue the monstrous tyrant. His body having been blessed by the *Tathāgata* Vairocana, his speech by Amitābha, his mind by Akṣobhya, his attributes by Ratnasaṁbhava and his deeds by Amoghasiddhi, the invincible Vajrapāṇi confronted the demon Maheśvara on the summit of Mount Malaya and overthrew him. The body of that proud spirit was cast down from the mountain with such force that his dismembered parts were scattered into the eight directions. Maheśvara's head landed in the south at a place called Body's End, his heart landed in the east at Sitavana, his intestines at Lankakuta to the west, his genitals at Padmakuta to the north, his right arm to the southeast at a place called Self-formed Mounds, his left arm at Secret Great Pleasure to the southwest, his right leg fell at Lokakuta in the northeast and his left leg at Creeping Great Laughter in the northwest. These sites subsequently became famous as 'the eight great charnel grounds' (*aṣṭamahāśmaśāna*), and thus the number of sacred places associated with this myth is raised to thirty-two.

With the overthrow of their lord Maheśvara, the various gods and demons who had been his subjects were converted by the power of Vajrapāṇi to the path of Buddhism. The twenty-four places under their control thus became incorporated into 'the kingdom of Buddhahood': the *maṇḍala* or sacred domain of the wrathful (*heruka*) *buddha*s. There can be no doubt that *yogin* devotees of this cult of wrathful *buddha*s undertook the arduous trek from site to sacred site around India as part of their devotional worship. Carrying tridents and wearing necklaces of bone, these tantric pilgrims (*kāpālika*, 'adorned with skulls') proclaimed the defeat of Maheśvara by mimicking his attributes and visiting those very places where once he held sway. There they would gather together and celebrate the rites of enlightenment and the triumph of good over evil.

Spirit of the earth

A simpler parallel to this story is told with regard to the conversion of Tibet. That country, it is said, was under the sway of an ogress who resisted every attempt by humans to introduce to her realm the teachings of the Buddha. In this case, however, the actual landmass of the country was said to be the body of the ogress who was finally subdued by the construction of *stūpa*s and temples upon her heart and limbs which rendered her immobile and thus incapable of further harm. Around the central temple upon her heart, an inner series of four constructions pegged down her shoulders and hips, an intermediate series pegged down her elbows and knees, and an outer series pegged down her wrists and ankles. Those original thirteen sites of her subjugation remain places of worship and pilgrimage to this day.

Sacred dimensions of architecture

As a map of the state of enlightenment, the tantric *maṇḍala* is generally square in form with the centre, marked blue, as its most sacred spot. Around this in the four directions stand the white, yellow, red and green courtyards spoken of above. These five areas comprise the floor-plan of a divine residence with four doors, before each of which stands a large triumphal archway (*toraṇa*). The palace is overhung with projecting roofs from which dangle an abundant array of precious jewels and it has an upper storey with a dazzling *vajra* spire rising skyward from the centre. It rests upon a solid, unshakable, foundation and is surrounded by circular rings of lotus petals, *vajra* lattice and mountains of fire.

Many attempts have been made to represent this ideal of sacred architecture in bricks and mortar and every Vajrayāna temple is equated with the *maṇḍala* in the minds of those who worship there. The large temple complex of Samye (bSam-yas, eighth century CE), the first of its kind to be built in Tibet, was conceived outwardly as a map of the cosmos with its central and outlying buildings standing for the *axis mundi* Mount Meru and its surrounding islands of habitation. Inwardly it was modelled on the divine architecture of the *maṇḍala* with different floors dedicated to specific deities of the Vajrayāna pantheon. Later temples at the dawn of the second wave of Buddhist traditions to enter Tibet followed this plan even more rigorously. In western Tibet, for example, the temple at Tabo built by Rinchen Zangpo has a specially built *maṇḍala* house and at Alchi stands the three-storeyed temple called Sumtsek, both of which were purpose-built for the bestowal of Vajrayāna empowerments.

For the purposes of general assembly, however, although ideationally perfect, the *maṇḍala* with its square design and radial symmetry is ill-suited to ritual requirements. The four-doored sacred prototype is generally found inadequate to cope with the need to position the images, the offerings and ritual paraphernalia, the senior monks, the musicians and the main body of the *saṅgha*, each in prescribed hierarchical order for the performance of the rites. For temples of assembly, then, the radial symmetry of the ideal *maṇḍala* plan quickly gave way to the more practical arrangements of bilateral symmetry about a single axis leading from the main door to the high altar. The radial plan remained, however, viable for special 'initiation chambers' within which few people were expected to gather at a time, or for small shrines and other buildings not intended for human entry. It also remained perfectly acceptable to the Hindu architects of India and Nepal who tended to construct one house as a temple for the god, into which the priest alone could crawl, and another (*maṇḍapa*) for the assembly of a congregation of worshippers. Such an arrangement could not meet the special requirements of the egalitarian Buddhist *saṅgha*, however, and thus Buddhist temples in general do no more than reflect the glory of the sacred *maṇḍala* palace in the minor decorative features of their architecture. Thus the triumphal archways of the *maṇḍala* are replaced in Buddhist temples of the Kathmandu valley by decorative plaques placed over the doorways, and rows of lotus petals, and ornamental carved friezes depicting loops and tassels of jewels are incorporated within the structure of the temple walls.

With the growing influence of Vajrayāna ideas, the architectural forms of *stūpa* and *maṇḍala* began to converge. One of the earliest extant representations of the *maṇḍala* form, in fact, is the ninth-century *stūpa* of Borobudur in Java, now recognised as a depiction of the Vajradhātu *maṇḍala*. In Tibet the 'great *stūpa* of a thousand images' (*sKu 'bum mchod rten chen po*) in Gyantse deliberately sets out to recreate in architectural form a vast array of *maṇḍala*s in over seventy chapels on five storeys. Countless temples, Buddhist and Hindu, epitomise the *maṇḍala* ideal in the jungles of Cambodia and throughout southeast Asia and each one of these magnificent edifices carries the transcendent notion of sacred space to the mortal realm of humanity.

The tantric *maṇḍala*, however, is not merely to be located in the mundane, external world. As the absolute paradigm of sacred place it is considered to embody a transcendent ideal, the roots of which are to be found in the heart of wisdom. The peaceful Buddha, surrounded by his retinue of *bodhisattva* sages, is taken to be the prototype of the peaceful *maṇḍala* assembly, while the wrathful *heruka* and his conquered retinue, consisting of former acolytes of Maheśvara, is the prototypical *maṇḍala* of wrath. The essential *maṇḍala* of buddhahood, in either peaceful or wrathful form, may be contemplatively generated in the mind on any occasion, for its true nature is an archetype of manifestation beyond manifestation itself. The pillars and beams, the foundation platform and the walls and so on of the divine palace, within which the *maṇḍala* deities reside, are constructed of sacred doctrine so that the entire edifice is a construct of truth, not of materiality. Its depiction in form, therefore, is a representation of *Dharma* in exactly the same way as the *stūpa* looked at above.

Unification of outer and inner

Taking the *maṇḍala*, then, as equivalent to all *dharma*s or aspects of realisation and its path, the *yogin* contemplates the eight great charnel grounds around the sacred periphery as the eight levels of consciousness (*vijñāna*) within his own nature. Recognising all appearances (eye consciousness), sounds (ear consciousness) and the rest as inherently perishable (*anitya*), empty (*śūnya*), unsatisfactory (*duḥkha*) and lacking a 'self' (*anātman*), he casts their impure natures out to the eight great charnel grounds and thereby purifies his perception of reality. As a pilgrim to the holy places of the external world, the *yogin* visits the *pīṭha* and is said thereby to achieve the first *bhūmi*, or stage of the *bodhisattva*'s path, called Joyous. Travelling to the *upapīṭha* he attains the Immaculate. As he reaches the *kṣetra* and *upakṣetra* he traverses, in turn, the stages called Radiant and Flaming. In similar fashion the *yogin* gains the stages called the Invincible, Manifest, Far-Reaching, Immovable, Excellent Intelligence and Cloud of *Dharma* as he continues on his pilgrimage to the *chandoha*, *upacchandoha*, *melāpaka*, *upamelāpaka*, *śmaśāna* and *upaśmaśāna*. These ten stages of the *bodhisattva*, together with the ten perfections (*daśapāramitā*) simultaneously accomplished on his journey, constitute the final stages of his path to perfect enlightenment (*samyaksaṃbodhi*) leaving nothing more to be achieved. By the placement of his body in sacred space the *yogin*'s mind has reached its goal, becoming liberated in the *Dharmakāya* where the minds of all *buddha*s reside.

For the sake of the world, however, in fulfilment of his Mahāyāna vow to liberate all beings, the *yogin* should strive to perfect the internal *maṇḍala* of his form (the *rūpakāya*). With the help of a manuscript 'traveller's guide' he may thus undertake an internal pilgrimage to those twenty-four sacred places where once dwelt the beings from the sky, the earth and the regions below the earth. These groups of places and the deities attendant upon them are contemplatively to be metamorphosed by the *yogin* and integrated within the subtle system of pathways (*nāḍī*) and energy nodes (*cakra*) within his body where they are to be thought of as the retinues of his mind, speech and form.

A tantric pilgrim's guide to medieval India

Pullīramalaya in the outer world are the 'mountains of abundance' (Paurnagiri), the Malaya range on the western Ghats abounding in sandalwood trees. Within the body this site is to be equated with the forehead from where a pathway carries energy (*prāṇa*) to the fingernails, toenails and teeth. It is guarded by the wisdom *ḍākinī* Pracaṇḍā and her male consort Śikhaṇḍakapālin, and the *yogin* on his pilgrimage should worship that divine couple there.

Jālandhara stands at the confluence of three rivers in the district of Kangra (Himachal Pradesh) where there are to be found sacred springs and a natural blazing of fire from the earth. The site remains popular to this day with pilgrims who go there to bathe in its holy waters (modern name: Jawalamukhi). The *yogin* should contemplate this site as the 'aperture of Brahmā' upon the top of his skull where heat rises and three pathways meet. Pathways radiate from that place, the home of Caṇḍākṣī and Mahākaṅkāla, carrying energy to the hairs of the *yogin*'s head and body.

Oḍḍiyāna in the west (now Pakistan) is a triangular area in the Indus Valley that has been blessed by countless *vidyādhara* and *ḍākinī*. The people of that region are said to be possessed of great wisdom and this corresponds in the body to the right ear, the abode of Prabhāmatī and Kaṅkāla, from which pathways carry subtle energy to the pores of the skin.

According to the ancient texts, Arbuda (Taxila, also known as Vajrakūṭa) was a peaceful, prosperous area of wooded slopes abundant with cattle. The abode of Mahānāsā and Vikaṭadamṣṭrin, it corresponds in the body to the spine from which flow pathways of energy for the flesh.

Godāvarī, across the valley to the west of the Vindhya mountains, is known as 'the place of the cow's gift'. It is said that in former times a Nepalese cowherd lost one of his cows in the hills and when he finally found the beast her udder was empty. Seeing a nearby hollow in the ground full of milk, he dug into the earth and discovered a buried Śiva *liṅga* and a black stone flask of nectar marked with the triangular sign of origination (*dharmodaya*). The correspondence of this in the body is the waxy hollow of the left ear from which radiate pathways to the muscles and tendons. It is known as the home of Viramatī and Svaravairiṇa.

To the east of Bodhgaya lies an area of forest where once the king Rāmeśvara had his city. There is a rock nearby, the shape of which reminds one of a horse's mane and it is said to be the abode of Kharvarī and Amitābha. Within the body it is the harmonious spot between the eyebrows from which radiate pathways to the bones.

Devīkoṭa, the abode of the goddess, is an ancient temple of Umā built by king Deśopāla within which are to be found two images of the goddess that look like eyes. It is situated at a distance of four *krośa* (a little over two miles) from the town of Pancapata in Bharendra and it is said that those who gaze upon the images sometimes see their own form. The abode of Laṅkeśvarī and Vajraprabha, its position in the body is the eyes from which flows a pathway to the liver.

Mālava in central India is a district made beautiful by white flowers, said to abound with horses. It corresponds to the shoulders, the abode of Drumacchāyā and Vajradeha, from where there is a pathway that flows to the heart.

Those eight sites of the sky-travelling ones are arranged in the body as a circle (*cakra*) for the mind. Now, with regard to the eight places of those who roam upon the earth, these constitute within the body a circle of speech.

In the hot place to the east known as 'the form of desire' (Kāmarūpa), there is a hollow shrine like an armpit within which the triangle of origination may sometimes be discerned upon the rock by those of much merit. Airāvatī lives there, together with Aṅkurika. Its place in the body is marked by the two armpits from which travel pathways to the eyes.

Oḍra in the kingdom of Daśaratha in the south is famous as 'the place of nourishment'. It is said that a deity once took residence there within a stone shaped like a breast and sustained the happiness and prosperity of the kingdom. Mahābhairavī and Vajrajaṭila dwell there now and their place within the body is the breasts which provide sustenance and joy. Pathways from there convey *pitta* ('bile', one of the three vital humours) to the rest of the body.

Triśakuni is the 'triple intersection' where the rivers Ganges, Indus and one of their tributaries meet. It is a most charming and agreeable place, constantly resounding with the calls of ducks, storks, geese, swans, parrots and other birds. There is a natural stone there in the form of the triangle of origination, the abode of Vāyuvegā and Mahāvīra. In the body it is located at the navel, the triple intersection of the three primary *nāḍī*, from where a pathway flows to the lungs.

Kosala in the west of India is just one *krośa* from the kingdom of Prasenajit. In the place of meditation there, there is a symbol (*liṅga*) with the shape of a nose. The home of Surābhakṣī and Vajrahūṃkāra, its place in the body is the top of the nose from where a pathway flows down to the garland of intestines.

Kaliṅga is in the area of Hastidhara ('having elephants', possibly Hastinapura), about twelve *yojana* (fifty miles) from Bodhgaya where meadow and forest meet. It is a region inhabited by *preta* (insatiable ghosts) and the abode of Syāmādevī and Subhadraguṇa. It corresponds in the body to the mouth from where a pathway travels all the way to the colon.

Lampāka is situated beyond the territory of Turkestan, a place inhabited by non-humans where water beats against the rocks. Its name derives from a certain neck-shaped rock in the vicinity that seems to hang down (*lamba*) from the side of the mountain. Subhadrā and Vajrabhadra live there and it corresponds in the body to the throat from where there runs a pathway to the stomach.

Of Kāñcī the ancient guidebooks say: 'At a distance of twelve *yojana* from Turkestan is the district of Kāñcī where there is to be found a large boulder in the shape of a heart'. Current opinion, however, identifies this city with modern Kanchipuram, not far from Madras. It is said to be a place of clarity where all the people are possessed of wisdom. Hayakarṇī lives there with Mahābhairava and their abode within the body is the heart from where a pathway moves downward for the elimination of faeces.

In the district of Himālaya there stands the sacred mountain Kailash from which the waters of our world (the Indian subcontinent) flow down. There, on the shore of lake Anavatapta ('never warm', now identified with Manasarovar), stands the sacred Jambu tree from which our world derives its ancient name of Jambudvīpa, 'the isle of Jambu'. Among the twenty-four places, Mount Kailash is possibly the most famous of all, a favoured destination of pilgrims from every school. Known among Hindus as the sacred abode of Śiva, this mountain has been the site of countless legends and miraculous events as recorded in the guidebooks of

Buddhists and non-Buddhists alike. From the mouth of an elephant to the south of that place is said to arise the Sutlej river which eventually joins the Indus. From the mouth of a horse to the east arises the Brahmaputra. From the mouth of a bull (or peacock) to the west arises the Karnali which joins the Gogra and ultimately the Ganges. From the mouth of a lion to the north flows the great river Indus. The *ḍākinī* Khagānanā lives there with Virūpākṣa and their abode in the body is the penis because water also flows out from there. A subtle pathway from that spot carries energy to the centre of the hairline.

Now, with regard to the eight sites formerly inhabited by those from the nether regions beneath the surface of the earth, these are to be understood within the *maṇḍala* as comprising the circle of the body.

The region of Pretapurī is a desolate and uninhabited area at the border of India and Tibet. It is very difficult to obtain food and drink there or to satisfy any desire. Mountains of rock tower ominously overhead and precipitous gorges loom beneath one's feet. The pathways are slippery and uneven and only those *yogin*s of the highest calibre venture there to meditate. It is known as the abode of Cakravegā and Mahābala and because it is a region of insatiable desire characterised by chasms it is equated in the human body with the vagina. Subtle pathways from there convey *śleṣma* ('phlegm', one of the three vital humours) to the rest of the body.

'The residence of the deity' (Gṛhadevatā) is an arbour of willow trees (or reeds) in Khotan marked by a sacred rock with the shape of a pyramid. It is the abode of Khaṇḍarohā and Ratnavajra which, in the body, is identified with the anus. Subtle pathways from that region serve to expel purulent matter from the body.

Saurāṣṭra is a place of great strength. Some identify it with Varanasi while others say that it is the city of Bumu in Turkestan. The land in that area is strong and supportive of all that is built upon it so within the body it is equated with the strong thighs that serve to carry the trunk. Sauṇḍinī and Hayagrīva live there and it is the seat of the pathways that convey blood throughout the body.

Suvarṇadvīpa is 'the golden island' of Sumatra that lies in the ocean to the east of India which some identify with the country of the glorious king Maṇicūḍa of China. It is said that one's prosperity greatly increases in that place. It is the home of Cakravarminī and

Ākāśagarbha. Within the body it is the shanks where the pathways of perspiration are to be found.

With regard to Nagara, some say that it is the city of the *rākṣasa* in Sri Lanka while others identify it with an area on the borders of India and Kashmir. The site is marked by an outcrop of rock resembling the five-fold hood of a *nāga* king and for this reason it is associated in the body with the five toes which project from the foot in a similar manner. Suvīrā and Marari live there and pathways from the toes convey fat.

Sindhu is the old name for the Indus valley which divides the areas of Jalandhara and Turkestan. It is famous as the abode of many *ḍākinī* and is given as the residence of Mahābalā and Padmanarteśvara. Its place in the body is the instep of the foot from where pathways convey tears.

Maru is an area of rocky caves situated to the north of Jalandhara. The caves particularly favoured by *yogin*s for their meditation in that place, are quite inaccessible from below and may only be reached by descending on ropes from above. It is the abode of Cakravartinī and Vairocana which, in the body, is the thumbs. Pathways from there convey watery spittle throughout the body.

Kulatā is another rocky area in the foothills around Lahoul. It is said to be a peaceful place of pleasant contact where the *yogin* should worship Mahāvīryā and Vajrasattva. In the body it is the knees from where pathways convey mucus.

With regard to these twenty-four sacred places of pilgrimage, the *yogin* (*siddha*) Saraha has said: 'I have visited in my wanderings *kṣetra* and *pīṭha* and *upapīṭha* for I have not seen another place of pilgrimage blissful like my own body' (*Dohākoṣa*). 'Pilgrimage' in this context is to be understood as the movement of the subtle airs and humours along the internal pathways of the body, experienced by the *yogin* as bliss. The various *ḍākinī* to be worshipped by Saraha at those sites are of the variety known as 'naturally-' or 'simultaneously-born' (*sahaja*). Other *yogin*s on the path would conjure up those partners in their minds and worship them in the form 'generated by meditation' (*samādhija*), or summon them by means of spells (*mantraja*), or seek them in the sacred places of pilgrimage in the external world (*kṣetraja*). In the light of the tantric theory of correspondences mentioned above, however, the truly enlightened *yogin*, whose residence is the central palace of the divine *maṇḍala*, moves freely within the sacred space of his own wisdom which pervades both inner and outer phenomena without distinction. There he enjoys the blissful company of the elements which are, for him, the best of consorts. Wherever he roams he remains at the epicentre of sacred space for his natural abode is always at rest at the foot of the tree of enlightenment.

FURTHER READING

Basham, A.L. (1954) *The Wonder That Was India*, London, Sidgwick & Jackson.

Bechert, H. and Gombrich, R. (eds) (1984) *The World of Buddhism*, London, Thames and Hudson.

Berkson, C. (1986) *The Caves at Aurangabad: Early Buddhist Tantric Art in India*, New York, Mapin International.

Boord, M.J. (forthcoming) *Maṇḍala Meaning and Method*, London, Kailash Editions.

Dahman-Dallapiccola, A.L. (ed.) (1980) *The Stūpa: Its Religious, Historical and Architectural Significance*, Wiesbaden, Franz Steiner Verlag.

Dorje, G. and Kapstein, M. (eds and translators) (1991) *The Nyingma School of Tibetan Buddhism: Its Fundamentals and History*, by Dudjom Rinpoche, Boston, Wisdom Publications.

Dowman, K. (1987) *Power Places of Central Tibet*, London, RKP.

Dutt, N. (1980) *The Early History of the Spread of Buddhism and the Buddhist Schools*, Delhi, Rajesh Publications.

Gomez, L. and Woodward, H. (eds) (1981) *Barabudur: History and Significance of a Buddhist Monument*, Berkeley, University of California.

Hazra, K. (1984) *Buddhism in India as Described by the Chinese Pilgrims, CE 399–699*, Delhi, Motilal Banarsidass.

Lamotte, E. (trans. Sara Boin-Webb) (1988) *History of Indian Buddhism*, Louvain, Institut Orientaliste.

Pal, P. (1982) *A Buddhist Paradise, the Murals of Alchi*, Basel, Ravi Kumar.

Slusser, M. (1982) *Nepal Maṇḍala. A Cultural Study of the Kathmandu Valley* (2 vols), Princeton, Princeton University Press.

Snellgrove, D. (1987) *Indo-Tibetan Buddhism*, London, Serindia.

Strachan, P. (1989) *Pagan Art and Architecture of Old Burma*, Whiting Bay, Kiscadale.

2. Christianity

Douglas Davies

Christians have many sorts of sacred places including cities, geographical territories, and churches. Some of these are pilgrimage centres, places where miracles are believed to have happened. Most are actual geographical locations as with Jerusalem, Rome, or the local church, but some, like heaven, belong to the realm of belief, imagination, and hope. It is very easy to discuss sacred places that can be located on ancient or modern maps, but it is much more difficult to talk about those 'places' that are often described as though they exist in a physical way but which belong essentially to the world of faith and certainly cannot be visited today. The Garden of Eden and Heaven might be two obvious examples.

When Christians talk about these 'places' they use language in a special way, often without realising it. This can be a problem because it touches the way different Christians interpret the Bible and talk about their faith. The major difference is between those who hold a literal interpretation of the Bible and those who bring to the text various other means of interpreting it and who, for example, are happy to see parts of the Bible as poetic, metaphorical, or theological expressions of belief.

This is not a particularly new problem in Christianity since in the early fifth century CE Augustine devoted chapter 21 of Book 13 of his remarkable work *The City of God* to the question of whether the Garden of Eden stories in Genesis should be interpreted in allegorical terms to refer to 'spiritual meanings' or in a more literal sense to refer to a real place. He concluded that it was perfectly proper to use the stories to derive additional meanings 'provided that the history of the true and local . . . paradise . . . be firmly believed'. Augustine was happy with the idea that Eden could represent the bliss of the saints or could stand for the church itself, or that the four rivers flowing from Eden could be seen as the four gospels, but whatever else was said he believed that Eden was an actual place where actual people lived. For him Eden lay at the heart of human history and the dealings of God with humankind. Some modern-day Christians would agree with him, but many other believers, who accept the modern world-view grounded in evolution, read the Genesis stories as theological truths about God and humanity rather than as literal accounts of human origins.

Jerusalem and Babylon

One of the best examples of this literal and metaphorical interpretation of sacred places focuses on Jerusalem, a city which makes its appearance in the Bible as the capital of Judah, and the site of the Temple or holy place of the Jews. As such it plays an important part in the history underlying the Old Testament and the account of God leading the Jews into the land divinely promised to them. In the sixth century before Christ it was overcome and many of its citizens were deported to Babylon. Psalm 137 expresses the hopelessness of the exiles in Babylon:

> By the waters of Babylon we sat down and wept,
> when we remembered thee, O Zion.
> They that led us away captive required of us a song,
> and melody in our heaviness, saying,
> Sing us one of the songs of Zion.

They find themselves quite dispirited as they ask, 'How shall we sing the Lord's song in a strange land?' In this poignant question Babylon symbolises alienation from the sacred place of Jerusalem or Zion. After the Exile, Jerusalem was rebuilt with its second Temple which served as an important centre for worship and a focus of Israel's identity. Yet further political disaster led to this temple being profaned in the second century BCE. The third Temple was established only in the generation before Jesus and plays a significant part in the New Testament accounts of his life. This temple, in its turn, was destroyed by the Romans in 70 CE, an event which marked the end of any centralised Jewish sacrificial worship.

Although these temples were interpreted by the Jews in terms of their faith as important sacred places for the worship of God, they all actually existed in a physical location. To this very day Jews in Jerusalem regard the Western Wall as part of the remains of Solomon's Temple, and it serves as a sacred place for prayer and lamentation over the downfall of Israel's temples.

The site of the last Temple is now partly covered by the Dome of the Rock, a sacred place for Muslims who believe that it covers the rock from which Muhammad ascended to heaven. This kind of interpretation shows how places come to play an important part in the practical life of religions even if beliefs associated with them cannot be proved historically or even in terms of the actual world in which we live. The idea of a heavenly Jerusalem in Christian thought offers a dramatic example of the way an actual place comes to function symbolically as an expression of faith and hope.

Heavenly Jerusalem and heaven

In the Book of Revelation, placed at the very end of the New Testament, there is a vision of 'a new heaven and a new earth', and of 'the holy city, new Jerusalem, coming down from God out of heaven' (Rev. 21:1–2). This image united together two features of Old Testament thought: the one spoke of the sky as heaven (Gen. 1:8), and also as the abode of God (Eccles. 5:2), while the other depicted Jerusalem as the earthly city where God dwelt in some symbolic way. By the first century CE heaven is widely seen as the place where God reigns and the faithful find their ultimate life (Matt. 5:12). Numerous other references occur in the New Testament (e.g., 2 Cor. 12:2–4) and are perhaps best summarised in the very opening words of the Lord's Prayer as presented in Matthew's Gospel: 'Our Father who art in heaven' (Matt. 6:9).

The link between the Christian idea of heaven and the image of Jerusalem is one of the strongest marks of the fact that Christianity emerged out of Judaism. It was developed by later Christians to the point where heaven came to be viewed as the actual place into which people passed after death. This belief is enshrined in many Christian liturgies, hymns and prayers. The biblical image of the descent of Jerusalem from heaven was, for example, taken by Bernard of Cluny in the twelfth century as the basis for his hymn 'Jerusalem the golden'. For him the heavenly Jerusalem – with milk and honey blessed – reflects the promised land of the Old Testament. He speaks of 'those halls of Zion, all jubilant with song', of 'the throne of David' surrounded by a triumphant 'martyr throng' of Christians who have 'conquered in the fight'. Christ is there as their Prince, surrounded by 'many an angel', while the daylight is serene and the 'pastures of the blessed are decked in glorious sheen'. Bernard ends his hymn with a prayer which says much about a type of popular Christian piety that probably extends from the days of the first disciples to the present:

O sweet and blessed country,
The home of God's elect!
O sweet and blessed country,
That eager hearts expect!
Jesus, in mercy bring us
To that dear land of rest:
Who art with God the Father,
And Spirit ever blest.

Very similar thoughts come from Thomas à Kempis (1380–1471), who is reckoned to have written 'Light's abode, celestial Salem'. This hymn speaks of heavenly Jerusalem as an image which serves as a vision that brings peace to the believer. It is a place of unending worship, as befits the dwelling of God, and in it the human body will ultimately be transformed:

O how glorious and resplendent,
Fragile body, shalt thou be,
When endued with so much beauty,
Full of health, and strong and free,
Full of vigour, full of pleasure,
That shall last eternally!

This hymn, like many other hymns of heaven, can help believers think about themselves by providing a framework for reflecting upon contemporary experience and giving life a sense of direction. At certain periods in the history of Christian movements, especially during times of evangelism and revival, the idea of heaven as a real place seems to become increasingly important to people. This was true in many parts of Britain and America during the later nineteenth and early twentieth centuries. 'Sacred Songs and Solos' was one famous hymnbook that grew out of that period of largely Protestant evangelism, and was used by many different Christian denominations. Of its approximately 1,200 hymns more than a hundred are devoted to the idea of heaven and to a heavenly life after death. The general outlook of many such hymns is expressed in one that runs:

> There's a land that is fairer than day,
> Any by faith we can see it afar,
> For the Father waits over the way,
> To prepare us a dwelling place there.

A chorus takes up this hope in the repeated refrain:

> In the sweet by and by,
> We shall meet on that beautiful shore.

Many of these hymns contrast the hardship and pain of life on earth with the joy and pleasure of heaven in quite a literal way.

Heaven on earth

It is quite easy to see these hymns as examples of a heavenly reward following earthly hardship or, as the popular expression puts it, as 'pie in the sky when you die'. It is probably true that many Christians and converts who have sung these hymns with gusto have had relatively low standards of living. What is interesting is that heaven as a future place is practically ignored in the Charismatic form of evangelism that emerged in many parts of Britain and the United States of America from the 1960s onwards, and which involved a kind of religious revivalism among people of relatively high standards of living. In 'Songs and Hymns of Fellowship', published from the late 1980s and much used by enthusiastic Christian groups, practically none of its six hundred items deals with heaven as a place. Instead tremendous emphasis is placed upon today's experience of God and the powerful presence of the Holy Spirit.

Another historical period, that of the Industrial Revolution in Britain, illustrates a similar yet slightly different attitude towards the idea of Jerusalem as God's special city. During the period of approximately 1750–1850, Britain shifted from being a largely agricultural to an industrial society. There were many consequences of this and one of them involved uncertainty and fear resulting from rapid change in customs and social habits. The change of the century in 1800 was one trigger to some people's imagination, and caused them to wonder if it heralded some portentous event such as the Second Coming of Christ and his thousand year reign on earth as part of the establishing of the kingdom of God. These millennial movements often took the idea of a new Jerusalem as a dominant theological motif. At just this time, in 1804, William Blake published his poem *Milton* which includes the section entitled 'Jerusalem'. This was, much later, set to music by Hubert Parry and has come to be one of the best known of all English songs, ending with the strident affirmation:

> I will not cease from mental fight,
> Nor shall my sword sleep in my hand
> Till we have built Jerusalem
> In England's green and pleasant land.

Here the Jerusalem of the Old Testament combines with the Jerusalem of Christian hope to fire and motivate an attitude to the land and society of England. He sets Jerusalem against the image of the 'dark Satanic mills' of the industrial revolution and in doing so he echoes a recurrent theme in Christian thought about the world as a sacred place. The issue focuses on contradiction between the belief that God is perfect, powerful and responsible for creating this universe, and the actual human experience of life as flawed and problematic. The world is both wonderful and terrible. It is aweful in the two senses of the word, it both strikes terror into us and draws our profound admiration. To explore this theme of the dividedness of the world we turn to the accounts of creation in Genesis.

The Garden of Eden

The myths of creation presented in the first book of the Bible (Gen. 1:1–2:3 and 2:4bff.) raise many themes founded on the basic belief that God made the universe and everything in it. God is said to have looked upon all that he had made and saw that it was good (Gen. 1:31), but the picture of perfection, of the whole world as a sacred place, is soon fractured and flawed through human disobedience. This act of human wickedness is often called the Fall, and is depicted in Genesis as having both moral and physical consequences for humanity. The mythical figures of Adam and Eve become ashamed of themselves before God (Gen. 3:10). Eve is told that she will have pain in bearing children (Gen. 3:16), and Adam is similarly told that only through the sweat of his labour will the ground yield any harvest. God curses the very ground because Adam disobeyed the divine command not to eat from the forbidden tree growing in the Garden of Eden (Gen. 2:15–17).

The Genesis story of Adam and Eve soon comes to a critical climax as the guilty pair are thrown out from this place of perfection which now comes to be protected by the heavenly creatures, the cherubim, and by a similarly supernatural flaming sword which guards the way to the tree of life (Gen. 3:24). All these features, events and characters are described in strongly mythical language and spell out the fact that God is responsible for the creation of the universe, that God is the source of commands that must be obeyed, and that humanity is imperfect and responsible for imperfection.

The promised land

The Book of Genesis continues its stories of Adam and Eve after their expulsion from Eden; the great flood is one episode through which God condemns evil. But God also establishes a covenant with certain chosen individuals, and with Abraham in particular God establishes a covenant and promises to give him and his descendants a land as their home and inheritance (Gen. 12). As the narratives of the biblical stories progress the descendants of Abraham come to feature as those who inhabit their promised land, who go into captivity in Egypt, who leave in a great exodus and wander as pilgrims in the desert before settling fully in their promised land. That land of Canaan comes to be viewed in some way as a sacred place.

Christianity, emerging as it did from Judaism and inheriting the Jewish scriptures, also inherited these images of divine covenant and promise. But in the process of time these motifs of faith were elaborated and developed into more abstract ideas. The promised land of the Jewish people is transformed through metaphor to become an image of heaven. Life on earth is taken to be a pilgrimage through a wilderness to the promised land of life after death.

One of the hymns to emerge from the creative work of William Williams in Welsh Christianity in the eighteenth century is entirely grounded in this image of pilgrimage to heaven as the promised land. 'Guide me O Thou great Jehovah, pilgrim through this barren land', pray the worshippers who acknowledge themselves to be weak and in need of God's powerful hand. The images of the Old Testament are then brought into play. The fire and cloudy pillar that led the Israelites through the wilderness (Exod. 13:21), and the supernatural rock that was the source of water, these must now succour the believer, as must the 'bread of heaven' or the manna that God provided (Exod. 16:15). The hymn-writer then uses the image of the river Jordan to symbolise death and asks that God will calm him, 'bid my anxious fear subside', and bring him safe to heaven, 'land me safe on Canaan's side'. The hymn typifies the Christian experience of life as transitory, as a pilgrimage, as a movement to heaven and to God. In the New Testament this is most clearly expressed in the Letter to the Hebrews where many of the themes we have already considered are closely linked.

The writer of Hebrews roots Christian understanding deep in the Old Testament, painting a picture of Abraham and Sarah as journeying to the land of God's promise but dying before they had attained the final goal, a goal which Hebrews sees as heaven itself, a better country which is itself symbolised by the heavenly city (Heb. 11:16). In one verse Hebrews unites these images, as Christians are encouraged and exhorted in their faith because, 'you are come to mount Zion, to the city of the living God, the heavenly Jerusalem' (Heb. 12:22).

In all these texts and hymns there is a kind of supernatural geography, a territory of faith, in which believers see themselves depicted as part of the great community of believers down the years all moving towards God's final sacred place. But on the way they encounter and are encouraged by actual and local sacred places which help them to their goal. But what are sacred places in Christianity? How did they originate? What purposes do they serve?

In answering these questions we also explore the rich diversity of Christian ideas of the sacred in sacred places.

Holy people and sacred places

The first three hundred years of Christian history were marked by sporadic persecutions which resulted in the deaths of many individuals who were regarded as martyrs. Their tombs were held by the faithful to be places of special significance and even of religious power. The anniversary of a martyr's death was often celebrated at the tomb as a kind of 'heavenly birthday'. A *martyrium* was a special building set up as a shrine for the site of death or for the body of a martyr; they often resembled the mausolea which pagans built to honour their dead. It was only after Christianity became the official religion of the Roman Empire in the early fourth century under the authority of Constantine that believers were able to express and practise their religion in a more public way. This included an increased access to martyrs' tombs. In later centuries they would become important for pilgrimages.

Relics

What made these sites especially significant were the actual physical remains of a martyr's body. These relics were often treasured as the central possession of a church and marked, in some physical way, the continuity of the faithful with those who had given their lives for their faith in Christ. At the level of popular religion these relics were often reckoned to possess special powers which could, for example, heal people. In twelfth-century Europe relics played an increasingly important part in popular religious life; indeed it was the century of relics. Many important churches kept lists of the relics they owned and which they obtained either as gifts or through exchange with other churches. The relics not only reckoned to include pieces of the bodies of martyrs, but embraced an extremely wide variety of things including, for example, 'Our Lord's shoe, his swaddling clothes, blood and water from his side, bread from the feeding of the five thousand and the Last Supper . . . the rods of Moses and Aaron, relics of St John the Baptist' (Bethell 1972: 67).

While some relics of saints and martyrs may have been genuine, it is probable that very many were not. But genuine or not, the relic could serve as a concrete expression of the faith of past believers and as a focus for the faith of the living. This tradition became particularly important in the Roman Catholic Church where, until the present day, it became customary for every new altar to have a martyr's relic within it. It even became customary for the priest to begin the eucharist with an acknowledgement of the relic's presence by kissing the altar. The importance of relics to the faith of the twelfth century was linked with the fact that the Crusades led to many relics being brought back to western Europe.

Relics are widely significant in the Greek Orthodox tradition. So, for example, a special cloth containing a relic in one of its corners is placed on new altars as part of the total process of consecrating a church. Relics in general play an important part in Orthodox life and in some ways function like an icon, as a medium through which a saint or other sacred person may influence the living in some beneficial way. The Second Council of Nicea, held in 787, established the importance of icons and pronounced an anathema, a denunciation or formal curse, on anyone who denied the significance of relics. That Council made relics necessary for the consecration of a church. So a Christian sacred place was intimately associated with sacred persons through their relics.

Relics still play a part in many religious and social activities in Orthodox and Catholic contexts. St Spyridon, for example, died in the middle of the fourth century CE. He is said to have suffered and survived the persecution of the Roman Emperor Diocletian and to have taken part in early Christian Councils. Various miracles were also associated with him, including the delivery of the island of Corfu from its enemies. His whole body is now kept as a relic on Corfu and on the Saturday before Easter Day it is carried around the streets of the city in a religious procession before being returned to the church where it normally remains. Thousands queue to kiss the feet of St Spyridon and to gain the benefit of so doing.

Sacred places for burial

Churches built over the martyred remains of the faithful served as points of attraction for Christians, not least as far as their own burial was concerned. It became desirable to be buried near a saint or a relic for a variety of reasons, but principally in the hope of gaining some sort of protection from them. To cope with the increased demand, many churches were expanded in size to accommodate the burial of larger numbers of Christians within their walls. As time went on churchyards and cemeteries immediately outside the church building took on the nature of sacred places for the burial of the dead.

The idea of consecrating ground specifically for the burial of the faithful emerged from the original desire to be buried near to a saint or relic whose very remains consecrated an area. Indeed, the first formal ritual for consecrating a church as a church, apart from the earliest practice of simply holding a eucharistic service there, came with the bringing of a relic to place in the new altar of a church. By the eighth and ninth centuries this pattern was established and in many respects it is based on the model of a burial. The symbolic 'burial' of a relic in the altar established the church as a sacred place for Christian worship, and for the subsequent burial of Christian people.

One of the most interesting examples of death in relation to sacred places is currently found in British crematoria. Crematoria have only become popular in Britain since the 1960s so that by the 1990s approximately seventy per cent of dead people are cremated. The crematoria themselves are not built, owned or run by the churches, but largely by local authorities. Still, funeral services are conducted in them, usually by ministers of religion, and research shows that increasing numbers of people say that they think crematoria are sacred places. The sense of sacredness seems to be associated with the dead and the rites performed for them. As individuals gain experience of crematoria by attending funerals at them, so they regard them increasingly as sacred places. In some respects this resembles the early Christian experience of building churches over the tombs of the celebrated dead.

Holy rites make sacred places

Baptistries provide another example of sacred space to emerge very early in Christian history. Baptism was the major ritual for entering the Christian religion and was interpreted as a form of death to an individual's old way of life and entry to the new life of faith. The octagonal architectural form of baptistries in the fourth and fifth centuries often followed that of a mausoleum, and this was usually intentional, as in St Ambrose's fourth-century church in Milan. Symbolically speaking, this was because the baptistry, as a place of spiritual rebirth, was also a place of death to the old nature.

Ritual often works in a way that adds many layers of meaning to objects used, to actions performed, and to the places where rites take place. The architectural significance of the baptistry as a form of grave is repeated in the water of baptism as representing the waters of the Red Sea through which God's chosen people were delivered from captivity, just as they are waters of cleansing, and waters of birth. For Christians the underlying significance both of baptism and of death lay in the death and resurrection of Jesus Christ. In theological terms the font of baptism represented death because it stood for the death which Christ had undergone, just as it also represented the tomb from which he rose from the dead.

Just as baptism unites believers with the death and resurrection of Jesus, so burial associates them with his death in anticipation of their resurrection on the pattern of his rising again to life. This demonstrates the important theological point that in Christianity sacred space is predominately Christ-focused.

Miracles make sacred places

Some places become sacred because it is believed that something miraculous took place there, as with the Holy Land, given that name because Jesus was born and lived there. Several important holy sites in Europe resulted from appearances of the Virgin Mary in visions to the faithful. One of the best known is Lourdes in southern France. There the blessed Virgin is believed to have appeared to a young peasant girl, Bernadette Soubirous, in 1858. In fact there were some eighteen appearances in all, lasting over a period of five months. When the girl asked the apparition who she was the Virgin identified herself as the 'Immaculate Conception'. Some of the faithful interpret this title as rather miraculous in itself since it was only four years earlier that the Pope, Pius IX, had formally announced the doctrine of the Immaculate Conception of the Blessed Virgin Mary, a doctrine that some think would hardly have been known to a poor miller's daughter in rural France.

Whatever was the case, the girl believed that she was commanded to build a church, and that the Virgin's appearance was marked by a miracle in the form of a spring of water. After a difficult period when she was, inevitably, questioned about all these beliefs, Bernadette's claims were widely accepted, so much so that Lourdes has become a major sacred place where many come for healing to the waters of that miraculously occurring spring. The Roman Catholic Church authorities also accepted the account of the visitation by canonising Bernadette in 1933.

Pilgrimage and sacred places

Today many thousands of people travel to Lourdes each year as pilgrims. As we have already said, one major reason for so doing is in the hope of being healed from physical complaints through the miraculous waters. But for many of those who are not healed other benefits are obtained, not least a sense of an increase or strengthening of faith. And, when people travel in groups, they also often sense a depth of unity with one another.

The desire to visit sacred places involves many reasons and touches deep desires in human life and religion. One important dimension in the pilgrimages of Catholic religion lies in the belief that merit can be gained through pilgrimage. The hardship of the journey, along with the devotion shown in the worship at shrines along the way and at the final pilgrimage centre, all bring merit to the individual. This merit can be set against their load of sin as far as the final judgement is concerned, an idea fostered in medieval Catholic life because pilgrims were able to procure indulgences from the Pope in respect of their pilgrimage. Various sacred sites were ranked in order of priority according to the merit gained from them. So, for example, two visits to St David's in Pembrokeshire in Wales were equal to one visit to Rome. Other major sacred sites of European pilgrimage included Canterbury, where the Archbishop Thomas à Becket was murdered in 1170 after being in conflict with King Henry II. Many miracles were recorded in relation to his shrine and he was, in fact, canonised in 1173. Chaucer's *Canterbury Tales*, written in the late fourteenth century, show how popular pilgrimage was at that time.

Modern Christian pilgrimage

One of the most popular modern pilgrimages in Britain is to the Shrine of Our Lady of Walsingham. It was believed that the Virgin appeared in 1061 to the Lady of the Manor at that village in Norfolk and commanded that a replica be built of Mary's house in Nazareth. Popular tradition adds that this house was built with the help of the angels. A priory was later built on the site, incorporating the house and close to miraculous wells of water. Walsingham became not only one of the leading British shrines, but also one of Europe's most important pilgrimage centres, but it was destroyed in 1538 by Henry VIII who had himself visited the shrine. One suggestion is that he was disappointed because he had not received the male heir to the throne which his visit and prayers had requested. Despite centuries of neglect, Walsingham has risen again in the twentieth century as a place of pilgrimage for both Anglicans and Catholics.

Another dramatic origin is described for the pilgrimage centre of Fatima in central Portugal. Three local children reckoned to have seen a lady appear on five separate occasions in 1917. She called herself 'Our Lady of the Rosary', and requested that a chapel be built there. Subsequently, many people have been drawn to that spot and have experienced a strengthening of their faith as a result of their visit. This, along with many other sites, such as Santiago de Compostella in Spain, where St James is supposed to be buried, still serve as sacred places where pilgrims go in hope and with many motivations. For some the desire is for physical answers to physical needs as in sickness, for others the need is to be associated with the saints of the past and their perspective on life. The Church of St Francis of Assisi in Italy is one example of a less dramatic saint who himself found his life changed after his own pilgrimage to Rome where he was touched by the poverty of some people there. He died in 1226 and was canonised in 1228. Many who visit Assisi as tourists will have in mind this man who lived simply and in harmony with nature. They are reminders of the fact that there was something of the tourist in the medieval pilgrims, just as some modern tourists may, occasionally, have a pilgrim spirit.

Power, merit and sacred places

But for the pilgrim proper there is always the underlying belief that sacred places are places of power. Standing out from other spots, they focus the piety and faith, power and merit, of Christian saints of the past, and trigger a faithful response in living Christians. In this way sacred places afford a concrete expression of the idea of the Communion of Saints, the view that all believers of all ages and places, and whether dead or alive, share together in the life of God. In a vague way people sometimes talk about places having a special 'atmosphere' or a power that enables them to express their faith and hope in a way that makes sense to them. This kind of 'power' has been widely discussed in the study of many different religions and seems to be an expression of human nature at large. The phenomenologist of religion, Gerardus van der Leeuw, used the experience of power as the basis for his extensive and influential study *Religion in Essence and Manifestation* (1933).

In theological terms sacred places are special because they speak of the power and grace of God that was evident in the lives of past believers. The stress is on God rather than on the individual saint. But in terms of practical religion among people at large, particular saints and particular places do come to have a special relevance of their own; the individuality of saints or of miracles comes to the fore and attracts the faithful of today. Here, once more, the relationship between formal theology and the piety of folk-religion is complicated and many individuals will bring their own interpretation to sacred places. This is perfectly understandable since experience is a very personal thing even if the church or group to which someone belongs tries to lay down a pattern for experience and faith. This is especially important as far as salvation is concerned.

Christianity is a religion of salvation. It teaches that God shared in human life through the person of Jesus of Nazareth and that he died to save human beings from the consequences of their sin. Salvation means that the individual is caught up into this divine work of love and mercy, though different Christian traditions explain and interpret how this is done in various ways. Some have taught that merit which influences personal salvation for good can be gained through pilgrimages and worship at particular shrines. It was an important feature of Catholic Christianity in the medieval period. Part of the outlook of the Protestant Reformation lay in a fundamental objection to special merit being gained in such ways.

ICONOCLASM

In some places it led to iconoclasm, to the destruction of sacred places of pilgrimage, and of relics. There was a great debate about this in the Orthodox Church during the Iconoclastic Controversy from about 725 to 842 CE, which resulted in the retention of icons as part of faith and worship. The Protestant Reformation, involving many political and economic reasons alongside religion, sought to remove these external sources of religious power and merit and to replace them with a doctrine of faith that lay in a personal and interior attitude towards God. The dissolution of the monasteries in England under Henry VIII in the 1530s brought to an end a whole world of monks, sacred places, relics, and pilgrimages. The influence of the Puritans in the early seventeenth century reinforced and extended these objections to a priestly way of life and control of popular religion. But, despite this, the human attraction to sacred places remained, albeit in a transformed fashion.

Protestant sacred places

The 'sacred places' of Protestant Christianity obviously involved churches, just as among the Catholics and Orthodox, and these will be described in detail below (see pp. 53–4). Here we return to a theme raised at the beginning of this chapter to discuss 'places' which are mentioned in the Bible and which function in the imaginative realm of faith, in particular the places associated with the life, and especially, the death, of Jesus. Having already considered the symbolic significance of Eden, Babylon, Jerusalem, and heaven, we now focus on Calvary, and the places of Christ's passion.

Although the Protestant Reformation retained the sacraments of baptism and the eucharist, along with an official ministry to lead the church, its stress lay on preaching and the Bible. Excessive emphasis on the lives of the saints, miracles, pilgrimages and sacred places gave way to a rediscovery of the stories of the Bible and the significance of the Bible for understanding God, the Christian religion and personal dimensions of faith.

The death of Jesus lay at the heart of Protestant religion. His life was interpreted as morally perfect and as a preparation for him to be the sinless sacrifice for the sin of the world. But equally important was the fact that God had become a particular individual in the process of identifying with humanity, and that one person was a man who lived in Palestine. He inhabited the holy land and was associated with the landscape of the Old Testament. He was, in other words, part and parcel of the sacred places of the Bible.

The Incarnation, the process of God incorporated with humanity through the flesh and blood of Jesus, brought an added quality of the sacred to the established location of the holy land. His passion and suffering in the garden of Gethsemane, and his crucifixion on the hill of Calvary added even more to their sacredness, and preaching developed the vision of God's acts in time and place and sought to catch up modern believers in those events. The sacred places of Protestantism were based on the locations of Christ's life, taken up into the imagination of believers through these sermons, Bible stories and, as time went on, especially in hymns. These are sacred places of a spiritual geography.

Religious experience and hymns as art

Religious experience underlies such spiritual geographies just as it does any physical sacred space. The Protestant stress on conversion involved a psychological sense of freedom from guilt and release from sin. It emphasised the crucifixion as the scene of salvation and encouraged the sinner to identify with the death of Jesus on the cross. Many hymns reflected on the experience of salvation from sin by describing the place and event of the crucifixion.

Mrs C.F. Alexander's children's hymn, written in the mid-nineteenth century, has become very popular with adults also. Its familiar lines tell their own story:

There is a green hill far away,
Outside a city wall,
Where the dear Lord was crucified,
Who died to save us all.

This and many other hymns ask the believer to imagine Christ's death and to enter sympathetically into his pain. The hymn replaces the relic as an object of meditative adoration, as it also replaces the icon as a medium of obtaining religious benefit. In the hymn, 'When I survey the wondrous cross on which the Prince of glory died', written in the early eighteenth century, Isaac Watts speaks of counting his richest gain as loss, and as pouring contempt on all his pride when he considers the pain suffered by Christ. The imaginative mind sets to work through the lines: 'See from His head, His hands, His feet, Sorrow and love flow mingled down', and bring the hymn-writer to decide that, 'Love so amazing, so divine, Demands my soul, my life, my all'.

One of the most direct expressions of the retrospective hymn is by J.R. Wreford and Samuel Longfellow:

When my love for Christ grows weak,
When for deeper faith I seek,
Then in thought I go to thee,
Garden of Gethsemane

There I walk amid the shades,
While the lingering twilight fades,
See that suffering, friendless one,
Weeping, praying there alone.

When my love for man grows weak,
When for stronger faith I seek,
Hill of Calvary, I go
To thy scenes of fear and woe.

Other hymns make similar points and show the attractive power of the poetic description of sacred places in the devotional life of believers. So even in churches where there would have been no pictures or stained glass windows giving an artistic portrayal of biblical scenes, those scenes would be created in the mind's eye of believers as they sang and as they heard sermons describing the death of Jesus. Their own experience of forgiveness would often be intimately linked with those images and, in many respects, that experience would help give a sense of the sacred to the picture. Their own awareness of God in the present would feed back through their belief to give the sense of God's influence in that picture of the passion of Jesus centuries ago.

The experiences of many Protestants would have taken place in religious buildings. Those buildings may have been devoid of Christian art and bare of ornament but, as we have suggested, they were filled with imagery through hymns. The power of music to fill a building and add yet another dimension to words must never be ignored when considering sacred places in Christianity. This is especially important for those situations where believers argue that their building is not sacred in any special way. Statements about the ordinariness of religious buildings raise an important theoretical problem in religious studies precisely because certain ideas, such as ritual and sacredness, carry particular meanings for some religious practitioners which differ significantly from those used by scholars of religion.

The sacred and ritual in theology and religious studies

Some Protestant groups, for example, identify ritual and sacred places with Catholic theological ideas from which they want to distance themselves. In practice, such a group might carry a Bible in a procession and give it a place of great honour but would strongly deny any suggestion that this constituted a ritual. For them ritual is something that Catholics or other people do, and which does not belong to true religion. To the anthropologist or student of religion anything can be a ritual, because for them the word bears no theological overtones. This obviously raises a technical problem in religious studies which will be considered below.

It is an intriguing fact that some Christians are extremely happy to say that their meeting places are sacred while others strongly deny it. We have already given the example of Catholics and Orthodox incorporating relics into their altars as one way of consecrating – or making sacred – their churches. By stark contrast there are contemporary groups of Christians, especially those who are said to belong to House Church Movements, who specifically use for worship buildings originally built for quite different purposes. One contemporary group meets in a disused cinema and specifically tries not to put religious signs or symbols into the building. For them the idea of a sacred place does not make much sense, they see the group of believers as the real focus of God's activity through the Holy Spirit and not the place as such.

One key to understanding the difference between Christians happy with having sacred places and those unhappy with the idea lies in the sacraments and the emphasis placed upon sacraments and upon an authorised priesthood trained to administer them. We saw much earlier in this chapter how sacred places emerged in Christianity in relation to martyrs and dead believers, and how baptism soon led to special buildings being used by Christian groups. Similarly, the early rise of the eucharist as a central Christian ritual meant that churches emerged as places invested with a distinctive significance. Alongside the rites of baptism and death there emerged a formal priesthood of people whose task it was to conduct the ceremonies and to minister to the congregations associated with the church. When these factors are taken together it is easy to see how the church building as the place for sacraments and priesthood came to be viewed as different in some respects from other public places.

But in addition to these ritual elements, the experience of the members of the congregation cannot be ignored. There is strong evidence from social anthropology to suggest that experience and ritual are closely related through a kind of awareness that comes from ritual and which grows and develops through practice and throughout life (Sperber 1975). Such 'symbolic knowledge' influences the emotional life of people and supports a pattern of moods which particular religious traditions favour. If people find that through particular rites within a church they gain a sense of God's presence and activity, it is to be expected that the place itself will be viewed in a special way as a place of encountering God. Many religious rituals are rites of intensification where the same behaviour is repeated over and over again on a regular basis; a particular building is likely to enhance and foster this pattern of feeling. People may even become so attached to a particular place and to the sacredness of it that they are unwilling to change their behaviour for fear that their experience will suffer.

Another dimension of human life closely related to patterns of experience concerns personal identity. One theory suggests that things which help confer a sense of identity upon individuals are themselves highly valued in return (Mol 1976). They may be valued to such an extent as to be sacralised and given a status beyond the normal range of mundane significance. When this occurs over long periods of time the dimension of history comes to be added to personal identity and individual experience, giving a place particular cultural significance and making it very sacred.

The sense of identity people gain through religious and cultural life comes through many channels but their own religious tradition is likely to focus it for them in some very particular way. Catholic theology has traditionally stressed the sacraments while Protestant and Reformed outlooks have emphasised the Bible and its teachings. One of the consequences of these differences lies in the way churches have been organised as far as their sacred dimensions are concerned.

Churches as sacred places

Because Christianity was from the beginning a congregational religion it engaged in church-building to provide meeting places for members as soon as was practicable and publicly possible. This has continued in the great majority of Catholic, Orthodox, Lutheran, Anglican, and Reformed traditions as well as among many independent and sectarian forms of Christianity. The actual theological and symbolic significance attached to these various buildings has differed quite considerably. Where the liturgy of the eucharist has been central, as in sacramental forms of the religion in Catholic, Orthodox, Lutheran, and Anglican traditions, the altar has been set apart and has become the most sacred part of the church building. With time the area around the altar came to be set apart as a specially sacred area, sometimes called the sanctuary. It is worth remembering that the word 'sanctuary' has been used not only for this area but also to describe the place reserved for the clergy, and also for a church as a whole. This indicates that the idea of a sacred place can vary depending upon circumstances and context.

The altar itself has occupied several different positions in Christian churches. When churches are built as rectangles facing the east it has often been the case that altars, their sanctuaries, and the preferred place for burials have been at the most eastwards part of the building, often interpreted in relation to the rising sun and the symbolism of the resurrection, but this is only one partial explanation. 'The eventual triumph of the east end has yet to be fully explained in either architectural or liturgical terms' (Colvin 1991: 128). In practical terms the eastward sanctuary of churches in many parts of Europe often allowed the nave, or the large central body of the church, to be viewed as less sacred and to be used for all sorts of non-religious purposes. In fairly recent centuries the naves of some churches have been used for meetings and even sporting activities.

But altars have also been placed in the centre of churches both in some early Christian buildings of a Basilica pattern derived from pagan buildings, and in modern churches such as the Roman Catholic Cathedral at Liverpool. When this is done the church becomes a much more obviously sacred building with relatively little scope for other activities unless the altar is portable. In churches of a strongly sacramental character, including Roman Catholic and Anglican churches, the consecrated communion bread or host is sometimes kept in a special tabernacle placed above the main altar or else in a Lady Chapel. Where this occurs it provides a focus for piety and devotion and constitutes the centre of the sacred place because it is believed that the real presence of Christ is located within that host.

The Lutheran tradition has retained the central focus of an altar but it also stresses the pulpit for the preaching of sermons which are focused upon the teaching of the Bible. The Anglican Church has also focused on the altar as the central sacred spot in a church, even though its Reformed strain of thought led to pulpits being added to every Church of England parish by law in 1604.

In the Reformed Protestant traditions of the more Calvinist perspective, the Bible and the preaching of God's word have assumed paramount importance; it is the pulpit and not the altar that assumes pride of place, as in the Church of Scotland and many Nonconformist churches. Often the pulpit is placed centrally, with a high vantage point, and above the table that is used instead of an altar for the eucharist. In the earliest Christian congregations it appears that sermons were given from the bishop's chair which was itself centrally placed and marked off from the rest of the building.

So we see that the Reformed tradition does not speak of a building as intrinsically sacred, even though the preaching and reading of the Bible are treated with great respect, and hymn- and psalm-singing are given an important place in worship.

Churches: sacred or not?

The difference between Christian groups over the idea of the sacred presents an interesting problem because religious studies regularly uses the category of the sacred in its analysis of religious behaviour. There are at least two ways of dealing with this issue. First, by not using the category of the sacred for those Christian groups which have no theological need for it or which specifically avoid it, their churches could simply be described as locations of ritual, and the very term sacred space be avoided altogether. In many respects this is exactly what tends to happen in the social anthropology and sociology of religion where the idea of sacred spaces and sacred places is largely ignored when analysing religious behaviour. Secondly, it is in the phenomenology and history of religions that the idea of the sacred is most often used when describing religious events. It is possible to retain this perspective by defining sacred places in a strictly descriptive way to apply to places where people gather for religious ritual irrespective of how those people define their own places. On this basis the former cinema in which a religious group now meets is as much a sacred place as an ancient cathedral. The terms are used by the scholar and not by the participant. As long as terms are defined and clearly used there is little danger of making a major error of judgement over the question of method. This example clearly illustrates the fact that serious study of religion involves an understanding of how the scholar's criteria of analysis relate to the way practising believers think about their religion.

The holy eucharist in sacred and secular places

The case of the eucharist provides another good example of the need to be precise over the categories used to analyse religious behaviour. In the phenomenology of religion, the temples of many religions are often interpreted as representing the centre of the world, or the point of axis and contact between the world of everyday life and the realm of the deity. Such places are reckoned to be sacred precisely because they are the point of contact between God and humanity.

This scheme can be applied to Christianity in several ways. The eucharist, for example, is a strong candidate for being a ritual that links heaven and earth. In the rite, the central history of the faith is recalled and focused in the life and earthly ministry of Jesus. Then in the prayer of consecration the priest asks that by the power of God's Holy Spirit the bread and wine may be to the worshippers the body and blood of Christ. In the medieval period the doctrine of transubstantiation was developed to give a philosophical explanation of how the elements of bread and wine actually came to be the body and blood; in modern life many Christians would not accept that kind of explanation but still find a deep sense of being at one with God through the rite. Although this ritual normally takes place in a consecrated church, it can be carried out anywhere by a suitably ordained priest, whether in someone's home or in a field or factory. In some churches it may even be conducted by someone who is not formally ordained. The significant point is that in this service believers are drawn both into the presence of God and into the history of the life of Jesus. The group celebrating the eucharist comprises the sacred community of believers without having to be in any church building. In other words, it is the community of believers that marks off a sacred territory rather than the other way around. In terms of popular theology this is often argued by saying that the church is people and not a building. As one Christian hymn expresses it:

> For Thou within no walls confined
> Inhabitest the humble mind.
> Such ever bring Thee when they come,
> And going take Thee to their homes.

But preaching is also seen by some, especially in the Lutheran tradition, as providing a moment of communication between God and the congregation. When the preacher addresses the people it is God, they say, who addresses them through the words of the sermon. So the sacred place is the place where the divine word is spoken.

A final example of the sacred place which changes the meaning of the word might be that of self-sacrificial service to one's neighbour. The Christian tradition of care in hospitals and schools and other agencies is an expression of the belief that to serve another human being is to serve Christ. A few Christian groups have seen it as necessary to turn away from formal religious buildings and traditional religious behaviour and expressions of faith in order to pursue a 'secular' meaning of the faith. The German theologian Dietrich Bonhoeffer, who was killed in 1945 because of his part in a plot to kill Hitler, is often seen as a pastor calling other Christians to live fully in a secular world as their Christian duty: 'Before God and with God we live without God'.

The decade of the 1960s was very much a period when phrases such as the 'secular gospel' were popular. The American theologian Harvey Cox's influential book, *The Secular City* (1965), went so far as to say that the Jewish–Christian tradition was the root cause of secularisation. Once Christian faith argues against petty forms of superstition, then it is only a step away from denying any distinctive and particular significance to religious buildings. Here we see the two poles of Christian views of the sacred. The one accepts that sacred places exist as distinct from the rest of life, the other says that all life is equally sacred because God in Christ has become part of it. The one elaborates and develops ritual as a way of focusing on God, the other abandons special Christian places so as to make all places Christian.

This diversity is part of the challenge to religious studies to do justice to what devotees of a religion say, while also describing their behaviour from a non-committed perspective. As a final example we try to do this for one less familiar religious group, The Church of Jesus Christ of Latter-day Saints. In this example we also incorporate many of the central topics introduced throughout this chapter on the sacred in Christianity.

Sacred places in Mormon life and belief

Perhaps the best example of sacred places developing in nineteenth- and twentieth-century advanced societies is found in the Mormon religion. In this final section we explore several important dimensions of 'sacred places' to show something of their variety and the way they operate in the lives of Mormons.

The Church of Jesus Christ of Latter-day Saints, as it is officially called, was founded in 1830 by Joseph Smith in New York State in the United States of America. He, as the first Prophet of the movement, believed God had restored fundamental truths to humankind which had been lost since the early days of Christianity.

Because of this Mormons called their church a Restoration movement. Its central message called men and women to serve God according to these freshly restored truths and religious rites or ordinances in a new land of promise in America. And it is here that the first idea of a sacred place appeared in Mormonism, as the Saints believed that Jesus would soon return and set up his kingdom which would be a kind of New Jerusalem or Zion and would be in America. Thousands of Europeans emigrated to the United States of America in response to this message, and the hymn, 'Come, Come, Ye Saints' gave voice to their hopes and served as an anthem for what were, in effect, migrant pilgrims as they journeyed to their land of promise.

> Come, come, ye Saints, no toil nor labour fear;
> But with joy, wend your way.
> Though hard to you this journey may appear,
> Grace shall be as your day.
> 'Tis better far for us to strive,
> Our useless cares from us to drive.
> Do this and joy your hearts will swell.
> All is well! All is well!

As time went on and the nineteenth century came to a close without the Second Advent of Christ, Mormons came to accept that the Kingdom of God would not take the form of a miraculous divine appearance but of a steady growth of the Mormon Church throughout the world. At the same time Mormons placed increasing stress on buildings they called temples in which special rites were performed. They already had several temples in Utah, notably the Temple at Salt Lake City, and, as the twentieth century unfolded, they began building temples in each continent across the world. As Mormons acknowledged that a geographical Zion was unlikely in the near future their temples assumed the role of being pure and sacred places within an otherwise corrupt world. Sacred buildings replaced the idea of a sacred land.

In the 1990s there are some forty-four Mormon temples distributed throughout the world where members may perform a wide variety of religious rites which cannot be carried out anywhere else. The temple is distinguished from ordinary churches and chapels of Mormonism by being closed to the general public and open only to Mormons who receive special permission to enter them because they live up to the expectations and rules of their faith.

The temple is distinguished from the local chapel or 'stake-house' in a way that many non-Mormons initially find difficult to grasp. The difference is absolutely crucial to understanding the temple as a sacred place and is grounded in the distinction Mormons make between time and eternity. Ordinary chapels exist in time and any rites that take place in them last for the period of life on this earth. So, for example, a marriage conducted in a local Mormon chapel is 'for time', or as it might be expressed in more traditional Christian language, 'till death us do part'. But in the temple things are different. Rites performed in temples are 'for eternity', their effect is for ever and extends into the heavenly domain. So, a marriage that is performed, or 'sealed' in a temple as the Mormons put it, lasts not only for time but for eternity as well. This also applies for other rites as, for example, in the Mormon practice of being baptised on behalf of the dead.

The temple shares in the world of eternity quite closely and is a kind of point of contact between eternity and time. It is not surprising, then, that some Mormons speak of experiencing God, and sometimes their departed ancestors, in more intimate ways in the temple than elsewhere. In this sense, the temple is a clear example of Mircea Eliade's analysis of sacred places as centre-points of religious significance where earth and heaven intersect.

What this also indicates is the fact that for Mormons the life after death involves another sacred place, that of heaven. In Latter-day Saint understanding, heaven is divided into several domains and it is only in the highest one, which they call the Celestial Kingdom, that the fullness of eternity and of encounter with God is possible. And the opportunity for this is available only for those Mormons who have been married for eternity in earthly temples.

We can now see a variety of ideas of sacred places in the history of Mormon religion. There is the idea of an American Zion in which Jesus Christ will appear in his Second Coming, then there are the temples which enshrine eternity, and finally there is the heavenly domain for those who have fullness of life after death.

Another distinctive teaching of Mormonism is that human souls live in heaven before their human life, and ultimately return to that realm after death to be with both God their heavenly father and a heavenly mother. The famous Mormon hymn 'O My Father' expressed this truth and was important in conveying it to many new converts who would not have met that idea in the churches from which they came. The hymn speaks of God as having 'with-held the recollection of my former friends and birth', and of believers occasionally feeling that they are strangers on earth. The idea of heavenly parents is put in the form of a question:

> In the heavens are parents single?
> No, the thought makes reason stare!
> Truth is reason, truth eternal
> Tells me I've a mother there.

The hymn continues:

> When I leave this frail existence,
> When I lay this mortal by,
> Father, Mother, may I meet you,
> In your royal courts on high?

Then the hymn ends by saying that Mormons will return to live forever with their heavenly parents, having accomplished all they had been sent to earth to do. For many Mormons the hymn takes on special significance in relation to Mormon temples where important rites takes place on behalf of the dead.

The sacred in religious places: a conclusion

When people criticise Mormons for the secrecy surrounding their temple rituals they often reply by describing the rites as 'sacred not secret'. This shows the depth of feeling Mormons have towards rites that mean so much to them. It also reflects the much wider religious phenomenon that believers often focus their cherished beliefs on some particular place. The sacred involves the personal and corporate significance of a place which enshrines and focuses vital beliefs, even beliefs that God can be known, worshipped and served at all times and in all places.

FURTHER READING

Augustine, St (1950) *The City of God*, London, J.M. Dent.

Bethell, D. (1972) 'The Making of a Twelfth-century Relic Collection', in G.J. Cuming and D. Baker (eds) (1972) *Popular Belief and Practice*, Cambridge, Cambridge University Press.

Biran, A. (ed.) (1981) *Temples and High Places in Biblical Times*, Jerusalem, Jewish Institute of Religion.

Colvin, H. (1991) *Architecture and the After-Life*, Yale, Yale University Press.

Cox, H. (1965) *The Secular City*, London, Pelican.

Davies, J.G. (1982) *Temples, Churches and Mosques*, New York, Pilgrim Press.

—— (ed.) (1986) *A New Dictionary of Liturgy and Worship*, London, SCM Press.

Leeuw, G. van der (1967) *Religion in Essence and Manifestation*, Gloucester, Mass., Peter Smith (first published, 1933).

Mol, H. (1976) *Identity and the Sacred*, Oxford, Blackwell.

Sperber, Dan (1975) *Rethinking Symbolism*, Cambridge, Cambridge University Press.

Turner, H.W. (1979) *From Temple to Meeting House: The Phenomenology and Theology of Places of Worship*, The Hague, Mouton Publishers.

3. Hinduism

Anuradha Roma Choudhury

As a religion Hinduism is heterogeneous in character. It is a synthesis of many different beliefs and practices, various sets of values and morals, culminating in a way of life. Strictly speaking, it is not a 'religion' in the accepted western sense. Religious and non-religious matters are never truly distinguished in Hinduism. Each and every activity of life is thought to have some kind of divine purpose in it. The ordinary daily chores which are usually seen as 'secular', can be seen by an orthodox Hindu as having some divine potential. Accordingly, the topic of 'sacred place', as the Hindus see it, covers a very broad and varied arena indeed.

As sacredness has a religious connotation, places that are considered sacred are often closely associated with religious worship. In that context, for a Hindu, family shrines, temples, places of pilgrimage, all are considered sacred and will be discussed later. In addition, there are places of natural beauty such as awe-inspiring mountains, vast oceans, peaceful woodlands, which are not directly linked with religious worship but which are still held sacred by the Hindus for their serenity, magnificence and conduciveness to calm and a philosophical mood. Hence, sacred places are not necessarily confined to religious buildings alone, but can be discovered in the context of nature worship of the ancient Hindus (see 'Hinduism' in *Attitudes to Nature* in this series).

Sacred natural environment

MOUNTAINS

Hindus of the past and present have always been attracted by the Himalayas (*Himālaya* = abode/*ālaya*, of snow/*hima*). Its snow-clad peaks, beckoning with undiscovered mysteries and overwhelmingly awe-inspiring height and grandeur, held the Hindu spellbound. The innate humility one experiences in front of such a massive phenomenon develops into the kind of veneration that Hindus feel for this mountain. Though there are other mountains (e.g., Vindhya, Nilagiri, etc.) in India, picturesque enough to inspire Sanskrit poets (e.g. Bhavabhuti of the eighth century in *Uttara-Rāmacharita*), yet *Himālaya* enjoys a special reverence that others do not. It has been revered from ancient times as the abode of the gods of the Hindu pantheon. Durgā, the Universal Mother, also known as Pārvatī (lit. of the mountain/*parvata*) is the daughter of *Himālaya* according to Hindu mythology. Her consort Śiva lives in Kailāsa, a peak in the *Himālaya*, where he performs his long and arduous meditation. There are numerous references of sages (*ṛṣis*) and saints engaged in penances (*tapas*) in the *Himālaya* in the epics *Rāmāyaṇa* and *Mahābhārata* and in various mythological episodes in the *Purāṇa*s (the ancient/*purā* narratives). The classical Sanskrit literature is full of praises for the *Himālaya*. Kalidasa, the most renowned Sanskrit poet, addresses *Himālaya* as *devatātmā* (the Divine Soul or the soul/*ātmā* of the gods/*devatā*) and elevates it to the status of divinity (*Kumārasambhava* I.1).

The symbolism of the mountains is evident even in the architecture of Hindu temples, which are modelled on soaring peaks of natural mountains. The architectural terminology also makes this connection. The crown of a temple is called *śikhara*, a word which also means 'mountain peak' or 'crest'. That a temple can be identified with a mountain peak is seen from the name of Kailāsa Temple in Ellora. In the north Indian style of temple architecture, a conscious attempt to imitate the gradual ascending pattern of a complete mountain range is noticeable in the various levels of a temple complex. The fact that the Hindus chose to model their religious structures on the mountains indicates the sacredness they attach to them. After all, a grand mountain is not just a visual spectacle, but its soaring height symbolises the spiritual height a Hindu hopes to achieve.

CAVES

In association with the mountains, the caves (*guhās*) are also often regarded as sacred places. As George Michell (1977: 69) points out:

> The cave is a most enduring image in Hinduism, functioning both as a place of retreat and as the occasional habitation of the gods. Caves must always have been felt to be places of great sanctity and they were sometimes enlarged to provide places of worship.

The rock-cut temples (e.g., in Elephanta caves), with their interior spaces skilfully hewn and decorated with sculpted images, indicate that the man-made grottoes were considered to be as sacred as their natural prototypes.

The sanctity of the caves is transposed to the innermost sanctuary of the temples, when it is kept deliberately unadorned, small and dark, with no vent for natural light, strongly resembling a natural cave. On entering a temple, the symbolic mountain, a pilgrim gradually progresses towards the interior, the symbolic cave, where the image or symbol of the deity is housed. The progression from light into darkness, from large open foreground, to the small confined sanctum, from elaborately ornate exterior to unadorned plain interior 'may be interpreted by the devotee as a progression of increasing sanctity culminating in the focal point of the temple, the cave' (Michell 1977: 70).

SEA AND LAKES

Just as the grandeur of a mountain humbles the human mind, so does the vastness of a sea. The tranquillity of the sea gives it a meditative and hence a sacred connotation. Peninsular India is surrounded by sea on three sides and there is a tradition of shore-temples built in this sacred environment. The famous temple of Jagannātha (a form of Viṣṇu) is situated in the sea-side city of Puri, in Orissa, on the eastern seaboard of the Bay of Bengal. Further south, by the Bay of Bengal, are the most renowned shore-temples of Mahābalīpuram and Rāmeśvaram temple; and at the confluence of the Bay of Bengal, the Indian Ocean and the Arabian Sea is the temple of Kanyākumārī. The western seaboard is also studded with temples of various dimensions and description, of which the cave temple of Elephanta is particularly eminent. In the epic, *Mahābhārata* (III.118:4), the sea is described as *lokapuṇya*, which literally means 'where people acquire religious merits' (people/*loka*, religious merit/*puṇya*) or in other words, 'sacred/holy to people'. Also, mention is made (III.118:8) of places of pilgrimages by the sea (*tīrthāni cha sāgarasya*). Like many others in search of spiritual realisation in the past, Swami Vivekananda, the Hindu monk of the late nineteenth and early twentieth centuries, chose a rock in the sea at the southernmost tip of India, near Kanyakumari, for his seat of meditation. It is now known as Vivekananda Rock, and it can be seen in the pilgrims' map.

Of the lakes in India, *Puṣkara* lake near Ajmer and *Mānasa Sarovara* near the Kailāsa peak of *Himālaya* in Tibet, are considered specially holy by Hindus.

RIVERS

Rivers in general have very special significance in Hinduism for their life-sustaining and purifying qualities, and the Ganges (*Gaṅgā*) is regarded as the holiest of them all. To Hindus *Gaṅgā* is known as the Mother who 'bestows prosperity' (*sukhadā*) and 'secures salvation' (*mokṣadā*). In *Brahma-vaivarta Purāṇa* (*Kṛṣṇajanma Khaṇḍa*, 34) it is said in praise of *Gaṅgā*:

> She is the source of redemption. . . . As fire consumes fuel, so this stream consumes the sins of the wicked. . . . If a man, at an auspicious hour of time, takes a dip in the holy river, he dwells cheerfully in Vishnu's heavenly world, *Vaikuṇṭha*.
>
> (Kapur Singh 1989: 47)

The water of *Gaṅgā* and its banks are held in such high esteem by Hindus that it is believed that dying at its bank liberates one's soul from the cycle of rebirths. Not so long ago, devout Hindus used to express as their last wish that they should be taken to the bank of *Gaṅgā* in their final hours of life. This final journey is known as *Gaṅgā-yātrā* (journey/*yātrā* to *Gaṅgā*). Such conviction and faith in *Gaṅgā* elevates the river almost to divinity.

Mythologically, *Gaṅgā*, the river of heaven, originated from Viṣṇu's toe. It was brought down to the earth by king Bhagīratha through severe austerities and penances, to wash away the sins of his dead ancestors. Śiva, the Great god (Mahādeva), agreed to hold the first thrust of the tumultuous river falling from heaven in his matted locks, thus softening its blow to the earth. Because *Gaṅgā* was led by Bhagīratha, one of its names is *Bhāgīrathī*. In reality, *Gaṅgā* originates from the Himalayas. At Hardwar (*Haridvāra*) it descends to the plains, and near Allahabad at Prayaga it meets the river *Yamunā*. The meeting point (*saṅgama*) of any two rivers is considered sacred; especially so is the confluence of *Gaṅgā* and *Yamunā*. Hindus gather from all over India to bathe there on auspicious days in order to acquire extra religious merit. All the places, cities and towns through which *Gaṅgā* flows are also considered to be sacred e.g., Haridvara, Varanasi (Banaras), Kalighat (Calcutta), etc.

WOODLANDS

Hindus have a long and ancient tradition of forest culture. Woodland is revered not only for its contemplative atmosphere, but also for the continuing process of renewal of life that goes on in nature. The vedic priests and poets worshipped the forest as *Araṇyānī* (*Ṛg-veda* X.146), the Goddess of the Forest. There is also a whole set of vedic texts called *Āraṇyaka*s (lit. related to *araṇya*/forest). They deal with life during *vānaprastha* (related to *vana*/woodland), the third phase (*āśrama*) of a Hindu's life, the period of retirement. The *tapovana*s (woodlands/*vana*, for religious austerities/*tapas*), frequently referred to in Sanskrit literature, are places where individual sages (*ṛṣi*s/*muni*s) have their hermitages (*āśrama*), and where the setting is ideal for the training of students in religious and philosophical pursuits. Thus, *tapovana*s and *āśrama*s, the seats of educational, intellectual and spiritual interactions, are considered by Hindus as places worthy of reverence. The epic *Rāmāyaṇa* has a whole chapter called *Araṇya-kāṇḍa* (*araṇya*/forest, *kāṇḍa*/chapter – *Rāmāyaṇa* III), where there are many descriptions of *tapovana*s and *āśrama*s of various sages, and references to how revered these places were. The same is true of the epic *Mahābhārata* where a whole chapter (chapter III) called *Āraṇyaka-parvan* (*āraṇyaka*/related to forest, *parvan*/chapter or episode) is dedicated to the life of the Pāṇḍavas, the five heroic brothers, in the forest. In later classical literature also there are ample examples of sacredness that people attach to such *tapovanas* or *āśramas*. For example, in the play, *Abhijñāna-Śakuntalam* (Act I) by Kalidasa, Duṣyanta, the hero says '. . . let us purify ourselves with a sight of the holy hermitage (*puṇyāśramadarśanena tāvadātmānam punīmahe*)'.

Some individual types of trees and plants are also considered by Hindus as sacred (see 'Hinduism' in *Attitudes to Nature* in this series). The *aśvattha* (Ficus religiosa) and *vaṭa* (Ficus Benghalensis) are particularly venerated as having benevolent influence on spiritually aspiring *yogīs* meditating under their shade. The Buddha achieved his enlightenment in Bodhgaya, in Bihar, under such a tree; it later came to be known as the *bodhi* tree (tree of knowledge). More recently, the nineteenth-century Hindu saint, Ramakrishna Paramahamsa, achieved his enlightenment under a *vaṭa* tree in Dakshineshwar in Bengal. The vicinity of these types of trees is considered meritorious. Similarly, as the small plant *Tulasī* (Ocymum sanctum) is worshipped as a symbol of Viṣṇu, the outdoor altar around it is treated with reverence in a Hindu household.

Considering the reverence Hindus attach to their natural environment – mountains, rivers, woodlands, etc. – it is not unreasonable to infer that the sense of such sanctity originated from nature-worship (see 'Hinduism' in *Attitudes to Nature* in this series). Sacredness of a place, therefore, for a Hindu, is not necessarily confined to religious structures made by people.

Places of pilgrimage

Pilgrimage to holy places is not an obligatory duty for a Hindu as the pilgrimage to Makkah is for a Muslim. Yet Hindus undertake long arduous journeys to places considered as sacred. The most commonly believed purpose of this practice is to cleanse away one's past sins and to acquire spiritual merit for one's future life after death. The more austere the journey, the more spiritual merit one gains.

The Sanskrit word for a place of pilgrimage is *tīrtha* (from the root *tṛ*/to cross over). It has several connotations, such as a ford, passage, stairs for descent into a river, bathing place and so on, but all of them are connected with water. In fact, a significant number of the sacred places are located on the banks of bodies of water. This association of water with *tīrtha*s, or sacredness in general, may have continued from a very early period, following from the vedic reverence for water or rivers. In the *Atharva-veda* (1, VI.2–4) water is upheld as the bestower of remedies and protection. At places of pilgrimage where there is no natural water supply, artificial ponds are cut, because physical cleansing of devotees prior to participation in rituals is important.

The term *tīrtha*, apart from having the primary meaning of crossing over water, also has a symbolic meaning. It symbolises the location of the intersection of two realms, the mundane and the spiritual, the profane and the sacred. In that respect, the physical journey to the *tīrtha*s is instrumental in the spiritual progress of the pilgrims.

The practice of pilgrimage (*tīrtha-yātrā*; *yātrā*/journey) must have gained religious significance from very early times. It is given prominence in the *Mahābhārata* and the *Purāṇa*s, where many *tīrtha*s, their presiding deities, the glories and fruits to be gained by visiting, are celebrated at length. In the *Mahābhārata* a major section of the *Āraṇyaka-parvan* (Book of the Forest) is devoted to a grand tour of pilgrimage sites in India (*Tīrtha-yātrā-parvan*, III, 80–93, 109, 114, 118–20, 129, 140–53). Several *Purāṇa*s glorify numerous shrines throughout India, as Morinis (1984: 50) points out (e.g., *Matsya Purāṇa* chapter 13, 103–12, 186–94; *Skanda Purāṇa* chapter 2 called *Tīrtha Khaṇḍa*; *Vāyu Purāṇa* chapters 105–12; *Kūrma Purāṇa* I, 30). In later texts, especially in the *tantra*s, more lists of sacred places and their characteristics appear. Although some of the *tīrtha*s named in the above sources have disappeared and some new ones have arisen (e.g., Puttapurti in south India has become a *tīrtha* this century because of the presence of Satya Sai Baba, the saint of miracles), many of the ancient sacred places named are still regarded as important *tīrtha*s for Hindus today (e.g., Varanasi/Kasi/Banaras).

HOW DOES A PLACE BECOME RECOGNISED AS A *TĪRTHA*?

As mentioned earlier, in India sacred places are often associated with regions of natural serenity and grandeur, especially mountains and rivers. The Ganges (*Gaṅgā*) itself has multiple *tīrtha*s along its banks. Yet not all scenic sites or miles of river-banks are revered as places of pilgrimage. There are several factors which contribute to the transformation of an ordinary site into a *tīrtha* – factors that initiate the development of some kind of religious activity. A *tīrtha* might be a place where an individual achieved recognised spiritual inspiration (e.g., Bodhgaya for the Buddha), or where realisation came to a devotee about his or her deity (e.g., Dakshineshwar for Ramakrishna Paramahamsa, who had visions of the goddess Kālī there), or where an image of a deity was unearthed or miraculously appeared under unusual circumstances, or where the water of a pond or a river was believed to cure diseases, and so on. Some charismatic individuals, both historical (e.g., the Buddha, Chaitanya, Ramakrishna Paramahamsa) and legendary/mythical (e.g., Rāma, Kṛṣṇa) become prominent enough to be remembered with reverence, and therefore the places associated with their lives (places of birth, spiritual enlightenment, preaching, etc.) come to be recognised as sacred.

When a place is considered worth visiting for one reason or another, eventually a temple is built there, dedicated to the deity popular in that region or associated with the individual concerned. Often it is the ruling prince or a wealthy benefactor who endows the land or provides funds for the temple. The erection of a temple itself helps to glorify the site of devotion. It is the prior recognition of the sanctity of a place (*sthāna-māhātmya*; *sthāna*/place, *māhātmya*/glory) that prompts the building of a temple and not the other way round, but once the temple is there, it becomes the focal point of religious activities, a centre for spiritual discourses, a meeting place for devotees. In its turn the temple helps to attract pilgrims from far and wide, making the region into a thriving *tīrtha*.

VARIOUS TYPES OF HINDU *TĪRTHA*

Tīrtha-yātrā is an age-old tradition with Hindus from every part of India. Yet it is possible to identify a body of sacred places of overall importance visited by all Hindus as opposed to *tīrtha*s which are important to the sub-sects of Hinduism and sub-cultural regions. The *tīrtha*s that are mentioned in ancient and classical religious texts are the most revered by all Hindus, such as the famous group of seven *tīrtha*s designated as *mokṣapurī*s (holy cities/*purī* where one gains liberation/*mokṣa*), i.e., Ayodhya, Mathura, Kasi, Kanchi, Avantika, Puri and Dvaravati. Then there are *tīrtha*s visited mostly by the devotees of individual sects: the Śaivas or devotees of Śiva (e.g., Varanasi); the Śāktas or devotees of Śakti/Kālī/Mother (e.g., Kamakhya) or the Vaiṣṇavas or devotees of Viṣṇu (e.g., Vrindavana). Even among the national *tīrtha*s, Kasi/Varanasi and Avantika/Ujjayini are more frequented by the Śaivas, as Śiva is the presiding deity of those two holy cities. Similarly, Ayodhya, Mathura and Puri are the most important *tīrtha*s for the Vaiṣṇavas, as these are the cities associated with either Rāma or Kṛṣṇa (incarnations of Viṣṇu). Other kinds of variations in *tīrtha*s are found on a regional sub-cultural basis. For example, in the Bengal region, which is a stronghold of Śāktas and Vaiṣṇavas alike, Tarapith (Śākta) and Navadvip (Vaiṣṇava) are the most important *tīrtha*s for Bengali Hindus, but may not be so for Hindus from other parts of India.

GROUPING OF *TĪRTHAS*

There is a tradition in India of grouping sacred places in various systems. The seven *mokṣapurī*s, the cities that bestow liberation on the pilgrims, are mentioned earlier. Then there is the group of seven *tīrtha*s (*sapta-tīrtha*, using the primary meaning of water), referring to the seven holy rivers that wash away sins and purify a Hindu, i.e., Ganga, Yamuna, Sarasvati, Narmada, Kaveri, Godavari and Sindhu. The group of four *dhāma*s (holy sites) comprising Badrinath, Kedarnath, Gangotri and Yamunotri, combine together as the *tīrtha*s in the mountainous Garhwal region of the Himalayas. Another version of four *dhāma*s group Badrinath, Dvaraka, Ramesvaram and Jagannatha-puri together. In south India the tendency is to group together *tīrtha*s with shrines of a particular deity, to make a cluster of shrines. For example, the five *bhūta-liṅga*s dedicated to Śiva, the six centres of the deity Murukān, the six *tīrtha*s of Ayyapan (as quoted in Morinis 1984: 46–7) and so on.

In north India, on the other hand, the practice of pilgrimage involves completing a holy circuit within the region of the main centre. For example, in visiting Gaya pilgrims can choose from several rounds consisting of five, eight, thirty-five or thirty-eight stations on the journey. In Banaras (or Varanasi/Kasi) pilgrims can choose from two routes of circumambulation of the city. One consists of five main stations (*pañcha-tīrtha*) and the other of a fifty-mile (*pañcha-kośī*) walk encircling the city, which is considered to be more meritorious than the former. Similarly, as Morinis states:

> A 600-mile course around the Himalayan sites above Rishikesh, including Gangotrī, Kedārnāth and Badrināth, is sacred for its inclusion of the sources of the three main branches of the Ganges: the Bhāgīrathī, Mandākinī and Alakanandā. The grandest circuit of all is that which covers the entire length of the Ganges, beginning on one bank at the source, travelling to the mouth, then returning up the other bank to the source again.
>
> (Morinis 1984: 47)

Different systems of pilgrimage for different sects

THE ŚĀKTAS (DEVOTEES OF ŚAKTI/DEVĪ/MOTHER)

The idea of *Śakti*, on the one hand, is that of a supreme female deity representing the creative energy (*śakti*) of the universe, and on the other hand, she is the protective Mother or Devī. As characteristic of all Hindu deities, *Śakti* has two aspects. As cosmic energy she is formless, boundless and beyond time, but as the Mother she has numerous forms and names (e.g., Kālī, Durgā, Umā, Satī, Pārvatī, Tārā, Chaṇḍī, Chāmuṇḍā, etc.) by which she is affectionately worshipped by the devotees (see 'Hinduism' in *Picturing God* in this series).

The places of pilgrimage of the Śākta sect are known as *pīṭha*s (seats). A *pīṭha* is regarded as the sacred seat where the unmanifest goddess makes herself manifest. It is believed that *pīṭha*s are the places where she is in residence, where she can be approached personally. *Pīṭha*s known as *siddha-pīṭha*s (*siddhi*/enlightenment) are considered particularly effective for acquiring spiritual power, wisdom and bliss (e.g. Tarapith in Bengal).

A myth that links most of the Śākta *pīṭha*s together and accounts for their sanctity is found in diverse Hindu texts, e.g., the

Mahābhārata (XII.282–3), *Brahma Purāṇa* (chapter 39) and several *tantra* texts. The myth is about Satī, who is the daughter of Dakṣa and the wife of Śiva. The narrative runs as follows.

Dakṣa, one of the sons of Brahmā, held a great sacrifice (*yajña*) to which he invited neither his daughter nor his son-in-law, due to some offence he had taken at Śiva's conduct. Satī was offended at this but nevertheless went to the sacrifice uninvited. She felt humiliated by her father who chose to insult Śiva in an open court and Satī took her own life in protest. On hearing this, Śiva charged the place of sacrifice, killed Dakṣa and retrieved the body of his wife. In inconsolable grief at the loss, Śiva placed Satī's body on his shoulder and began his dance of fury (*tāṇḍava*). The whole of creation was threatened by his wild dance. Viṣṇu was asked by the gods to appease Śiva and save the creation. To detach Satī from Śiva, Viṣṇu dismembered Satī's body with his discus (*chakra*). Without the body of Satī Śiva calmed down. The scattered parts of Satī's body fell to the earth and all the places where they landed became the sacred *pīṭha*s.

The list of these *pīṭha*s varies with different versions of the myth, but most commonly known are the fifty-one *pīṭha*s. Each *pīṭha* is identified by the part of Satī's body and the name and form of Devī in which she is worshipped there (e.g., in Varanasi-*pīṭha* where her ear-lobe fell, Śakti is worshipped in the name of Viśālākṣī). These *pīṭha*s are scattered geographically over a large region: Kanchipuram in the south, Hingula in Beluchistan in the west of Pakistan, Kashmir and Nepal in the north and Assam in the east. As Morinis (1984: 20) points out, the myth 'which unites the diverse and dispersed temples of the various goddesses strengthens the unity and organisation of the Śākta sect. The unity is expressed in the concept of each Śākta *pīṭha* sharing in the body of Satī'. The myth also helps to emphasise the sanctity of these *pīṭha*s, each having been energised by the contact of the flesh of the goddess.

Not all the *pīṭha*s mentioned in ancient texts are active places of pilgrimage today and not all the present-day *tīrtha*s are mentioned in the early texts. More recent well-visited Śākta temples are getting recognised as places of pilgrimage. For example, the Kālī Temple of Dakshineshwar, near Calcutta, built in the nineteenth century, is now established as a place of Śākta pilgrimage, due to the association with the saint, Ramakrishna Paramahamsa, for whom Kālī was a living deity.

The images or symbols of the goddess in the Śākta *pīṭhas* are not always in human-like forms. Sometimes they are rocks embedded in the floor of the temple (as at Labhpur, decorated with painted eyes and smeared with vermilion paste) or rough, uncarved stones (as in Tarapith, stored inside a hollow human image of the goddess).

The sect of Śakti is related to that of Śiva. Śiva and Śakti are conceived symbolically as a wedded couple. In every Śākta *pīṭha* Śiva is installed as a *liṅga* (phallic symbol) in a small shrine next to that of the goddess. There he is also visited by the pilgrims but holds a secondary status to that of the goddess.

THE ŚAIVAS (DEVOTEES OF ŚIVA)

Śiva, primarily the destroyer in the Hindu Trinity, is also revered as the supreme ascetic. The Śaiva sacred places are often busy refuges for wandering ascetics/*sādhus* and *yogīs*. In most places Śiva is worshipped in the form of a *liṅga*, a stylised phallic symbol. The *liṅga*-worship may have originated from the pre-Aryan fertility cult which was absorbed by the Aryan Hindus into their cult of Rudra (a vedic god)-Śiva in the post-vedic period. The *liṅga*, as the principal symbol of Śiva, represents his vast generative energy. 'It is said that the symbol has been a conventional image of the god for so long that most of his devotees do not realise that it has any sexual significance' (Cavendish 1980: 24).

The places of Śaiva pilgrimage are known as *kṣetras* (fields). As in the Śākta tradition, the Śaiva tradition also recognises a unity among its holy sites throughout India. The number of Śaiva *kṣetras* varies – five, twelve or sixty-eight. *Śiva Purāṇa* (XXXVIII, 17–20) is the source of detailed accounts of Śaiva places of pilgrimage. It describes twelve *kṣetras* of sacred *liṅgas*, together with their names and the names in which Śiva is known there. For example, in Varanasi Śiva is *Viśveśvara* or *Viśvanātha*, in Ujjayini he is *Mahākāla*, in Saurasthra, *Somanātha* and so on.

In some Śaiva *kṣetras*, *liṅgas* are not installed by humans but are discovered as though they have risen up from the ground by themselves. These are considered to be most sacred *liṅgas*, known as *svayambhū* (self-born) *liṅgas*. For example, in Amarnath, the Himalayan *tīrtha*, the natural *liṅga* made of ice melts away every summer and is naturally reformed in winter.

THE VAIṢṆAVAS (DEVOTEES OF VIṢṆU/KṚṢṆA/RĀMA)

According to Hindu texts (e.g., *Daśāvatāra stotra*) Viṣṇu, the preserver of creation in the Hindu Trinity, is believed to have appeared in earthly forms through various incarnations (*avatāras*) to save the creation from extinction. Rāma and Kṛṣṇa are both described as Viṣṇu's incarnations at different times. Rāma is the legendary hero of the epic *Rāmāyaṇa* and Kṛṣṇa plays an important role in the epic *Mahābhārata*. The sites that are associated with these legendary figures are revered by the Vaiṣṇavas as *tīrtha*s. Viṣṇu himself is said to have visited Gaya and left a two-foot long footprint (*Viṣṇu-pada*) there, which has led to Gaya's sacredness. It can be said that Vaiṣṇava *tīrtha*s are mostly associated with divine individuals.

The Vaiṣṇava sacred places are known as either *dhāma*s (abodes) or *līlā-bhūmis* (*līlā*/play/sporting, *bhūmi*/ground). Places where Rāma led his life are marked as *dhāma*s, e.g., Ayodhya (birthplace), Chitrakuta, Nasik, Sitakunda, etc. But the most holy and most visited are the places of *līlā* (divine play) of Kṛṣṇa. Vrindavana, Gokula, Mathura and Dvaraka are the places in north India where Kṛṣṇa 'played' his role among humans as a youthful cowherd and later as a princely ruler. The historical personage, Gautama Buddha, is also regarded by Hindus as an incarnation of Viṣṇu and thus the sites of important events in his life are revered by the Vaiṣṇavas.

In the Vaiṣṇava pilgrimage tradition there is a second type of personage whose associations are no less important than those of the divinity. The well-known *bhakta*s (devotees) of Viṣṇu/Kṛṣṇa, the saintly individuals who led an exemplary life according to the ideals of Vaiṣṇavism, are held in high esteem, sometimes to the point of deification. Among such celebrated *bhakta*s, Sri Chaitanya (fifteenth century CE) is the foremost. His contribution to the Vaiṣṇava sect by rejuvenating the *bhakti* (devotion) tradition is so great that places associated with him have become Vaiṣṇava *tīrtha*s. Chaitanya was born in Navadvip in Bengal but spent much of his time visiting places of pilgrimage throughout India. The Jagannātha (a form of Viṣṇu) temple of Puri is rendered holy not only by the presence of the deity, but doubly so by its association with Chaitanya. Similarly, all the Vaiṣṇava sacred places that were visited by Chaitanya on his pilgrimage have become enhanced in importance and sacredness. Such places are marked either by a shrine or by an annual festival or fair (*melā*) that developed there. Another Vaiṣṇava *bhakta* who is commemorated by an annual fair (in Kenduli in Birbhum) is Jayadeva, the poet who composed *Gīta-Govinda*, a marvel of Vaiṣṇava literature.

The dust (*dhūli*) from a sacred place has a special significance for a Vaiṣṇava. Gathering the dust off the feet (*pada-dhūli*) of a holy man is a symbol of humility. While visiting *tīrtha*s, the pilgrims rub the dust of the holy place on their forehead and body as a mark of humble devotion.

All three sects – the Śāktas, the Śaivas and the Vaiṣṇavas – however, share some common features in their attitudes to pilgrimage. All hold that visiting a sacred place, or living in one, is meritorious (acquiring spiritual merit/*puṇya*). Even dying in a *tīrtha* is desirable, as it is thought to liberate the soul. This explains why Hindu *tīrtha*s have a significant association with death. *Tīrtha*s like Varanasi, Gaya and Hardwar/Haridvara are celebrated for death-related rituals and acts. As *tīrtha*s are regarded as the crossing points from the mundane to the spiritual world, as the meeting points of humans and the divinity, as places where divinity is in residence and accessible to devotees, all sects recommend pilgrimage to sacred places as a means to spiritual ends. But in reality, only a minority seek liberation (*mukti*/*mokṣa*). The majority seek more earthly rewards such as health, happiness, children, success, cure from diseases, etc.

To discourage people from making pilgrimage for material reasons, all three sects emphasise the purity of mind and intention rather than the actual physical journey itself. Pilgrimage, as an act of devotion, must result from a devotional frame of mind. *Devī-Bhāgavata* (VI, 12.26 – quoted in Labye 1973: 370), a Śākta text, states that 'purity of mind is the best Tīrtha, more holy than *Gaṅgā* and other sacred places'. It is probable that, because the Hindu tradition attaches paramount importance to the spiritual effect of pilgrimage, some thinkers strongly oppose mere observance of geographical pilgrimage. It is easier to venture on a physical journey than to achieve a spiritual discipline. If the soul of the pilgrim has not been led along the path of God, the pilgrimage is futile. The essence of this theme comes through again and again, not only in Hindu scriptural texts, but even in vividly worded folk songs of simple people close to the soil. The *Bāul*s (wandering bards) of Bengal are well known for their concept of God as *maner mānuṣ* (the person living within one's own mind) and the human body as the living temple of resident God.

Sacred buildings: the temples

As sacred buildings, Hindu temples present a vast variety of architecture, sculpture, size and location, depending upon the period, the region and the religious sect of the people building the temple. Nowadays, when the theme of Hindu sacred places is mentioned, non-Hindus immediately think of magnificently ornate temples. It may seem strange, then, to learn that 'not a single text of the revealed scriptures of the Hindus refers to images or temples, and even the epics do not' (Chaudhuri 1979: 90). The early form of Hinduism was without image-worship and without temples. Vedic worship, with its sacrificial fire, was an open-air activity. Even during the compilation period of the two epics, temples do not seem to be around as there is no mention of people visiting temples. Yet there are numerous references to people praying to deities, practising meditation in the Himalayas or in woodland retreats (*tapovana*s), or visiting places of pilgrimage. As mentioned before, the *Mahābhārata* has a whole chapter on pilgrimage (*Tīrtha-yātrā-parvan*). It is most likely that image-worship was introduced by the cults of Śiva, Viṣṇu/Kṛṣṇa and Śakti/the Mother. By the time the cults took firm hold, possibly by the beginning of the Christian era, image-worship in temples was established. It is hard to imagine Hinduism now without the image-worship and temples with which it is identified by the non-Hindu world.

In the Indus Valley excavations, no specific structure was found that can be identified as a temple, though the archaeologists found many examples of female figurines (which, according to some, are examples of image-worship of a Mother cult). N.C. Chaudhuri (1979: 52) points out that the earliest structure which can be regarded as a temple was actually found in Afghanistan.[1] It has been dated as early as the second century CE. It is not certain whether it was a temple for a God or for some kind of imperial cult, like that of the Roman emperors. Two other temples, both dedicated to Viṣṇu, thought to be the earliest specimens of temples in India, are in

Deogarh and Bhitargaon. They are dated approximately between the fifth and seventh centuries CE. An important point of contrast to be remembered in this context is that, whereas south India is known for its profusion of temples that survived through the ages, there is a curious absence of particularly old temples in the Gangetic plains in the north. This is due to the historical fact that they were systemically destroyed by the Muslim conquerors who very seldom invaded the south in the early days.

STATUS OF TEMPLES

Though worship of images in temples is a widely known and accepted practice, it is interesting to note that it is wholly optional. Most Hindus do not need to go to temples, because the worship could just as well be done at home. They visit temples only on special occasions. Moreover, Hindu theologians often maintain that real Hinduism lies in the pursuit of spiritual depth, and worship in temples is only for simple people for whom the highest expression of Hinduism is too abstract to comprehend.

However, the most important point about temples is that they are not, strictly speaking, places of worship, at least not in the same sense as a church is to a Christian on a Sunday. A temple is the 'residence' of a deity. The Hindu term for a temple is *mandira* which literally means 'an abode', 'a dwelling'. In Hindu temples there is installed an image or symbol of a deity who is in residence there. It is the daily duty of the priest, symbolically speaking, to awaken the deity in the morning with musical chantings or songs of praise (*bhajana*s) and then to bathe and to adorn the image. With ritual worship (*pūjā*) food is offered to the deity. In the afternoon the deity is put to rest and the activities quieten down. In the evening the deity is welcomed again with ceremonial prayer with lamps (*ārati*) and entertained with devotional music and dance. (Most classical forms of Indian dance originated from temple-dance. Temples had dedicated female dancers who were married ceremonially to the deity of the temple. See 'Hinduism' in *Worship* in this series.) As Chaudhuri (1979: 90) points out, the 'whole routine of daily worship in temples is only a replica of the daily life of the Hindu king'. A temple is, therefore, not a place where devotees congregate to worship at a particular time on a particular day, but is a place where devotees come to pay their homage to the deity at his/her home at any time of the day they wish.

THE HOUSE OF GOD

Terms like *devagṛha* (*deva*/God/deity, *gṛha*/house) and *devālaya* (*ālaya*/house), denoting temple, clearly point to the belief that, in the house of God, God makes himself/herself accessible to humans in the form imagined by the worshippers. The sacred image or symbol of the deity is housed within the temple in a small sanctuary called *garbha-gṛha* (womb-chamber), a term indicating that it contains the kernel and essence of the temple. The sacred images or symbols are not identified with the deities but considered as the temporary forms in which they manifest themselves after being invited into them by the priest or devotee. The image is not live until the deity is welcomed into it by necessary rituals. Elaborate rituals of consecration of the image are performed before it is ceremonially enshrined. A temple is revered only because it houses the deity or deities. If the rituals are not performed and so the deities are not present, then 'the temple lies dormant as the deities are not "in residence"' (Michell 1977: 62).

THE STRUCTURE OF A TEMPLE

The structure of a Hindu temple is guided by sets of instructions from ancient texts on temple architecture. The architectural rules are dictated by rigid rules of mathematics and symmetry. The shape and the height of the temple, the location of the sanctuary in the temple, the direction in which the temple should face, all are decided by the metaphysical considerations made by ancient Hindu theologians in relation to the cosmos and its creation. The ground plan of a temple is a sacred geometric diagram known as *yantra* (further developed in Buddhism as *maṇḍala*) that symbolises the essential structure of the universe. It is usually a square divided into a number of smaller squares by an intersecting grid of lines. The central square, dedicated to Brahmā, or a prominent deity associated with creation, is to be the base of the sanctuary, which is the focal point of the temple. Around this square are the other squares, dedicated to the planetary divinities, including the Sun and the Moon, guardians of the directions of space, all playing their roles in the universe. By constructing the temple as a miniature of the universe and placing the image of the deity at the focal point in the sanctuary, a symbolic representation is created of the creative energy emanating from the centre. The central square is, therefore, the most significant part of the plan, 'as it is here that the worshipper may experience transformation as he comes into direct contact with the cosmic order' (Michell 1977: 72).

The outer appearance of a temple often resembles a mountain peak (see p. 63 above). Some temples with several tiered arrangements suggest the visual imitation of a mountain range. With the development of building techniques, the tendencies in temple-building to extend upwards seem to aspire also to represent the soaring heights of the mountains.

The tip of the temple, the summit of the symbolic mountain, is positioned precisely over the sanctuary or womb-chamber (*garbha-gṛha*). The highest point of the elevation of the temple is aligned with the most sacred part, the sanctuary that holds the image of the deity. The metaphysical significance of the link between the summit and the sacred centre along an axis is that the forces of energy radiating from the centre project upwards. This upward projection, in its turn, symbolises the 'progression towards enlightenment, and the goal of this journey is identified with the crowning finial of the superstructure of the temple' (Michell 1977: 70). The axis also symbolises the supporting pillar between heaven and earth, and is known as *Meru*.[2]

The womb-chamber (*garbha-gṛha*) also, similar to the axis *Meru*, is a significant feature of temple architecture and probably plays the most important role in temple worship. It symbolises a cave. A cave is regarded as a place of sanctity by Hindus (see above, p. 64). Generally, in Hindu temples the sanctuary, the holy of holies, strongly resembles a cave. It is 'small and dark as no natural light is permitted to enter, and the surfaces of the walls are unadorned and massive' (Michell 1977: 69–70). The analogy of the sanctuary with a cave seems consistent with that of the temple with a mountain. However, later temples do not always follow this convention and in modern temples particularly, the images of deities are placed in well-lit focal points.

While visiting a temple it is customary for a worshipper to go round the central structure of the temple on foot in a clock-wise direction to complete the circle before gradually penetrating inwards. This circular journey is known as *pradakṣiṇa* (circumambulation). Because of the importance of this journey, many temples are furnished with ambulatory passageways, e.g., in the temple of Ramesvaram, one has to walk through a series of enclosures which become increasingly sacred as the sanctuary is approached. Usually the approach to the sanctuary is along an east–west axis. As the direction of the approach is important for reasons of ritual, most temples face east. The worshipper enters the temple from the east, then walks along the ambulatory passage clock-wise in the order, east, south, west, north and back to the east before approaching the interior.

In front of the doorway leading to the sanctuary, there is often a pillared hall called *maṇḍapa*, serving as an assembly hall for the devotees. As Percy Brown (1942: 72) points out, some of the earlier temples indicate that the *maṇḍapa* was a detached building, isolated from the sanctuary by an open space (e.g., in the shore-temples of Mahabalipuram – about 700 CE). Later on it became the custom to unite the two buildings.

According to the Hindu texts of temple architecture, to have the desired effect of energy emanating from the sanctuary, the whole structure of the temple has to be precisely measured and accurately symmetrical. That is why mathematics is considered to be a sacred subject by Hindu theologians. Mathematical schemes are often introduced by theologians and philosophers to describe the celestial or even the ethical world. According to them, if a temple is to function in harmony with the mathematical basis of the universe, it has to be constructed correctly according to a mathematical system. Thus, the welfare of the community and happiness of its members can result from the erection of a correctly proportioned temple that generates desired harmony.

However, measurement is not confined to temple architecture alone; the sacred images of the deities have to be carved according to the strict mathematical discipline of iconometry, the geometry of image-making. The face-length is used as the module (*tāla*) for the figures. Appropriate facial expressions (*bhāva*s, e.g., *raudra*/anger for Kālī), postures (*bhaṅgī*, e.g., *tribhaṅga*/tri-flexed for Kṛṣṇa), hand gestures (*mudrā*, e.g., *abhaya*/security for protection), colour (*varṇa*, e.g., *kṛṣṇa*/dark for Kālī and Kṛṣṇa), garments (*vasana*, e.g., *pīta*/

yellow garment for Kṛṣṇa) and even weapons (*āyudha*, e.g., *chakra*/discus for Viṣṇu) of individual deities are all prescribed by strict iconographical texts. Only a correctly made image will be able to invite the deity to reside within it. Therefore, the texts stress that the worship of an image not made according to prescribed rules is fruitless.

PROTECTION OF THE TEMPLE

To ensure the security of a temple and to avert accidents, each stage (e.g., selection of the site, drawing of the plan on the ground, laying of the foundation stone, etc.) in the building process is initiated with appropriate rituals. Once completed, the temple continues to need protection from negative forces. Much of the temple art, for example the motifs and symbols (e.g., *svastikā*s – see the notes section in 'Hinduism' in *Worship* in this series) that decorate the doorways, provide such protection. Hindu temple art is full of minor deities, guardians and attendant figures (e.g., *yakṣīs*/*apsarā*s or semi-divine creatures, tree-nymphs and *dvārapālas*/door-guardians) which surround the sacred image once it is installed, offering their protection. Images of secondary deities are placed in key positions, in elaborately decorated niches, especially at the centres of the north, west and south walls of the sanctuary, facing outwards. Some occupy the four corners of the walls as well. Guardians of eight directions are often depicted as protecting the temple from all sides. Demonic mask motifs over doorways are also used for warding off evil forces.

Some temples in the south are protected by perimeter walls with tall gateways called *gopuram*s (cow-gates). While the walls themselves have the appearance of a fortress with very little aesthetic value, the tall pylon-like monumental entrances or *gopuram*s have considerable architectural character with rich sculptural embellishments. A typical *gopuram* is oblong in plan, rising up into a tapering tower often over one hundred and fifty feet in height, with a doorway in the centre of its long side. The lower storeys are built of solid stone masonry providing stable foundation for the superstructure made of lighter materials like bricks and plaster. On the flat summit rests the distinctive barrel-vaulted uppermost storey with gable-ends. Often the actual temples inside the perimeter walls are retained in their original humble forms, without any structural alterations, keeping their religious antiquity and sanctity undisturbed. The surrounding high walls emphasise their sanctity and ensure their security while the imposing *gopuram*s appear like watch-towers.

ART IN TEMPLES

Hindu temples, whether in India or in Southeast Asia, are well known for their ornate stone carvings, especially on the outside. Intricate terracotta reliefs are also found in the few existing brick-built temples. As most Hindu art forms have originated from religious roots (see 'Hinduism' in *Worship* in this series), it is no wonder that religious buildings are profusely decorated with appropriate art of sculpture.

The most frequently used decorative motifs are often taken from nature, e.g., flowers (particularly lotuses), trees, creepers and birds. But the themes of the large-scale sculpture on the outside walls of temples are based on various deities, with their individual characteristics as described in Hindu mythology. These images of deities are not meant for worship but are purely artistic representations of popular mythological personages. Another favourite theme seems to be scenes from the epics, *Rāmāyaṇa* and *Mahābhārata*, usually depicted in series of panels.

But not all the temple art themes are religious by nature. There are some temples where secular themes found their place as evidence of pure art. The most frequently mentioned temples of Khajuraho in Madhya Pradesh are of this kind. It is believed that at one time eighty-five temples existed in this region but only twenty have survived. These temples 'are known for their elegance, graceful contours and rich sculptural treatment' (Narain 1982: 14), and also for their treatment of varied and sometimes unconventional themes. The themes depicted in stone are often secular, e.g., groups of dancers and musicians, sculptors at work, warriors marching, hunting parties, teachers and disciples, domestic scenes, etc. But the most talked about scenes are those of amorous couples and their sexual exhibitionism. The controversial sculpture of an erotic nature on temple walls has puzzled spectators as to how sex and religion co-exist in Hindu temple art. As Narain (1982: 7) explains, 'the large time gap between the building of the temples and our modern assessment of them, and the almost total change in cultural values has resulted in some misunderstanding' and bewilderment. Several explanations for the depiction of sexual motifs in religious buildings are available.

One commonly used explanation is that these erotic figures are a reminder of sexual desires that have to be conquered if one wishes to attain spiritual heights. In that context, the outside walls of a temple work as an aid to screening out people who are not yet spiritually ready to enter a sacred place and can easily be tempted away by sexual scenes. Devotees who are unperturbed by the erotic scenes of the exterior are worthy of entering the interior of the temple. Another explanation is that, because in most ancient societies the primary concern of religion was the conservation and generation of life, the sexual activities gained a religious and mystical connotation. Particularly in Hinduism, where there is no concept of 'original sin', most of the deities are coupled with their consorts (e.g., Śiva–Durgā, Viṣṇu–Lakṣmī, etc.). Hindu mythology is full of the amorous play of gods and goddesses. As a temple is regarded as the personal dwelling place of a deity, living there in human fashion, all the normal occurrences of everyday human life, including sexual activity, find their way on to the temple walls.

Moreover, it is not only art in temples, but also the classical literature of the Hindus that is full of amorous sports of heroes and heroines, who are often the divine personalities from Hindu mythology. In addition, several treatises were written on sexual behaviour, *Kāma-sūtra* (well-known in the West) being just one of them. All these factors indicate that social attitudes towards sexuality were in general fairly liberal.

Not only in Hindu temples, but also in Buddhist religious monuments (e.g., at Sanchi and Bharhut in central India) there are numerous carvings of amorous couples in pilasters and panels. Mild amorous depictions of male and female figures standing very close with arms around each other 'were considered auspicious and were used as *alankāra*s (decorative elements). They are in no way connected with the Buddhist religion but are simply a reflection of the artistic tradition of the time' (Narain 1982: 32).

It is a possibility that the sculptor artists used these temple walls as permanent museum galleries or exhibition spaces to show their intricate artistry in the popular art form of the day, knowing that stone-work would outlive all other mediums. Although, with changed moral values, one might find it difficult to associate eroticism with religion, yet these magnificent pieces of sculpture demand appreciation in their own right as pure art. Nude figures and life-drawing have been accepted as an important theme in art all over the world, and Hindu art is no exception.

Whatever may be the reason for the co-existence of erotic art in Hindu religious buildings, one is reminded by these findings that in Hinduism religion is never compartmentalised as a separate activity. Religious and secular activities are intertwined, and often inseparable, in Hinduism, as every secular activity is somehow linked with the will of God.

Small shrines

WAY-SIDE SHRINES

Compared with the magnificently ornate temples, considerably less spectacular in appearance and insignificant in size, but no less important in sacredness, are the way-side shrines that can be found in abundance in rural and urban India. It is often a symbolic stone or a lump of clay daubed with red vermilion paste, or a Śiva-*liṅga*, placed at the root of a tree (most commonly a *vaṭa* or *aśvattha*, known as sacred trees – see above p. 67) that makes a basic shrine. Passers-by pay their homage to the deity of the shrine with a flower or a small amount of money. Though they may look insignificant, these road-side shrines are the nerve-centres of rural religious life and are intimately linked with local people's everyday life of vows and thanksgivings, births and deaths. Their deities may be regional, deities who avert diseases prevalent in the area (e.g., the deity *Śītalā* in Bengal, for small-pox), yet their sanctity is no less than that of the temples of Viṣṇu or Kālī. People's simple faith makes them into living sacred places.

TULASĪ-ALTAR

Many Hindu families, especially in rural India, cherish in their courtyard an altar with a *tulasī* (Ocymum sanctum) plant in it.

Tulasī is revered as a symbol of Viṣṇu, and it is watered regularly, and a lamp is lit in the evenings at its altar. This outdoor *tulasī*-altar is treated as a sacred place in a Hindu household.

FAMILY SHRINES

Hindus, generally speaking, have a home-shrine placed in the midst of the family hubbub, connected with the daily chores of secular activities. It can be a whole room or a little corner in a room. It can be a big wooden or brass throne-shaped structure with a canopy on top, or even just a wooden stool on which images or symbols of deities are placed. Whatever the size, however gorgeous or humble in decoration, this shrine is the most sacred place for a Hindu family. Nobody touches the shrine unbathed. Usually twice a day, morning and evening, a lamp is lit, incense burnt in reverence to deities who co-exist happily in Hindu households. Members of the family sing songs of praise (*bhajana*s) or chant from the scriptures, sitting on the floor in front of the shrine with faith in God's presence there. This is the most intimate sacred place for a Hindu.

No need for a sacred place

There are Hindus who consider no specific external space as sacred but believe only in internal sacredness. Such Hindus do not need even a family-shrine, or a temple to go to, but feel that any place is sacred enough in which to meditate. Then there are others, for example the *Bāul*s (wandering bards) of Bengal, who maintain that the human body is the only sacred place, as it houses the God within.

Variable sacred places

The concept of a sacred place, therefore, is variable in Hinduism. To different people it brings different visions. A place is sacred if one feels sanctified within oneself by being there. Some feel sanctified by visiting distant places of pilgrimage, some by paying homage to the local temple, some by sitting quietly in front of the family-shrine, and some just by possessing an invaluable human body that uniquely holds an immortal soul within.

NOTES

1. 'They were discovered at a place called Surkh Kotal in 1951 by Schlumberger, who was then the head of the French archaeological mission at Kabul' (Chaudhuri 1979: 52).
2. The axis *Meru* is a significant concept in Hindu geology and even in human physiology. The earth's axis of rotation is known as the axis of *Meru* and, accordingly, the North Pole and South Pole are named as the north and south end of the axis Meru: *uttara*(north)-*meru* and *dakṣiṇa*(south)-*meru* respectively. The word *Meru* has the connotation of being in the central position around which everything else revolves. Again, *Meru* or *Sumeru*, is the mythical mountain that is at the centre of the earth, storehouse of gold and gems, and hailed as the abode of gods.

   The spine of a creature is called *meru-daṇḍa* (rod/support), which is vitally important for its physiology and consciousness. Especially in a human body, according to the tantric cults, *meru-daṇḍa* plays the role of a central channel along which the spiritual consciousness awakens and moves upward towards the experience of liberation or *mokṣa*.

FURTHER READING

Brown, P. (1942) *Indian Architecture: Buddhist and Hindu Periods*, Bombay, D.B. Taraporevala Sons.

Cavendish, R. (1980) *The Great Religions*, London, George Weidenfeld & Nicolson for W.H. Smith.

Chaudhuri, N.C. (1979) *Hinduism: A Religion to Live By*, London, Chatto & Windus.

Eck, D.L. (1983) *Banaras: City of Light*, London, Routledge and Kegan Paul.

Labye, P.G. (1973) *Studies in Devī-Bhāgavata*, Bombay, Popular Prakashan.

Michell, G. (1977) *The Hindu Temple: An Introduction to its Meaning and Forms*, London, Elek Books.

Morinis, E.A. (1984) *Pilgrimage in the Hindu Tradition: A Case Study of West Bengal*, Delhi, Oxford University Press.
Narain, L.A. (1982) *Khajuraho: Ecstasy in Indian Sculpture*, New Delhi, Roli Books International.
Singh, K. (1989) *Pārāśarapraśna*, Amritsar, Guru Nanak Dev University, Department of Guru Nanak Studies.

4. Islam

Clinton Bennett

Unity of the sacred and the secular

The whole Islamic system, whether we are thinking about its theology, its politics or its epistemology, develops from the fundamental concept of *tawḥīd*, unity, balance, or making one. While it is often stated that Islam makes no distinction between 'religion' (*dīn*) and 'world' (*dunyā*), it is probably more accurate to say that it aims, in all spheres of life, to maintain a balance between these two dimensions, to achieve such a degree of integration, or inter-relatedness between them, that any real distinction between the 'sacred' and the 'secular' becomes irrelevant. Initially, *tawḥīd* refers to the Unity, or Oneness of the divine reality, God. The affirmation that 'there is no god but God' forms the first statement of the declaration of faith, the *shahādah*, that every Muslim testifies as part of the first pillar of Islam. Next, *tawḥīd* refers to the essential unity of all creation. Everything that God has made is by definition 'good' and has no existence apart from him. Islam rejects the concept that anything is inherently evil. Rather, rebellion against God (*kufr*) is unnatural, obedience (*islām*) is natural. To be a 'muslim' is as natural as it is for an autumn leaf to fall from a tree. This is why Muslims call their religion *dīn-al-fiṭr* (the religion of nature).

Pursuing this logic, it is perfectly possible to argue that, for Muslims, no place, or building, is especially more sacred, or holy, than any other. However, Islam is a practical religion whose realistic view of human nature includes a profound awareness of the importance of symbolism. It knows full well that, although in theory the sacred is to be found everywhere, if people lack anything on which they can specifically focus their awareness of the sacred, it will be too diffuse, too general, to fulfil their spiritual and psychological needs for nourishment. In practice, if everything is sacred, nothing will be, so Islam, like other religious traditions, does have its concept of the 'sacred place'. However, while Islam does, as we shall see, designate certain places as 'sacred', it never loses sight of its fundamental conviction that all space is sacred place, and, through worship, architecture and traditional city planning, tries to sacralise all space by extending the 'sacred' into the 'secular'.

Transforming space

Islam's concern to hold different spheres in harmony extends to a profound respect for nature, and embraces the desire to interrelate man-made and natural environments so that mosques especially are not seen as

> holy space separated from natural space but an extension into a man-made environment of the space of virgin nature which, because it is created by God, is sacred in itself and still echoes its original paradisial perfection. Light and air can easily enter into the mosque and other buildings, and birds even fly around within the sacred edifice during the most solemn moments of a religious ceremony.
>
> (Nasr 1987: 245)

Similarly, because Islam wants to affirm the essential sacredness of any *ḥalāl* (permitted) activity, the traditional mosque often opens out into commercial, educational and even into recreational space, therefore also sanctifying these activities. 'Spaces, through their interconnection, proximity and multi-faceted use, enable men to experience this intertwining of work and leisure, of making a living and perfecting one's mind and soul through study and worship' (Nasr 1987: 247). Traditional Islamic architecture values ubiquity of function as another expression of the falsehood of any total divide between 'sacred' and 'mundane' space. In fact, Muhammad and his wives lived in the archetypal mosque at Madinah (see below); Christians were once allowed to use a corner for worship, while the courtyard was where the poor were cared for, judgements pronounced, political and social meetings took place. Ubiquity of function means that, when necessary, any building can serve as a place of prostration (a mosque, or, more properly, *masjid*): 'Whether a Mosque exists or not . . . a Muslim can construct a sacred space set apart for prayer in any place – in his own or another's house, or outside in the street if he wishes' (Gilsenan 1990: 179). We shall add a further note about the ubiquity of function later in this chapter when we explore how the archetypal 'sacred place' extends even into mundane space.

Even the most economically busy area in a Muslim town or village, the central market, is often regarded as a sacred, or *ḥarām*, place; a forbidden and sacred place where no weapons can be carried and no blood spilled. Anthropologists Michael Gilsenan and Ernest Gellner describe how, in many north African villages, the *marabout*'s settlement (the settlement of the Ṣūfī master), adjacent to the market, sacralises that space so that visitors from outside the tribe must first deposit their arms at the shrine before trading and bartering. Often, they will be accompanied by one of the *marabout*'s representatives as a guarantee of safe passage. These settlements, too, are usually located at significant boundaries, which enables these holy men to serve as arbitrators between the various tribes and as regulators of trade between them, guaranteeing peace and good relations (see Gilsenan 1990: 174; and Gellner 1981: 121).

For our purposes, this excellently illustrates how Islam succeeds in using respect for the sanctity of holy person and holy place (both of which symbolise the presence of the vertical dimension within the horizontal) to ensure good inter-tribal relationships. Here, the sacred is not 'other worldly', divorced from the business of life, but part and parcel of social interaction, indeed, of social control. As *ummah*, as a political–economic–religious system, Islam has a legitimate concern for peace-keeping. Another anthropologist, Clifford Geertz, who has undertaken fieldwork in Morocco and Indonesia and elsewhere in the Muslim world, describes what he calls the 'religious perspective of looking at the world' in the following terms, which many Muslims find congenial. It is not, he suggests, the theory that

> beyond the visible world there lies an invisible one . . . rather, it is the conviction that the values one holds are grounded in the structure of reality, that between the way we ought to live and the way things really are there is an unbreakable connection. What sacred symbols do for

> those to whom they are sacred is to formulate an image of the world's construction and a programme for human conduct that are mere reflections of one another.
>
> (Geertz 1968: 97)

Sacred place and sacred time sanctify all places and all time

This fundamental commitment to *tawḥīd*, to 'making one', to holding in balance 'world' and 'religion', means that Muslims are encouraged to integrate those activities that especially focus their thoughts on the divine, which we can call *'ibūdāh* (worship), with their more mundane day-to-day chores. This is one reason why *ṣalāh* (prayer) is said at five set times during the day. These set times help sanctify the time spent between prayer, at work or at leisure: 'Both time and space are punctuated, given a series of complex rhythms and movements . . . within which the sacred takes on an everyday nature as well as marking the extraordinary' (Gilsenan 1990: 179). The story of how Muhammad received the divine instructions regarding prayer excellently illustrates that the Islamic ideal is to pray without ceasing, to dedicate all time to remembering God. It was during his Night Journey (see pp. 103–4 below) that God told Muhammad to instruct his followers to pray fifty times daily. Later, during the prophet's descent back towards the earthly sphere, he met Moses, who asked 'How many prayers have been laid upon you?' When he heard 'fifty', he advised, 'your people are weak. Return to the Lord and ask him to lighten the load'. This process repeated itself several times until only the five prayers remained. This incident indicates, first, Islam's conviction, expressed at *sūrah* 2:185, that God does not place burdens on people that they cannot bear; secondly, the ideal that all time is sacred time. Islam's commitment to holding in balance 'religion' and 'world' results not only in the blurring of the distinctions between 'secular' and 'sacred' place, 'mundane' and 'sacred' time, but also blurs any dualism between 'flesh' and 'spirit'. Muslim prayer involves the worshipper's body, mind and soul which, as we shall see below, implies the sacralisation of the human body.

Consequently, five times every day are set apart for prayer, and, theologically and historically, three cities, together with the generic 'mosque' and 'shrine', are regarded as particularly significant foci of 'the sacred place'. Interestingly, the Arabic word used to describe a sacred place, city, or building which, as we have seen, can be a village market, is the word '*ḥarām*'. This is usually translated as 'prohibited' and refers to those acts, or foods, that are forbidden, as opposed to those which are *ḥalāl*, permitted. Applied to the three sacred cities, the word is extended to mean 'sacred'. It is especially forbidden for any *ḥarām* act to defile their sanctity. This is why the visiting tradesmen, in Gellner's description above, were required to deposit their arms at the shrine of the *marabout*. Similarly, no blood can be shed within the precincts of a sacred place.

THE ACQUISITION OF SANCTITY

In this chapter, we shall explore the significance of these three sacred places, the role they fulfil in Islam, and the meaning of the symbolism, rituals and buildings associated with them. However, since the concern of this chapter is less with the particular, more with the generic, before we turn to examine in detail these particular examples, or expressions, of 'sacred place' in Islam, a further gloss on the meaning of 'sacred' in Islam will aid our exploration. As we examine the significance of particular places, and how they function as 'sacred place', we shall see that although there are some very specific reasons for regarding these as 'holy', one common factor is that all have been sanctified by use. Use, or function, itself sanctifies. It can be said that a mosque is intrinsically no more sacred than any other building. It is not consecrated by a special service performed by a special person – although popularly something very much like this may happen. Yet Muslims speak of the mosque as 'consecrated space'; because mosques are 'set aside' for prayer, people do not enter them without performing ablution, and prayer is habitually and regularly offered there. It is this use, or function, that consecrates and sanctifies mosques so that, in practice, few Muslims view them as simply 'another building'. There is, too, a real sense in which, because they replicate the symbolism associated with the prophet's mosque at Madinah, all mosques, in a special, even unique way, participate in something of Madinah's sanctity.

Similarly, shrines of Ṣūfī *pir*s (teachers) or of Shi'ah *Imām*s (male descendants of Muhammad who led the early Shi'ah community), and places associated with Muhammad's life, function as holy space in part at least because of their past, or sometimes present, association with people who were, or are, considered so 'holy' that something of their sanctity, blessing (*barakah*), or grace (*karāmāt*) is transferred to that place. A mosque where Muslims have prayed for centuries, a place where a holy man has lived and died, a place where Muhammad lived, or visited, becomes holy, or sacred, by a process of association. Once regarded as sacred, and declared *ḥarām*, the inherent sacredness of such places is thereafter reinforced by the ritual ablutions and regular prayers of generations of worshippers. Here, Muslims' awareness of the vertical axis within the horizontal is heightened by the sanctity that these buildings, or places, have acquired.

This acquisition of sacredness reinforces the point already registered, that, fundamentally, no place is more sacred than any other: 'Revile not the world', said Muhammad, 'for the world is God' (*ḥadīth*). This suggests that those places which are regarded as especially sacred fulfil, primarily, symbolic functions. You do not acquire salvation, merit, or grace, simply by visiting a sacred place. Rather, their powerful symbolism and historical associations outwardly reflect the Muslim's inner, personal experience of *īmān*. Even the *ḥajj*, the pilgrimage at Makkah, itself an obligatory religious duty, is valueless unless accompanied by the inward *ḥajj* of the heart and soul. In practice, though, there is a very thin line between viewing ritual, or a visit to a special place, as merely symbolic, and the very often popularly held conviction that visits (*ziyārah*) are of themselves sacramental. As we shall see, 'sacred places' in Islam become associated with miracles, blessings and with other extraordinary supernatural happenings. Both this acquisition of sacredness, and the belief that at such places the divine and the human meet, fits well Mircea Eliade's definition of 'sacred place' as meeting points between 'heaven' and 'earth'.

Makkah as archetypal sacred place in Islam

Most Muslims, if asked to name their sacred place *par excellence* would reply 'Makkah'. Not only is Makkah closely associated with Islam's prophetic messenger, Muhammad, who is the universal prophet, and the best interpreter of God's final, complete revelation, the Qur'ān, but it is also associated, in the Qur'ān, with the ancient patriarchal figures of Abraham and Ishmael. The verses linking Makkah with Abraham and Ishmael give scriptural sanction to the idea that Makkah is a sacred place:

> And when we made the House at Makkah a resort for mankind and a sanctuary, saying: take as your place of worship the place where Abraham stood to pray. And we imposed a duty upon Abraham and Ishmael, saying: purify my house for those who go around and those who meditate therein and those who bow down and prostrate themselves in worship.
>
> (*sūrah* 2:125)

At *sūrah* 5:2, the *Ka'bah*, the shrine containing an ancient meteorite known as the Black Stone referred to in the above quotation as the 'House', is called the 'Inviolable Place' and a 'sacred territory' while at *sūrah* 2:144 it is declared the direction (*qiblah*) that all Muslims must face during their five daily prayers. To these scriptural references, Islam adds an oral tradition, which, almost certainly reflecting ancient pre-Islamic Arab lore, associates the *Ka'bah* with Adam. This association is suggested by *sūrah* 3:96, which calls the *Ka'bah* 'the first sanctuary appointed for mankind'. Eliade observes that sacred places are 'never chosen by man', but are 'discovered by him, in other words, the sacred place in some way or another reveals itself to him' (Eliade 1958: 369). In fact, according to Islamic tradition, the *Ka'bah* marks the site where human life began, where the Garden of Eden was located, where Adam named the animals, where all the angels but one, 'Iblīs, bowed down to primeval man (see *sūrah* 2:30–37). Thus, it was, says tradition, Adam who first built the *Ka'bah*. It was rebuilt by his son, Seth, by Abraham and Ishmael, and, later, by descendants of Noah. Finally, it was rebuilt by Qusayy ibn Qilab, whose tribe then became its guardians. Muhammad himself was a member of a sub-sect of the Quraysh. Eliade shows how the archetypal sacred place is often associated with the beginning of life, since such places obviously connect 'heaven' and 'earth'. The *ḥajj* pilgrimage, already popular in pre-Islamic Arabia was also associated with events in the life of Abraham, Ishmael and Hagar.

The axis of the universe

As we continue to explore the origins, and symbolic associations of Makkah, we shall see how Eliade's thesis that archetypal 'centres' replicate themselves elsewhere is sustained by the way in which Makkah serves as the paradigm for subsequent 'sacred places', especially for shines and mausolea. In a sense, this is an example of *tawḥīd*, understood as 'making one': all 'sacred spaces' in Islam are extensions of the one 'sacred place'. There is one 'sacred place', not many, but the one manifests itself plurally. As Islamic theology and cosmology developed, the Muslim theologians' understanding of *tawḥīd* informed their concept of 'oneness of being'. The 'there is no god but God' of the *shahādah* becomes 'there is no reality but the reality'. Everything that exists is a manifestation of God; different horizontal dimensions, or worlds, radiate out from the divine Being, or reality. Each world is also, essentially, an expression of the one reality which permeates everything vertically. As the nursery of human life, Makkah is the paradigmatic place on earth where the vertical axis connects with the horizontal. The *Ka'bah*, with the Black Stone at its centre, is 'not merely the central point of the earth; directly above it, in the centre of heavens, was the "gate of heaven" . . . the ka'bah, in falling from the sky made a hole in it, and it was through this hole that a communication could be effected between earth and heaven. Through it passed the *Axis Mundi*' (Eliade 1958: 227). This axis is also referred to in Muslim metaphysics as 'the *Quṭb*', which, as we shall see, is both 'axis' and 'spiritual centre'. It can manifest in a person, as well as a place.

The Tree of Life

Another symbol, used especially by the Muslim mystics, the Ṣūfīs, to describe this connection between heaven and earth is the image of the 'Tree of Life' – often inverted, the Tree has its roots in heaven and its branches on earth. However, for ibn Arabi (1165–1240) the *Ka'bah* represented 'Being' itself. Eliade explains how 'The sacred place is a microcosm . . . because it reproduces the Whole . . . the idea of a "centre", of absolute reality – absolute because it is the repository of the sacred – is implied', he says, 'in even the most primitive concepts of the "sacred place" and, as we have seen, such conceptions always include a sacred tree' (Eliade 1958: 271). As the Adamic temple, the *Ka'bah* is the first temple of humankind. As the temple of the last religion, it is also the final temple, linking not only heaven and earth but also the past, the present and the future.

The *ḥajj*

Performance of the *ḥajj* also becomes a living link between sacred past and present faith. After his final victory over the Makkans, and after destroying the idols that profaned the *Ka'bah*, Muhammad claimed the pilgrimage as Islam's fifth pillar, or obligatory duty. Thus, as pilgrims circumambulate the *Ka'bah*, 'they know that they are treading in the footsteps of angels and prophets, of princesses and paupers, and of past believers and believers yet to be born' (Gumley and Redhead 1990: 73). Originally, the *ḥajj* probably fulfilled various vicarious functions by which, drawing on the sanctity of the patriarchs, blessing, or even forgiveness, could be obtained. Something of this continues in its Islamic form. As Muslims re-trace the pilgrim steps of Muhammad, of Abraham, and probably of Adam, they 'hope by the *ḥajj* to cleanse themselves of present sin and to ensure in the future a more faithful and wholehearted submission to God' (Gumley and Redhead 1990: 70).

Madinah as sacred place replicated

Unlike Makkah, there is no qur'anic reference to Madinah as an 'inviolable place', or as containing a 'house of God'. Nor are there any traditions associating Madinah with other revered patriarchal figures in Arabia's religious past. Rather, it is regarded as sacred because it clearly participates in something of the sacredness of Makkah. Partly, this sacredness was transferred there by the fact of the *hijrah*, Muhammad's migration, with his companions, from persecution in Makkah, to eventual success and power in Madinah (622 CE). It is this event that marks the real birth of Islam, the beginning of the Islamic calendar, the organisation of the *ummah*, the community of Islam which, under the rule of the prophet and his immediate successors, represents the ideal human society: 'the best community given to mankind' (*sūrah* 3:110). Madinah thus became another place where heaven touched earth. As noted, the *quṭb*, the vertical axis, can also manifest itself in people, in those of such obedience (*islām*), faith (*īmān*) and virtue (*iḥsān*) that they serve as living links between the divine and the human. Muhammad was such a living link, as were the first four *khalīfah*s (his successors as temporal leaders of the *ummah*), as were subsequent Ṣūfī saints (*walī*s, or friends of God), as, for Shi'ah, were their *Imāms*.

Muhammad's burial place, and, nearby, those of his relatives and of the first two *khalīfah*s, continue to be regarded, popularly, as a place where the vertical axis touches the horizontal. Elaborate ceremonies, special prayers at different stations of the prophet's mosque, all non-canonical but hallowed by centuries of use, accompany the pilgrims' visit usually after, or before, performing the official *ḥajj*. These prayers take qur'anic warrant from the injunction at *sūrah* 33:56 to 'bless' (*ṣalah*) Muhammad. Sometimes, his two hundred honorific titles, or names, are recited. The petitioners' expectation is that Muhammad, because of his proximity to God, will intercede on their behalf. This expectation is reflected in popular prayers, such as al-Basiri's ninth-century *Mantle Prayer*, which depicts Muhammad as a bridge between earth and the hereafter:

> Muhammad, Lord of two worlds, and of the two species having weight [people, and *jinn*] and of the two human groups, Arabs, and non-Arabs, Our Prophet, who issues commands and prohibitions, and there is no one more justified to say 'no!' or 'Yes!'. He is Allah's beloved, whose intercession is to be hoped for . . .'
>
> (extract from the *Mantle Prayer*)

Andrew Rippin observes how such popular portraits of Muhammad show him as an extremely important persona in the salvation of his community, someone far more significant than simply the recipient of the revelation of the Qur'ān (Rippin 1990: 43). This reverence for Muhammad's shrine and expectation of *barakah* (blessing) subsequently transferred itself to the shrines of Ṣūfī *pīr*s and of the Shi'ah *Imāms*, who, believed by their disciples to stand in an initiatic chain with Muhammad, also function as points of contact between earth and heaven. As we shall see, based on the architecture of the shrine known as the Dome of the Rock in Jerusalem, the physical structure of Ṣūfī shrines reflects the metaphysical system that undergirds the Ṣūfī's quest for union with the divine reality.

The archetypal mosque

However, before we discuss the significance of Jerusalem, and of the Dome of the Rock, as the third expression of the sacred place in Islam, we have by no means exhausted the symbolic significance of Madinah. In Islam, just as Muhammad is the model for all human behaviour, just as Madinah under his rule is the model society, so his mosque at Madinah serves as the archetype for all mosques. As the Muslim empire expanded, mosques evolved in various styles. The detailed development of their architecture is not our concern in this chapter but their basic plan always resembles the original quite humble structure that Muhammad had inhabited. For example, although much elaborated, the *mihrāb* (niche marking the *qiblah*, or direction of prayer) is based on the simple stone indicating the *qiblah* in the prophet's mosque, while the often equally elaborate *minbar* (pulpit) evolved from the rudimentary wooden platform (it may have been a stool) from which Muhammad preached. Perhaps the tree-trunks supporting the original roof were later stylised into the elegant columns, or graceful arches, of the later monumental mosques. The typical spacious courtyard, too, which often contains fountains for ritual ablution, as well as helping, as Nasr has pointed out, to integrate natural and human environments, also replicates Muhammad's courtyard where, as noted above, he often taught, passed judgement and spent time with his companions. Lacking, though, was the minaret, which first appeared towards the end of the first *hijrah* century, and also the characteristic dome, or cupola. The symbolic significance of domes will be explored further below, when we discuss Jerusalem, but Muslims usually see them as symbolising how the grace of heaven falls upon the worshippers. If we look at a mosque such as Istanbul's Blue Mosque, its series of domes seem to soar, almost to cascade upwards towards heaven, perhaps suggesting movement from earth to heaven along the vertical axis. The Blue Mosque's internal dimension exactly equals its external volume which can be interpreted as an architectural expression of *tawḥīd*, understood here as 'harmony' or as 'balance' as well as 'making one', or 'unity'.

Perhaps, too, the graceful arches of a mosque such as the Great Mosque at Cordoba, Spain (now a cathedral), as well as stylising the tree-trunks of Madinah, draw on Islam's conviction that geometric forms and patterns reflect 'the archetypal and intelligible world . . . the origin of geometric forms and patterns, as well as mathematical rhythm, is none other than the angelic world' (Nasr 1987: 244–5). Cordoba's arches, says Burckhardt, convey the impression 'that space itself seems to be breathing and to expand outwards from an omnipresent centre', a description which this writer, from his own visit, fully endorses (Burckhardt 1976: 125). As architectural styles developed, typical mosques, with arches and domes and mathematically placed minarets (uniquely, for example, six grace the Blue Mosque) were consciously built to reflect their intended role: to be places where the human can enjoy contact with the divine. The dome's 'undifferentiated plenitude' evokes 'peace and submission', while the minaret 'leaping audaciously towards the sky . . . is sheer vigilance, and active attestation (*shahāda*) to Divine Unity' (Burckhardt 1976: 159). Of course, the typical dome owes some debt to Byzantine architecture: compare San Sophia with subsequent Ottoman mosques and the ecclesiastical source of the architect's inspiration will be obvious. To this day, the inner ceiling of many an Orthodox church's cupola is decorated with a night sky, symbolising the vault of heaven.

Islam's sacred art

Madinah's lack of any representational art, of any images, due to Islam's conviction that God is incomparable, similarly means that Islam has discouraged any form of visual icongraphy. Instead, calligraphy and geometric patterns, reflecting the forms and language of the angelic realm, decorate Islam's mosques and other public buildings, especially its ancient mosque–universities. Arches, concentric circles, geometric patterns, all represent the 'point' that is both nowhere and everywhere, or that which has no beginning or end: 'The circle surpasses all other geometric patterns as the symbol of cosmic unity, its inner core or hidden centre becoming the timeless moment of the revolutions of time and the dimensionless point of the encompassing space' (Critchlow 1976: 58). This also suggests harmony, balance, equilibrium – all of which reflect the *tawḥīd* of

God, and of his creation. Such patterns and arabesque forms must 'not be confused with mere decoration or cosmetics in the modern sense'. Rather, the intent is to 'make cosmic-like, or to bring out the correspondence of something with the cosmos and cosmic harmony . . . the mathematical order and harmony which underlie the appearance of the corporeal world' (Nasr 1987: 224). A mosque's often very spacious interior, too, represents infinity – God's limitlessness. Visiting Ottoman mosques in Turkey, this writer was overawed by their spaciousness: massive cupolas rest as if by magic above huge interiors, uncluttered by any supporting structures. This invoked in me a profound sense of peace and of infinity (see Burckhardt 1976: 141–53).

Nor are the colours used in Islamic art and architecture accidental – green, the prophet's favourite colour, is the colour of life, and therefore of paradise. Blue, the colour of sea and sky, is the colour of infinity, of God's eternal mercy. Gold, the colour of precious coin, is the colour of sun and of the night moon reflecting the sun's light. This represents knowledge, which Muhammad himself once compared with 'necklaces of jewels, pearls and gold' (*Ḥadīth*, quoted in Robinson 1991: 14). Sacred art is itself a channel between cosmic realms: 'The world of imagination', says Nasr, 'occupies an intermediate region in the hierarchy of cosmic existence between the material and purely spiritual worlds. Its forms, sounds, colours have an objective reality' (Nasr 1987: 230).

As places which represent the connection between heaven and earth, between the human and the divine, mosques and shrines also share something of the essence of the revelation to which they bear witness, itself 'sent down' (*tanzīl*) by God. In fact, Muslims believe that the revealed, written Qur'ān is a replica of the *Kalām* (word) that existed from eternity within the mind of God, first transcribed to a 'heavenly tablet' (*sūrah* 85:21–2), then sent down, or revealed (*waḥy*). Thus, 'the function of sacred art is parallel to that of the revelation itself as a means of causing repercussions on the human soul in the direction of the Transcendent' (Lings 1976: 14). This is especially true of calligraphy, which flows with graceful brush stroke and beautiful symmetry from the walls of mosques and public buildings alike. As God's *Kalām* (word), each beautifully decorated text connects with the inner essence (*ḥaqīqah*) of the revelation itself, which, by definition, is a channel between the human and the divine (see Burckhardt 1976: 46).

Islamic realism

The conviction that God is incomparable and that no image, or visible symbol can properly serve as a representation of God, also informs what has been called, in art and architecture, Islamic realism. In this context, 'realism' means that every material object, or substance, should be respected for what it actually is, not substituted for, or treated as, something else. Wood should be treated as wood, stone as stone, not disguised. Substances should be 'treated and respected in such a way as to bring out their character as part of God's creation' (Nasr 1987: 244). Islamic realism also helps to explain why 'space' itself should be respected, rather than forced to fulfil only one limited function determined by furnishings, or shape. Instead, 'the different components of the space' should be 'born from the conception of the structure as a whole and possess a plasticity of usage derived from the multiple functions which most spaces serve' (Nasr 1987: 234). In the domestic context, Gilsenan describes how the *maglis* (reception room) traditionally fulfils a multiplicity of functions. It is perhaps the domestic equivalent of the market, and therefore also quasi sacred space:

> The *maglis* is the key area in the symbolic and social world. It may be used for prayer, the men lining up behind the prayer leader facing Mecca. . . . On all other ritual and general social occasions, such as funerals and marriages, food will be served to the guests. The reader will chant from the Qur'ān from the place of honour in the *maglis*, and if a family wishes to hold a *mulud* (services in honour of the Prophet Muhammad) that is where it will be performed . . . .
>
> (Gilsenan 1990: 182)

Yet if public religious observances mark the *maglis* as 'sacred', perhaps the most sacred space, the inner sanctum, the *sanctum sanctorum*, is the *ḥarīm*, or woman's quarters – another word derived from *ḥarām* which therefore carries the dual meaning, doubly significant in this context, of 'sacred' and 'forbidden'. Here, it is forbidden for the outsider to see: 'Not being seen save by the privileged and authorised few is one of the things that separates out the most sacred and dangerous in life – the women in the house, the secret and inner knowledge of things that only the shaikh can see' (Gilsenan 1990: 190). This curious mixture of metaphors – referring to women as both sacred and dangerous, refers both to their being capable of betraying honour, and of giving, as well as receiving, great satisfaction and pleasure. In Muslim thinking, the most intimate act of sexual relationships within the sanctum of the *ḥarīm* qualifies as *'ibādāh* (worship), and 'is considered to be a Divine Mercy, even sacramental . . . as can be seen from the literature of Islam, sexual union readily prefigures the felicity of paradise, and eroticism within marriage is condoned'. Ibn Arabi (*d.* 1240) said, 'The most intense and perfect contemplation of God is through women, and the most intense union in the world is the conjugal act' (Glassé 1991: 357–8). As heaven touches earth in the marital bed, archetypal sacred place extends into the family home and fulfilment of one of the most basic human desires becomes an act of the profoundest religious significance. In fact, the Ṣūfīs go further: sexual intercourse reintegrates husband and wife into their original, prototypal state of *tawḥīd*. The female principle becomes 'infinitude' in the face of the Absolute, while the male principle dissolves into the infinity of the female principle. Merged, unified, duality ceases and they become a single Self. Burckhardt actually suggests a link between ritual purity, and this process of sacralising human sexuality: 'there is a link between the sacralization of the body, as realised by ritual purifications, and the Islamic conception of sexuality' (Burckhardt 1976: 85).

The ideal city

This sacralisation of human sexuality can easily be seen as a logical extension of Islam's fundamental aim: the bringing under God's rule of all human life, and, by implication, because humans are God's vice-regents on earth (*sūrah* 2:30), of the worlds of flora and fauna as well. This is why, as we have already noted, traditional Islamic city-planners attempted to harmonise human and natural environments, 'The countryside is always nearby, and the rhythms of desert and mountain penetrate into the city' (Nasr 1987: 245). Territory that had been claimed for Islam, understood as having been brought under the authority of the *khalīfah* irrespective of whether the majority of inhabitants had accepted Islam as their faith or not, became known as *dār-al-Islām* (the world, or abode, of Islam). As such, everything under the rule of the *khalīfah* is submitted to the will of God as expressed in the Qur'ān, through the inspired life of Muhammad, and as interpreted in the *sharī'ah*, or Islamic law. In a real sense, the whole of *dār-al-Islām* participates in the sanctity of Madinah as ideal human community. Today, as Muslims strive to create legitimately Islamic societies after the disruption of colonial rule, or after centuries of rule by Muslims who disregarded much of the *sharī'ah*, many aim to replicate, to re-create, Madinah.

Throughout history, Muslims have revered Madinah as the ideal city or, in the work of philosopher al-Farabi (879–950), as the virtuous or good city. In this work, al-Farabi asserts that 'happiness' can be achieved 'through the political life and the relationship between the best regime as Plato understood it and the divine law of Islam . . . the good city resembles a sound body in which all the members co-operate and of which the ruling member is the heart' (Schacht with Bosworth 1974: 420–1). Similarly, Ibn Rushd (*d.* 1198) in his paraphrase of Plato's *Republic*, taught that a succession of enlightened rulers could re-create the ideal society. This concept of the philosopher-king, while clearly owing much to Plato, also draws on traditional Muslim belief that Muhammad was a 'perfect man' and that the Muslim who completely submits to Allāh's will, whose intellect, in philosophical thought, has merged with Cosmic Intellect (God), can also achieve perfection. By extension, the whole society governed by such a 'perfect man', is, as a totality, a sacred enterprise. Not only its geographical territory, but every aspect of its life, from the public transactions of the market place to the private intimacies of the bedroom, is sanctified by virtue of this perfect at-one-ness with God's will. For such a society, even the need to consider certain places especially sacred alongside more mundane spaces becomes obsolete. Non-Muslim territory, however, known as *dār-al-Ḥarb*, the house of war, or of rebellion, remains unsubmissive to God's will and, by definition, profane.

Jerusalem's Dome of the Rock – archetypal shrine

The third expression of 'sacred place' in Islam is Jerusalem. Muslims also call Jerusalem '*al-Quds*', which translates as 'The Holy'. As with Makkah, qur'anic references declare Jerusalem a 'sanctuary': 'whose precincts we have blessed' (*sūrah* 17:1). This verse also mentions Muhammad's *mir'āj*, or Night Journey: 'Glorified be he who carried his servant by night from the Inviolable Place of Worship to the Far Distant Place of Worship'. This mystical experience is usually dated at about 620 CE, two years before the *hijrah*, when persecution against Muhammad was at its zenith. Muhammad was transported on a winged donkey, accompanied by *Jibrā'īl*, to the Temple Mount in Jerusalem where, until 70 CE, the Jewish Temple had stood. There, he met with Abraham, Moses and Jesus before ascending through all the spheres of creation into the divine presence where he received the instructions about prayer described earlier in this chapter. 'Tradition says that, on the Temple Mount, Muhammad saw a ladder rising from the temple of Jerusalem (the "centre" par excellence) into heaven, with angels on the right and on the left . . .' (Eliade 1958: 107). This ladder represents the *Axis Mundi* along which he travelled through the cosmos. As the place where, according to Hebrew scripture, God had made his Name dwell, Jerusalem, already a meeting place between heaven and earth, is thereby claimed for Islam – by Muhammad's meeting with his predecessors, as well as by his ascent into the heavenly spheres. Thus, Jerusalem's origin as 'sacred place' in Islam draws partly on its ancient sanctity, not only as the site of the Jewish Temple but also as the location of so many events associated with the life of Jesus, whom Islam holds in high esteem. To this, Muhammad's mystical visit and ascent into heaven adds a direct link with Islam's primary 'centre', Makkah, and, of course, with its own prototypal 'perfect man'.

As well as possessing its own sanctity, something of Makkah's sacredness transfers itself to Jerusalem as a result of the prophet's visit. It becomes doubly holy. When Jerusalem fell to Muslim conquest in 638 CE, it was already considered Islam's third sacred place, and in 683, when Makkah was seized by a rival *khalīfah* to the Umayyads, Khalīfah al-Malik declared that the *ḥajj* was to be performed at Jerusalem, not at Makkah, and built the Dome of the Rock in 688. Its colonnaded passages actually allow for *ḥajj*-type circumambulation. This extraordinary episode suggests that the 'sacredness' of Jerusalem almost substitutes for Makkah's, since it perfectly mirrors the archetypal sacred place. Nor is it insignificant that until the revelation at *sūrah* 2:142f, Jerusalem had served as the *qiblah*, or direction of prayer. According to Rippin, Jerusalem's importance to a triumphant early Islam cannot be overstated. Its conquest represented supremacy over the earlier, superseded religions, Judaism and Christianity. Little wonder, he says, that Muslims soon built a shrine there to rival in beauty any Byzantine church possessed by their Northern rivals: 'the desire of the builder was not only to rival but to outshine all other buildings and, most significantly, to symbolise the triumph of the conquerors over the land and over rival religions. The Dome of the Rock embodies the arrival of nascent Islam and underlines the religion's rising presence.' This, he says, 'is why the building is so important to any understanding of the rise of Islam' (Rippin 1990: 54).

While we are not concerned here with trying to understand Islam's meteoric rise to a numerical and military success, historically unrivalled by any other empire, it is interesting to speculate why this very significant, and, as we shall see, architecturally symbolic building, was built as a shrine and not as a mosque. The fact that its architecture became the archetype for all Muslim shrines, wherever they are found, suggests that the inspiration behind its design was the emerging metaphysics that informs Ṣūfī (mystical) symbolism, rather than the Prophet's mosque at Madinah. This metaphysics, with its layers of creation emanating outwards from the divine unity, was first developed in the late Umayyad period, although it did not reach its classical formulation until later. Its inspiration also owed much to traditional accounts of Muhammad's Night Journey. Rippin suggests that the association between the Dome of the Rock and Muhammad's *mir'āj* was a later development: 'Such an interpretation is clearly late, however, for no part of the inscription of 'Abd al-Malik found in the building makes any reference to this journey; nor do any of the texts which are found in the colonnade inscription . . .' (Rippin 1990: 53–4). Perhaps, though, what was so obviously a reason for building the Dome was omitted because it was taken for granted.

The silence of the texts may support Rippin's argument, but why a shrine? The fact that the building's style became the universal style for entombing those thought to be friends of God, sometimes regarded as *quṭb*, suggests that it was designed as a 'spiritual centre', and, as such, mystically enshrines something of Muhammad's influence, his *barakah*, if not his physical presence. Decorative features of the Dome fit Rippin's thesis that it celebrates Islam's victory over the two superseded religions; the beautiful qur'anic inscriptions around the main octagonal structure, and those inside the colonnades, proclaim the *tawḥīd* of God, that he has sent many prophets to call humankind back to the 'straight path', that Jesus was his 'word' and a 'spirit from him' (but not divine), and that Muhammad is God's final messenger. Built on the very site of the Jewish Temple, the claim that Islam has succeeded to 'the Davidic heritage' as well, is also implicit.

To this, though, we must add the architectural symbolism of the total edifice, which draws, I suggest, on the imagery of Muhammad's ascent into heaven and deliberately represents the *Axis Mundi* along which the seeker must travel to gain union with the divine. We have already noted how Islamic metaphysics developed to include a complex understanding not only of the relationship between the individual soul and the creator, but also between creation and God. Early Muslim interest in astronomy, in the movement of the stars and planets, aided their formulation of this elaborate system. Below, we shall explore how the Dome's construct reflects this metaphysical cosmology.

The Dome as cosmos in microcosm

Eliade suggests that 'sacred place' is a 'microcosm' of the Whole; because they are centres of the world, they 'stand at the very heart of the Universe and constitute an *imago mundi*' (Eliade 1958: 271). Arguably, the Dome of the Rock symbolises the whole structure of the Universe, and the path along which the soul must journey in order to reach its centre. First, the octagonal shape. In Muslim understanding, the number 'eight' is a primary step in the mathematical progression from 'square', which represents 'fixity', the earthly realm's station in the cosmic order, to 'circle', which represents heavenly perfection. The temple mount, or rock (with its well-like cave from where Muhammad's ascent is believed to have occurred), actually an oblong of about 18 by 14 metres, stands for the 'earth'; the earthly origin of the seeker's quest for union with ultimate Being. The Dome's octagonal base thus marks the beginning of the ascent upwards, along the *Axis Mundi*. The golden dome, or cupola, itself a perfect circle, represents the heavenly spheres, and Muhammad's successful ascent. Gold, as the colour for knowledge, can represent the realisation that the 'knower' is none other than 'the known', another formula used by Muslim philosophers. Muhammad himself, as 'perfect man', represents this link between heaven and earth. This configuration quickly became the model for all tombs and shrines, whose occupants were believed, like Muhammad, to have completed the journey. In fact, since they were also believed to share something of Muhammad's *barakah*, by virtue of their initiation as masters of his esoteric teaching, the link between any Ṣūfī shrine and the Dome is metaphysical as well as symbolic. We can also identify another interesting symbolic link between the Dome of the Rock as the archetypal shrine and its numerous 'replicas' – the forty pillars and columns which support the cupola represent 'the number of saints who, according to a saying of the prophet, constitute the spiritual "pillars" of the world in every age' (Burckhardt 1976: 13).

The symbolism replicates

Consequently, shrines and mausolea throughout *dār-al-Islām* replicate this symbolism, in its general, if not always in its total configuration. More often than not, though, a shrine's square, or cubic, base supports first an octagon, then a cupola, thus symbolising the saint's complete journey along the *Axis Mundi* to union with God: a 'passing away' (*fanā'*) of the self into the divine oneness. Perhaps the most exquisitely beautiful example of the full configuration that this writer has seen is Chisti's tomb at Fatehpur Sikri, built by Emperor Akbar (*d.* 1605). Its white exterior conveys a profound sense of peace, of at-one-ness with the Reality to which it bears witness. Several significant shrines are associated with the Shi'ah *Imāms*. At the tomb of Shah Ni'matullah Wali (*d.* 1431), a Ṣūfī saint, at Mahan, near Kirman, Persia, the dome's inner surface has twelve triangular segments representing the twelve Shi'ah *Imāms*, merging Ṣūfī and Shi'ah symbolism. The number twelve has mystical significance: 'The profundity of twelve has echoes in the 12 Imams of Sh'ia Islam . . . Twelve is . . . the greatest number of evenly distributed points on a single spherical surface which, when connected by lines, result in equilateral triangles' (Critchlow 1976: 50). Twelve disciples of Jesus, twelve months of the year, twelve tribes of Israel, all draw on this same tradition. For Shi'ah, the sanctity of Karbala, where Muhammad's grandson, Husayn, was martyred (680 CE), where this event of cosmic significance in Shi'ah theology is commemorated in the ritual passion play, even surpasses

Makkah's. According to Husayn's son, God created Karbala 24,000 years before he created Earth. At the Day of Reckoning, Karbala will be restored to Paradise as the dwelling place of the prophets and saints.

Shrines and cosmic order

Not only do the architectural features of shrines replicate the archetypal symbolism of the Dome of the Rock, as a place where heaven and earth meet, as metaphors of the soul's journey along the path (*tarīqah*), or axis (*quṭb*) towards the goal of union with the real, but, through the *pīr* who is buried there, they are believed to be directly connected with the cosmological structure itself. We have already noted how the *quṭb*, the vertical axis that interlinks all the horizontal layers of creation, can reside in a person as well as in a place. Ṣūfī *pīrs*, having completed the journey, themselves become indispensable parts of the total pattern. As *walīs*, saints, or friends of God, they form a spiritual hierarchy that itself helps to maintain cosmic balance: 'God has lifted the heavens up high, and has set up the Balance' (*sūrah* 55:7). R.A. Nicholson explains:

> The saints form an invisible hierarchy on which the order of the world is thought to depend. Its supreme head is entitled the *Qutb* (Axis). He is the most eminent Sufi of his age, and presides over meetings regularly held by this august parliament. . . . Below the *Qutb* stand various classes and grades of sanctity. Hujwiri enumerates them, in ascending series, as follows: three hundred *Akhyār* (Good), forty *Abdāl* (Substitutes), seven *Abrār* (pious), four *Awtād* (supports) and three *Nuqabā* (Overseers).
>
> (Nicholson 1963: 123–4)

From the beginning of their own journey as a seeker or traveller (*sālik*) under the guidance of their chosen master, the Ṣūfī saint first becomes guide and teacher, then founder of their own order, then, as *walī*, or *Quṭb*, they are themselves caught up by, and become part of, the metaphysical structure on which their scheme is based. Also, initiated into a succession, or *silsila*, that begins with Muhammad and Islam's own origins as the final religion, the straight path for humankind, they enjoy a direct, not only a symbolic or metaphorical, link with the 'perfect man'. This title, originally reserved for

Muhammad, is also used of the *walī*. Thus, says Nicholson, the station of the *Quṭb* is the station 'of the Perfect man'. He becomes

> the centre of the universe, so that every point and limit reached by individual human beings is equally distant from his station, whether they be near or far; since all stations revolve around his, and in relation to the *Qutb* there is no difference between nearness and farness.
>
> (Nicholson 1963: 164)

Saints have the right to guide others to God, and enjoy the ability to bestow grace (*karāmāt*) and blessing (*barakah*). Indeed, these functions are associated with Ṣūfī masters before they die. The *quṭb* of the age may be living, and several eminent Ṣūfī masters are believed to have been 'the *Quṭb*', such as al-Misri (*d.* 859), and al-Jilani (*d.* 1166), who promised his disciples that he would always leave the 'Unseen' (his principal work was called *Revelations of the Unseen*) to aid them if they called upon him – hence his title as *Ghawīth al-A'ẓam* (the greatest succour). Saints, then, during their lifetimes, are often believed to possess special powers, usually to heal, but other extraordinary abilities also manifest their sanctity, such as

> walking on water, flying in the air . . . rain-making, appearing in various places at the same time, healing by the breath, bringing the dead to life, knowledge and prediction of future events, thought-reading, telekinesis, paralysing or beheading an obnoxious person by a word or a gesture, conversing with animals or plants, turning earth into gold or precious stones, producing food and drink.
>
> (Nicholson 1963: 139)

Nicholson's book, though still a useful guide to Ṣūfī (mystical) thought and practice in Islam, suffers from its dated scholarship. Nicholson's own sense of incredulity constantly intrudes personal opinion into his text: for example, 'To the Moslem, who has no sense of natural law, all these violations of custom, as he calls them, seem equally credible'. Since Muslim physics, medicine, science and astronomy had, by the European middle ages, developed far in advance of any that the Christian world could offer, his statement that Muslims have no sense of natural law is woefully inaccurate. Similarly, he writes,

> The beginning of wisdom, for European students of Oriental religion, lies in the discovery that incongruous beliefs – I mean, of course, beliefs which our minds cannot harmonise – dwell peacefully in the Oriental brain; that their owner is quite unconscious of their incongruity; and that, as a rule, he is absolutely sincere. Contradictions which seem glaring to us do not trouble him at all.
>
> (Nicholson 1963: 130)

This polarisation of the Western over and against the Oriental mindset, as a device for interpreting data to highlight the assumed rationality of the West over and against the supposed irrationality of the Orient, has been well explored, and exposed, by writers such as Edward Said in *Orientalism* (1978, Routledge and Kegan Paul) and *Culture and Imperialism* (1993, Chatto and Windus). The details of this critique cannot concern us in this chapter; what is relevant, however, is to point out that what we are actually dealing with is not some innate Muslim inability to distinguish between the 'natural' and the 'supernatural', but the conviction that in people and at places where the horizontal and vertical dimensions have merged, the extraordinary, indeed the supernatural, can and does manifest itself within the natural. '*Barakah*', says Gilsenan,

> is therefore the key to practices that in a fictive way transform things into their opposite (as do so many miracles) and enable the passage to be made from the ordinary world to the realm of the sacred. . . . Oppositions are transcended, miracles produced, the individual's own biological and emotional nature momentarily dissolved into a 'higher' state of being.
>
> (Gilsenan 1990: 91)

Miracles at Christian shrines may equally be explained in exactly the same way. Of course, there is always the tendency to so idealise and mythologise saints, Muslim and Christian, that the boundary between fantasy and fact blurs. Nevertheless, the numerous miracles associated with such saints and shrines, with Muslim and Christian manifestations of 'sacred place' should invite serious investigation rather than scholarly incredulity.

What is undeniable is that throughout the Muslim world Ṣūfī shrines have become important 'spiritual centres' where pilgrims believe that they can 'break through' into that which, alone, is really real. In fact, as places where the *pīr* teaches his disciples, they often become centres of learning, and, as Sufism teaches that serving others is a step towards realising the selfishness of selfhood, hospices, schools, libraries and hospitals are also popularly associated with Ṣūfī centres. Whether or not miracles of healing occur, expert, though perhaps more conventional, medical help may very well be available. Modern anthropological studies testify to the continuing vigour of such Ṣūfī centres within the contemporary world (see Gilsenan 1990: 238).

Tawḥīd revisited

Some Muslim mysticism is in danger of too Hellenic a dualism between 'spirit' as eternal and 'flesh' as finite. The qur'anic teaching itself stands firmly in the Semitic tradition of belief in the resurrection of the body (see *sūrah* 75:3–4). Qur'anic descriptions of *al-jannah* (literally 'the garden', or paradise) imply that paradise, where the good will eternally reside, is a restitution of the paradise that once was where Adam and Eve dwelt: 'Gardens of Eden that the All-merciful promised his servants in the Unseen' (*sūrah* 19:61). At *sūrah* 56, verses 35–8 seem to refer to Adam and Eve's creation: 'Perfectly we formed them, perfect and we made them spotless virgins, chastely amorous, like of age, for the companions of the Right', while earlier verses of the same chapter seem to refer to the good entering the 'garden' on the day of judgement: 'When the event befalleth . . . those on the right hand . . . will be brought nigh. In gardens of delight a multitude of those of old' (*sūrah* 56:1–13). Other descriptions of paradise promise a place of milk and honey, with silk couches, vessels of gold and silver (*sūrah* 76), 'wide-eyed houris as the likeness of hidden pearls' (*sūrah* 56:22–4). However, the expression 'this is the similitude of Paradise' at *sūrah* 47:15, makes it possible to argue that these passages are allegorical, not literal descriptions. On the other hand, an Islam that ultimately wants to celebrate the essential goodness of flesh and blood existence can also teach that, when all the levels of creation are rolled back into their source, matter will continue to exist within the infinite ultimate Presence that is the one and only Reality. We have already noted how Shi'ah believe that the sacred spot of Karbala, itself created before Earth, will eventually be restored to the place of highest honour within paradise itself.

This process is sometimes called 'apocatastasis' (restoration) by Muslim philosophers: the idea that 'creation' will return to its source, duality will cease, and nothing besides the Absolute will exist, the 'knower' will become the 'known', the 'lover' the 'beloved'. The divine reality may be hidden behind successive 'envelopes', or layers of creation (the Five Presences of God), but it also envelops everything else, as, in reality, it is the only Reality, the Whole. Some Muslim philosophers, for example al-Kindi (*d.* 870), argued that what God has created he can un-create, but another understanding is that creation, as a manifestation or emanation of God, will return, or be restored to, its original Oneness. Muslims, however, do not view this oneness simplistically, but allow complex possibilities within the being of God – many attributes (*ṣifah*) and qualities (*awṣāf*), for example. An inner, indeed a mystical plurality, does not compromise external Unity.

In this restoration, even hell, *jahannam* (the fire), is sometimes said to return to its source. Arguably, say some Muslims, as long as hell exists, punishing those who have rebelled against, instead of obeying, God, hell and punishment represent the ultimate denial of God's Absoluteness. An *ḥadīth* says, 'By the God in whose hands is my soul, there will be a time when the gates of hell will be closed and watercress will grow therein' (quoted in Glassé 1991: 44). In this view, hell will join heaven, rebellion will cease, and only 'sacred place' will exist. The whole cycle will then be 're-set' to begin again, resembling the Hindu notion of an eternal cosmic process of generation, decay, destruction and regeneration.

Conclusion

For our purposes, this brings us full circle to this chapter's opening observations, that, in Islam, ideally, everything that exists is 'sacred', nothing, and nowhere, 'profane'. 'Sacred place' in Islam fulfils, ultimately, a 'making-one' function as an earthly manifestation of divine *tawḥīd*. Replication of Islam's archetypal sacred place throughout the Muslim world, in mosques, mausolea, shrines, as well as in living links with the cosmic order, who themselves represent a replication of the archetypal model, Muhammad, is part of a process by which everything that exists is being restored to its original perfection. Thus, a market place, the reception room in the family home, the most private inner sanctum, all function as 'sacred place'. In fact, wherever *ḥalāl* (permitted) acts, which, by definition, constitute *'ibādāt*, worship (the root of the word is *'abd*, a slave, a Muslim, one who obeys God), are practised, that place becomes sacred. As it is the duty of Muslims to strive (*jihād*) to bring their whole lives, their whole society, and the whole earth under the rule of God's law, so the cosmic plan aims to restore everything that exists to their original state of pristine purity. How else could God's power be limitless? Until everything is 'wrapped back' up into the ultimate oneness, 'profanity', anything not yet 'made sacred' represents a profound denial of divine absoluteness.

FURTHER READING

*Burckhardt, Titus (1976) *Art of Islam: Meaning and Message*, London, World of Islam Festival.

*Critchlow, Keith (1976) *Islamic Patterns: An Analytical and Cosmological Approach*, London, Thames and Hudson.

Eliade, Mircea (1958) *Patterns in Comparative Religion*, London, Sheed and Ward.

***Geertz, Clifford (1968) *Islam Observed*, New Haven, CT, Yale University Press.

***Gellner, Ernest (1981) *Muslim Society*, Cambridge, Cambridge University Press.

***Gilsenan, Michael (1990) *Recognising Islam*, London, I.B. Tauris.

*Glassé, Cyril (1991) *The Concise Encyclopaedia of Islam*, second edition, London, Stacey International.

**Gumley, Frances and Redhead, Brian (1990) *The Pillars of Islam: An Introduction to the Islamic Faith*, London, BBC Books.

*Lewis, Bernard (ed.) (1992 edn) *The World of Islam*, London, Thames and Hudson.

*Lings, Martin (1976) *The Qur'anic Art of Calligraphy and Illumination*, London, World of Islam Festival.

Nasr, Seyyed Hossein (1987) *Traditional Islam in the Modern World*, London, KPI.

Nicholson, Reynold A. (1963) *The Mystics of Islam*, London, RKP (originally published, 1914; paperback edition, 1975).
Robinson, Neal (1991) *The Sayings of Muhammad*, London, Duckworth.
**Rippin, Andrew (1990) *Muslims: Their Religious Beliefs and Practices*, London, Routledge.
Schacht,
Joseph with Bosworth, C.E. (1974) *The Legacy of Islam*, Oxford, Clarendon Press.

Note: Books marked * have excellent illustrations and chapters, or entries, relevant to the focus of this chapter. Those marked ** are good general introductions to Islam. Those marked *** are especially good anthropological studies with some material on 'sacred place'.

5. Judaism

Seth Kunin

This analysis discusses the biblical, rabbinic and modern understanding and use of sacred place in Judaism. The first half of the chapter examines two interrelated aspects of sacred place, i.e., the Temple in Jerusalem and the relationship of the land of Israel to the rest of the world. The Jewish understanding of pilgrimage and the modern understanding of land of Israel are discussed in the context of these two elements. The second half of the chapter discusses the two key elements of modern sacred place, i.e., the synagogue and the home. A case study comparing the differing use of sacred place among the Orthodox and the Progressive Jewish communities is presented to highlight the key aspects of sacred place in Judaism.

In order to understand properly the use of sacred space and place in Jewish thought and culture, the concept must be examined on two interrelated levels: the ideological and the functional. The ideological level is based on an abstract understanding of the structure of reality as it is realised in the Israelite and rabbinic understanding of geography and in the structure of the Temple and *mishkan* described in biblical and rabbinic texts. Although this level has its basis in biblical and rabbinic thought, it is still relevant to the understanding of the modern Jewish attitude toward sacred space, though it functions entirely on the abstract level. The functional level is found in the structure of the synagogue and in the place of the home as the replacement for the Temple.[1] The functional level which we find today developed as a response to the diaspora and destruction of the Temple. It has been continually transformed over the last two thousand years to remain in alignment with the needs of Jewish culture as it developed during that period.

This chapter shows that the conceptualisation of diaspora and pilgrimage, as two aspects of sacred space, can be understood only through the interaction of the ideal and functional levels. It also presents a comparison of the use of sacred space in Progressive and Orthodox synagogue architecture and religious services as a case study for the practical application of the concept of sacred space in Judaism.[2] The comparison also indicates ways in which the concept of sacred space is transformed in respect to transformed cultural needs (or perceived needs).

Ideological sacred space

The clearest depiction of the rabbinic model of sacred geography is found in the following text taken from Mishnah Kelim:[3]

> There are ten degrees of holiness: the land of Israel is holier than other lands. . . . The walled cities of the land of Israel are still more holy . . . within the walls of Jerusalem is still more holy. . . . The Temple mount is still more holy . . . the rampart is still more holy . . . the courtyard of the women is still more holy . . . the courtyard of the Israelite is still more holy . . . the courtyard of the Priests is still more holy . . . between the 'sea' and the altar is still more holy . . . the sanctuary is still more holy . . . the Holy of Holies is still more holy, for none may enter therein save only the High Priest on the Day of Atonement.
>
> (*Kelim* 1:6–1:9)[4]

This text presents a model for organising space into a coherent pattern. The model works from the outside in. Israel is contrasted with the rest of the world, Jerusalem is contrasted with the other cities of the land, the Temple is contrasted with Jerusalem, and the Holy of Holies is contrasted with the Temple. The text combines two levels of geography. It presents the relationships within macro-space, i.e., the world, Israel, Jerusalem and finally the Temple. It then presents micro-space which is a recapitulation of macro-space, i.e., the various areas within the Temple. The micro level focuses on an association of space with humanity. All people can enter the Temple Mount yet as we move inward the groups of people who are allowed to enter are progressively reduced.

The text presents space as consisting of progressively smaller opposing domains. Each ring of the set of concentric circles is

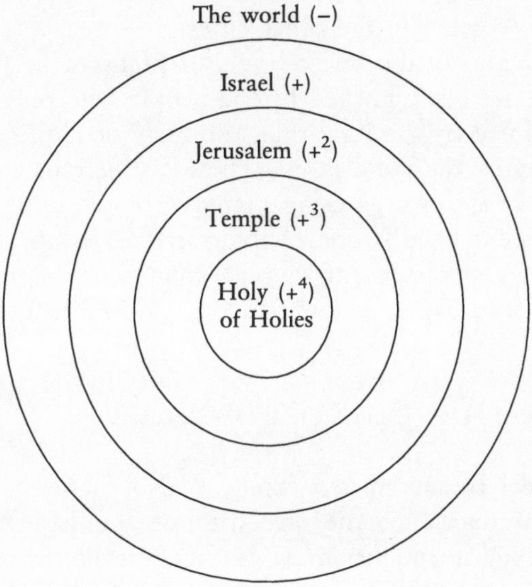

Figure 1 The abbreviated structure of rabbinic ideological sacred space

qualitatively compared (in terms of holiness) with its two adjoining rings. It is qualitatively positive with respect to the ring outside it, and qualitatively negative regarding the ring inside it. The negative and positive qualitative values are the degree of relative holiness.

It might be thought that this pattern of progressively wider domains of holiness extends beyond the circles listed here. This, however, is unlikely. The text itself compares Israel (i.e., the land of) to the world (i.e., everything other than Israel). The structure of sacred geography is presented in Figure 1. Notice that while the inner rings are progressively more holy (indicated by additional + signs), the outer ring, the world, is profane (indicated by a – sign).[5]

This text from the Mishnah brings together several other significant elements. At each level the text offers examples from other cultural domains which distinguish that level from the previous level. With respect to the distinction between Israel and the world, the text states that offerings from agricultural produce, e.g., barley, are brought from Israel but not from the other parts of the world. Similarly, Jerusalem is distinguished from the other cities by the fact that although the lesser holy things and the tithe may be eaten there, they may not be eaten in the other cities.

As observed above, the micro-levels of holiness, i.e., the Temple and its courts, are distinguished by the people who may enter them. This is exemplified by the final ring, the Holy of Holies, which may be entered only by the High Priest. These distinctions emphasise the role of sacred space in organising many levels of culture. They also reveal that sacred space is one of many related cultural hierarchies which organise experience into cultural manipulatable domains. We shall return to this aspect below (see pp. 119–22 below).

THE BIBLICAL MODEL OF IDEOLOGICAL SACRED SPACE

A similar model of sacred geography is also found in the biblical text, especially regarding the structure of the Israelite camp as described in Exodus and Leviticus. As in the rabbinic model, space is divided into a pattern of progressively smaller concentric circles. The camp is distinguished from the world. This distinction is found in the association of pure and impure with these two domains. Pure objects or people could remain within the camp and impure objects had to be removed from the camp. This separation of the camp from everything outside it supports the argument that the concentric circles of the rabbinic text also end with the borders of Israel, which are analogous to the boundaries of the camp. Israel and the camp are holy (albeit to a lesser degree than the inner circles) while the world and outside the camp are impure and profane. The enclosure was distinguished from the camp, the tent of meeting from the enclosure and the Ark from the tent of meeting. As in the division of pure and impure found between the camp and the outside world, the individuals permitted into each sacred space are progressively limited, culminating in the High Priest being the only person allowed into the presence of the Ark. The biblical model is depicted in Figure 2.

The ideological structure of sacred space found in these texts is in many ways analogous to a segmentary opposition model. Each circle or space comes into play depending on what is being opposed to it. The Land of Israel is used in opposition to the world. At smaller levels of opposition smaller spaces are compared. As in the segmentary opposition model, like must be opposed to like and the

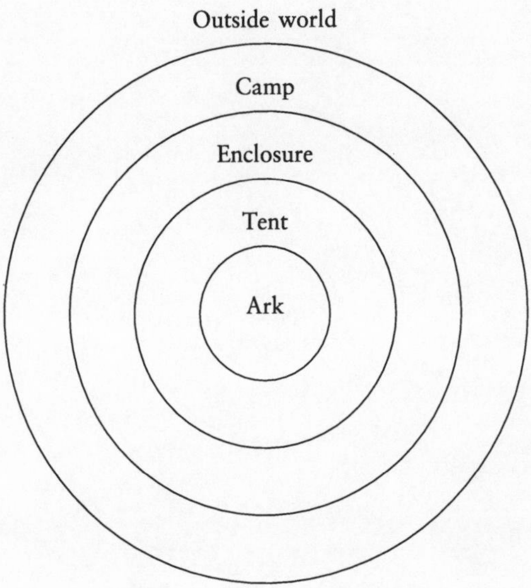

Figure 2 The biblical model of sacred space

smaller units come into play (as relatively more sacred) only when working on a micro- rather than a macro-level. Ultimately the comparison is between Israel and the rest of the world.

Structure and sacred space

We have already observed that space, like other aspects of experiential reality, is culturally structured to fit into an overarching pattern. Both the biblical and the mishnaic texts implied divisions within humanity and the Israelite community which mirrored those in geography. The pattern allows individuals within the cultural community to give meaning or value to particular events, people or places. The structure of space, e.g., into sacred or profane, is closely related to more general structural patterns, and therefore must be examined in the context of general cultural structures. This synthetic approach is especially relevant as it explains the relationship between the various circles in Israelite sacred geography.

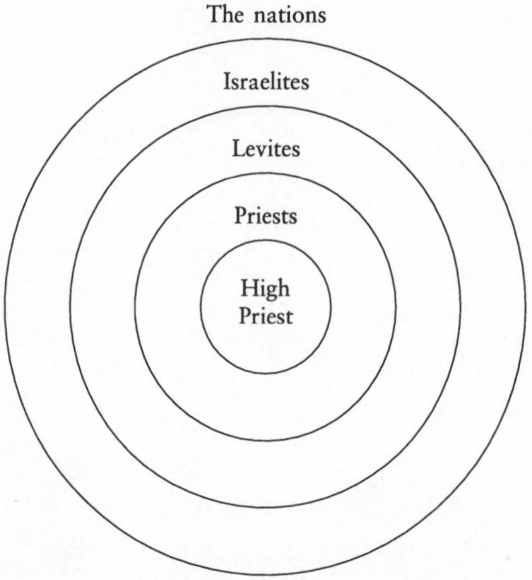

Figure 3 Structural model of humanity

Structuralist analysis suggests that Israelite social structure can be depicted by two related models. On the one hand the Israelites, as indicated in the above discussion, could be sub-divided in relation to holiness, e.g., who was allowed to enter various holy spaces or eat specific holy foods. Figure 3 illustrates this model of humanity. Notice that the outer circle of 'the nations' corresponds to the circle of the world in the geographic models.

It is, however, with the second model for humanity that the relationships in the other models can be clarified. This structure is based on a segmentary opposition model in which each smaller level is qualitatively more positive than the previous level. The model relies on a strong association of a preferential rule of endogamy with the family being the smallest unit. Although one was legally obligated to marry beyond the basic family unit, ideologically the preference was to marry as close as possible. Each level of kinship further away was less ideologically preferable. This system of increasingly large and negative concentric circles is limited. The rule of endogamy ultimately defines a boundary of inside and outside –

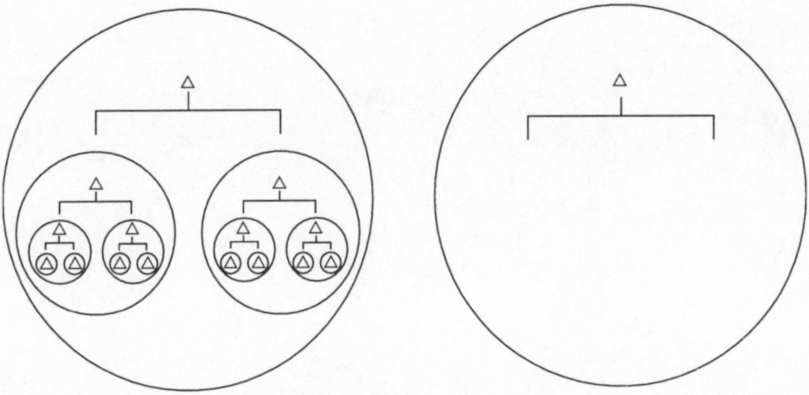

Figure 4 Genealogical model for sacred space

people considered inside are acceptable marriage partners and those considered outside are unacceptable partners. Thus, the ring of concentric circles logically ends with the culturally defined border of membership in the Israelite or Jewish people.

The model of sacred geography as well as the other models already presented are based on an identical structural pattern. Within a certain boundary, i.e., in respect of geography, the borders of the land of Israel, there is a pattern of graded holiness with the inner circles being progressively more holy. Yet in each case there is a clear boundary between sacred and profane. Regarding sacred geography both in biblical and rabbinic thought, sacred space ends at the borders of the divinely ordained space for Israelite occupation. In the rabbinic text sacred space is static; it is associated with a specific land and progressively more holy places within that land. In the biblical text discussed here, sacred space is mobile. It is the space in which the Israelites live, surrounded by the wilderness – a barren land associated with the rest of the world and non-Israelite humanity.

The model of geography and the sociological model of segmentary opposition ultimately grow from a simple structural equation: A not B. Thus the various models are based on non-overlapping circles which are united in opposition to larger circles. This pattern can be best understood using a standard genealogical table to exemplify the relationships. Figure 4 presents such a table. At the lowest level each

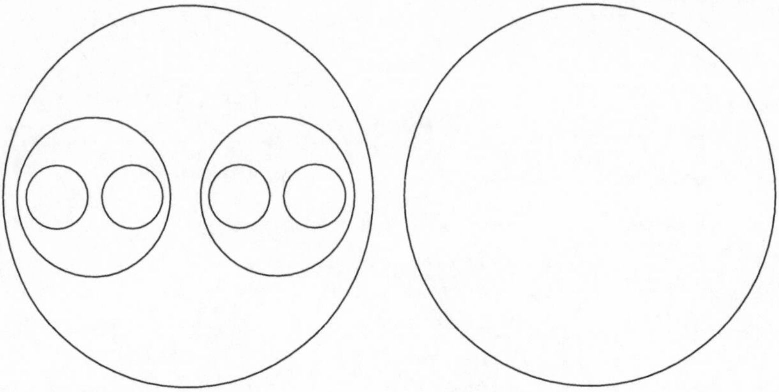

Figure 5 Abstract model of ideological sacred space

'brother' is a single circle in opposition to the other brothers. At the next level the brothers together form a complete circle in opposition to cousins, etc. Figure 5 illustrates this pattern in a more abstract form. The two largest circles are Israel and the world respectively. The smaller circles within the Israel circle are the next two smaller units. From the macro-perspective, the basic opposition is between Israel and not-Israel which is progressively mirrored on the micro-level. It is due to this recurring pattern that the micro-structure mirrors the macro-structure. The first half of the mishnaic text presents a macro-view of sacred space. In the second half of the mishnaic text and in the biblical text the Temple and the Tabernacle represent one aspect of the micro-level.

Alternative models of sacred space

This model of sacred space and place, however, is not the only one found in the biblical text. Several narrative texts suggest some related and some contradictory models for organising space. The two related models presented above are associated with a qualitative understanding of directions on the horizontal (i.e., north, south, east and west) and the vertical planes (i.e., up and down). The models of sacred place which contrast with the two models presented above are associated with the identification of competing holy places.

THE STRUCTURAL SIGNIFICANCE OF EAST AND WEST

There appears to be an association between the directions of the compass (at least regarding East and West) and the ideological quality of the events which take place or move in those directions. In Genesis all events which move in an easterly direction are qualitatively negative. In the early chapters of the book, movement in an easterly direction represents the descent of humanity into degradation. When Adam and Eve are expelled from the garden by God for eating the forbidden fruit, they leave the Garden of Eden towards the east (Gen. 3:24). After killing Abel, Cain moves to the east of Eden where he founds the first city. This ties the origin of civilisation to the descent into sin (Gen. 4:16). The founding of civilisation is logically opposed to the discovery of spiritual realities by the descendants of Seth who remain in the west. In later chapters the men of Babel move east before building their doomed city. The move to the east is associated with a challenge to God's power and leads to the confusion of language and conflict between people (Gen. 11:1–9).

There is also an association of 'east' with the nations other than Israel. When Abraham[6] and Lot divide the land, Lot chooses the east side of the Jordan, leaving the west bank to Abraham and the Israelites who came after him. Similarly, Abraham gives his descendants, other than Isaac, lands to the east (Gen. 25:6). The text therefore makes a double association: the west is equivalent to holy and is the proper setting for Abraham and his chosen descendants, while the east is associated with evil and is the proper setting for the other nations. It is likely that this qualitative categorisation of east and west is due to the geographic position of Israel. Its placement on the shore of the Mediterranean, the boundary of civilisation, meant that it was, in a sense, as far west as possible, while the preponderance of the nations with which the Israelites fought were to the east of Israel.

This qualitative understanding of direction, however, has not survived the transformation of the Israelites into a diaspora people. With the movement into Europe, to the west of Israel, east lost its symbolic power. In fact, the qualitative characterisation of east has been inverted; it now has a positive qualitative value.[7] The Ark, the most important part of the modern synagogue, is placed on the eastern wall, and services in a synagogue are conducted facing east, i.e., towards Jerusalem and the Temple. It should be noted, however, that west has not been equally inverted. It has little or no qualitative value in the modern Jewish understanding of space. The west's primary occurrence in modern Jewish sacred geography is the Western Wall which is one of the retaining walls of the Temple Mount in Jerusalem. In this particular case, west does have positive symbolic value.

THE STRUCTURAL SIGNIFICANCE OF UP AND DOWN

The vertical directions, i.e., up and down, are also given qualitative value in the biblical text. Perhaps because they have no direct or necessary historical association, this value has been retained. Up is consistently portrayed as a positive direction in opposition to down. This opposition is best illustrated by comparing two narrative texts: Genesis 22 and Genesis 37. In Genesis 22 Abraham is commanded by God to sacrifice his son Isaac upon a certain mountain which God will show him (the text actually initially says 'place', which turns out to be a mountain). Abraham prepares to offer his son as a sacrifice, and when he is stopped God blesses him because his actions showed his faith in God.

The positive value of the upward direction is indicated in several aspects of this text. God commands Abraham to bring Isaac to the top of the mountain, and to set him upon a raised altar. The actual act of sacrifice is called in Hebrew *laHa'alot*, i.e., 'to raise up'. Sacrifice must be understood as a positive and purifying death, and thus supports the positive value of the upward direction. Thus, movement in the upward direction is qualitatively positive and ultimately brings a blessing and fruitfulness – God promises Abraham a multitude of descendants.

Similarly, mountains and the direction up are qualitatively positive in several other key biblical texts. Moses, for example, receives the Ten Commandments (and the entire Torah) upon Mount Sinai, and the Temple in Jerusalem is built upon a mountain. It is significant that the sacrifice of Isaac is said to have occurred on the site of the Temple.

In Genesis 37 we find the association of down with evil. In this text Joseph's brothers, acting, in a sense, against God's command, attempt to murder their brother by placing him in a pit. Whereas in

Genesis 22 the upward motion is associated with positive death, i.e., sacrifice, in Genesis 37 the downward movement is associated with negative and polluting death, i.e., murder.

The negative association of downward movement is illustrated in two other elements of the text. First, Jacob tells his sons that Joseph's death will cause him to 'go down to *Sheol*', that is, cause his own death. Secondly, Joseph's journey into slavery is called a descent, and later, when he was sent to prison by Potiphar, the text referred to it as a descent. Thus, 'up' and 'down' should be understood as standing in qualitative opposition, with 'up' being qualitatively positive and 'down' negative.

THE ROLE OF THE LIMINAL IN SACRED SPACE

Both of these directions share a significant element in relation to the Israelite understanding and categorisation of space. Both should be considered liminal spaces (i.e., movement in either direction, up a mountain or down into a pit, is movement into a liminal space). The direction 'up', especially in regard to mountains, joins the domains of earth and the firmament, or perhaps the divine space. It is in this intermediate area that most communication with God occurs. Sacrifice, therefore, is doubly positive in biblical thought. It involves an actual raising of the object sacrificed and, at least during the Second Temple period, was performed only in Jerusalem on the Temple mount.

The direction 'down' also joins two domains, the surface of the earth which is the place of the living and the underworld which is portrayed in the idea of '*Sheol*' as the place of the dead. Thus, downward movement is symbolically the opposite of upward movement. The negative aspect of the depths is found throughout the biblical text. Two examples of this negative value are Psalm 30 and Jonah 2.

In the anthropological literature, liminal spaces are usually regarded as ambiguous. They are the places where opposing domains meet and perhaps overlap. This ambiguity is especially relevant in the context of the material discussed here. As we have observed, a basic pattern of Israelite structure is 'A not B'. The structure relies on a clear and complete distinction between A and B. A cannot be B, B cannot be A, and they similarly cannot overlap.

Such an overlap would diminish the distinction between the two. Thus, liminal spaces are structurally problematic. Israelite mythology and ideology cloud or remove this structural crisis by transforming the liminal spaces into non-liminal spaces, i.e., they transform or remove the ambiguity. The two directions, up and down, are transformed, not surprisingly, in opposite directions. Up is moved to positive, semi-divine space and down becomes negative space, the domain of the dead or sinful.

The text exemplifies the nature of these two different types of space through associating them with different types of death. We have already noted the association of up with sacrifice, positive, transformative death. On the most basic level, through sacrifice sin is removed and the giver or sacrificer transformed. On a mythological level – especially in respect of Genesis 22 – the sacrificed, or symbolically sacrificed, is transformed or divinely reborn as a result of the sacrifice. The direction 'up' is also associated with several other positive deaths. Both Moses and Aaron die on mountains after transferring their blessing or mantle on to the next generation. Both these deaths fit into the transformative aspect of sacrifice. The fact that the location of Moses's tomb remains secret or unknown also suggests a bodily transformation to spiritual space.

The aspect of sacrifice and transformation from human to semi-divine is most apparent in the case of Elijah. 2 Kings 2:11 states:

> And it came to pass, as they still went on, and talked, that, behold, there appeared a chariot of fire, and horses of fire, which parted them both asunder; and Elijah went up by a whirlwind into heaven.

This text and the verses before it contain all the aspects of the positive and divine aspects of the direction 'up'. As in a sacrifice, Elijah is transported to heaven by means of fire and wind. The element of fire is emphasised by being mentioned twice. Fire is tied to sacrifice directly in the texts about Elijah; see, for example, 1 Kings 18:20 and following. The transformative aspect of sacrifice is found on two levels. First, Elijah is transformed from an earthly being into a divine being. This element is emphasised in later Hebrew mythology, with Elijah becoming the precursor of the Messiah. Secondly, the transformation also occurs on the human level. Elisha is given Elijah's mantle and is transformed into a prophet and miracle worker.

The transformation of down from ambiguous to negative is also exemplified by types of death in the biblical text. The symbolic murder of Joseph is only one such example. The clearest example of this usage of the direction 'down', an example repeated throughout later books of the Torah, is the fate of Korah. He and all his followers are swallowed up by the earth. Thus, due to the needs of Israelite structure, liminal spaces are transformed into non-ambiguous spaces. Up is positive and transforming, while down is negative and polluting.

Conflicting models of sacred space

There are, however, examples of sacred space which are based on a different model than the segmentary model which organises the majority of textual material. Throughout Genesis there are a number of texts which highlight sacred spaces other than Jerusalem. Two examples of this type of text are: Genesis 28:10–22 and Genesis 35:1–14. Both of these texts establish Beth El as a holy place. In the first, Jacob dreams of God's presence and declares that the place is the house of God. The second text gives an explanation for its sacredness. Both of these texts justify Israelite worship at Beth El, and possibly explain the establishment of a dream cult at that Temple. There are many similar texts in the Bible which either justify the position of a place as sacred space or reveal the use of such places. One such text is 1 Kings 18:20–40. That text makes it clear that Elijah rebuilt the altar of God, implying that Mount Carmel was an established Israelite holy place. One attribute which many of these alternative sacred spaces share is their raised position, fitting in with the liminal and sacred aspects of raised places. This alternative version of sacred space can also be understood using the segmentary opposition model. Yet there is a clear difference between the model used in this approach and that presented above. This model never culminates in a single space which is distinguished from the rest, and it probably has no necessary outside boundary and is not based on the equation 'A not B'. Both these elements are basic to the primary understanding of sacred space. As suggested below, the primary distinction between the two models emerges from a different attitude towards endogamy. The multiple holy place model emerges from a society which does not emphasise endogamy, and the single sacred space model emerges from one which does.

It is likely that the two models, i.e., a single sacred space and multiple sacred spaces, are tied to a more general transformation in Israelite culture. With the return from the Babylonian exile in 538 BCE, the Temple, which was rebuilt in Jerusalem, became the political and religious centre of the re-established community in opposition to the centres which had been established during the exile by those who remained, e.g., the Samaritans. It is likely that several boundaries which became dominant in Judaism were established during this period. These new mechanisms included a strong emphasis upon endogamy. The new emphasis is an essential element of the basic structure discussed above. This transformation is equally reflected in an emphasis on the Temple in Jerusalem in opposition to any competing holy place.

What makes space into sacred space?

Thus far we have concentrated on the organising aspect of sacred space but have not addressed the question of what makes a space sacred. We find a pattern of evolution of this concept within the biblical text. In some texts, especially in regard to the Tabernacle and the Ark, God is viewed as actually dwelling in these objects or places. Similarly, there are texts which describe God in anthropomorphic terms, and thus almost physically present in a specific place at a specific time. Thus, the sacredness of the space is due to God's presence there as opposed to God's being anywhere else. In other texts, however, there is a gradual transformation and displacement. In Deuteronomy there appears to be a clear theological transformation in the understanding of the Ark and the Temple. The text emphasises that it is God's glory which is present, rather than God's actual physical presence. Presence of God's glory in one space is not mutually exclusive; God's glory can be present elsewhere as well.

This type of transformation continues throughout the development of Jewish thought. Rabbinic texts emphasise that although God was present in the Temple in Jerusalem, this did not prevent him from also being present, perhaps in a slightly less concentrated form, everywhere else. This idea is developed in the following rabbinic metaphor: God's presence in the Temple was like the sea in a cave.

The cave can be full of the sea without reducing the amount of water in the sea as a whole (Urbach 1979: 46). Thus, the rabbis preserved the pre-eminence of the Temple (while it still existed) as a sacred place, due to God's concentrated presence, while also allowing other places to be sacred by emphasising that God's substance and presence were not diminished by its concentration in the Temple. Other rabbinic texts even further emphasise God's omnipresence – i.e., suggesting that sacred places were not such by particular divine presence. They stated for example: God is the place of the world, the world (and therefore any specific space) is not God's place (*Genesis Rabbah* 1:18).

Other texts develop an even more fundamental understanding of God's relationship to space, and therefore the nature of sacred space. Many rabbinic *midrashim* suggest that God, as it were, went into exile with his people. Thus, God's presence is not tied to a specific place. Instead, it is tied to the presence of God's people, i.e., Israel, who bring God's presence to wherever they are. This dynamic aspect of God's presence, and therefore dynamic understanding of sacred place, is also illustrated in the following text from the Mishnah: 'If two men sit together and occupy themselves with the words of the Torah, the *Shekhinah*, God's presence, is in their midst' (*Mishnah Avot* 3:2).[8] The rabbis took pains to emphasise that this understanding of God's presence did not suggest that God could be divided or that there were many *Shekhinot*.[9] The metaphor of water (discussed above) was one such attempt. A second metaphor, i.e., the sun, was also used to similar purpose: 'it [the sun] shines on each individual and, at the same time, upon the world as a whole' (Urbach 1979: 48, adapted from *T.B. Sanhedrin* 39a).

The second aspect of the rabbinic understanding of the relationship to time and space is fundamental for the functional and modern Jewish use of sacred space and place. Both of the rabbinic concepts depend on a significant ideological innovation. The rabbis distinguished between two aspects of God. The essential essence of God is ultimately distinct from the world and transcendent. Yet one attribute of God, his presence or *Shekhinah* – coming from the Hebrew word meaning 'dwelling', or 'indwelling' – is immanent and present both with Israel and in the Temple in Jerusalem. As is seen, the *Shekhinah* itself is not necessarily tied to one place or location but can be found in any place. A second version of the text cited above (i.e., 'If two men . . .') gives the number as ten men. Ten men (a *minyan*) were seen by the rabbis as the minimum number of people needed to make a community. Thus the sacredness of a place depends on the presence of a community of people who allow God, or God's *Shekhinah* to enter.

The implications of ideological sacred space

In the beginning of this discussion we made a distinction between ideological and functional sacred space. The former is abstract in two respects. On the one hand, sacred space is an abstract hierarchical categorisation of geography. On the other hand, the centralisation of sacred space in Jerusalem and the Temple is also primarily ideological rather than functional. By the time that the rabbinic texts were written, the Temple in Jerusalem had been destroyed and Jews were forbidden to live in Jerusalem itself. A large proportion of the community was already living in other parts of the world, e.g., Babylon, Rome, etc.[10] Even in the biblical text describing the Tabernacle, it is likely that there is a similar ideological element. These elements come from texts which were probably written during the Babylonian exile and thus describe a situation which no longer existed or never existed.

It seems likely that this second aspect of ideological sacred space and place has messianic implications. This possibility is supported by the use of Jerusalem in the Passover *seder*. At the conclusion of the *seder* the words 'next year in Jerusalem' are read. Jerusalem in this context is always understood to be the heavenly or messianic Jerusalem rather than the material city of Jerusalem as it exists today.

This messianic understanding of the ideological levels of sacred space is significant in the transition to functional sacred space. We have already observed one aspect of that transition, i.e., the dynamic aspects of the *Shekhinah*. A second implication of this understanding is found with respect to pilgrimage. Although throughout the centuries Jews have made pilgrimages to Jerusalem and other holy places in the land of Israel, such pilgrimages are not obligatory in Jewish law. Return to the Holy Land, as a religious expectation or obligation, is left to the time of the Messiah. There is no special merit, as there is in Islam, for pilgrimage. On several occasions in Jewish history mass movements to the Holy Land have been associated with messianic movements or expectations. Secular Zionism called for a return to the land, not because of its (the land's) sacredness, but for nationalist and cultural reasons. The relationship of secular Zionism to sacred space is discussed below (see pp. 140-41 below).

There is a spiritual distinction between ideological, messianic space and functional space. The rabbis considered prophecy to be possible only in the Holy Land. Although they considered prophecy to have ended in the fifth century BCE, it is primarily associated with the transition between the Temple and the synagogue, or between an ideological space and a functional space. By the time they determined which would be the canonical books of the Hebrew Bible, the Temple had been destroyed for over one hundred years. It is likely that the rabbinic view of prophecy was shaped as much by political authority as by theological considerations. It does, however, reflect a significant transformation in the rabbinic view of the nature of Israel (the people). Whereas the Temple and prophetic period were based on a hereditary caste of priests and a group of individuals in direct personal, idiosyncratic communication with God through prophecy, the rabbinic model was non-hierarchical within Israel, and any properly trained person could be involved in the process of halakhic, 'legal', decision-making. In essence it was non-priestly. This transformation is especially significant with respect to the traditional understanding of the synagogue. This aspect is discussed below in the examination of the nature and role of the synagogue as a sacred space (see pp. 133-6). The distinction between the Holy Land and the lands of the diaspora is strengthened by medieval Jewish thought. Judah HaLevi, for example, states that prophecy and direct communication with God were limited both to the people of Israel and to the land of Israel (Altmann et al. 1981: 64–70).

Functional sacred space

Functional sacred space brings together many of the elements of ideological sacred space which are discussed above. With the transformation of the community from one based in the Holy Land to a diaspora community, and with the destruction of the Temple in Jerusalem, functional sacred space became primarily dynamic – following the community rather than being a specific place or places.

Sacred space in the diaspora is focused on two separate domains, the home and the synagogue.

THE HOME AS A SACRED SPACE

In rabbinic thought the home replaces the Temple as the central locus of sacred space. The family table and the family meal are seen as replacing the altar in the Temple and the sacrificial cult. Similarly, the two loaves of bread, the *hallot*, are symbolically associated with the Shew Bread which was part of the Temple ritual. The rabbis call the house a *mikdash maat*, a 'small sanctuary', using the same word, *mikdash*, which is used in the biblical text to refer to the Temple and the Tabernacle. Thus, the rabbis make a direct association between the two. During the Passover *seder*, the leader of the service, in imitation of the High Priest, washes his hands, linking the *seder* with the Paschal sacrifice in the Temple. Many other aspects of home ritual make a similar analogy between the home and the Temple cult.

A second aspect of the spiritual importance of the home is its place in the *halakhah*, the Jewish legal system. Probably with the exception of the synagogue, the home is the focus of more laws than any other location. Thus, the role of the home as a sacred space may also be tied to this legal concentration. The home is holy because through being in it, eating in it, one can fulfil God's laws.

The home as a sacred space fits in with the structural patterns discussed above. It is the logical extension of the pattern of structural opposition. Structural opposition is ultimately based on the smallest unit of the system. In this case the household is the smallest unit. Thus, by making the home a sacred space the system brings together key elements of both the social and spiritual systems. The unity of the two areas means that they mutually support each other: the sacredness of the home justifies the focus on the family, and likewise the focus on the family unit gives additional strength to the holiness of the home.

MACRO- AND MICRO-STRUCTURE

The transformation of sacred space from one to many, from the Temple to individual homes and synagogues, reflects a general change in Israelite/Jewish culture. During the biblical period (as reflected in biblical myth and law) we find two related structures: macro-structure and micro-structure. Macro-structure used the equation, 'A not B', to distinguish between Israel and the nations. This level is tied to the Israelite preference for endogamy. On the spatial level this structure is reflected in the distinction between the Land of Israel and other lands. Micro-structure is tied to structural opposition and is focused on the individual family and the preference to marry as close to the family structure as possible. This level of structure may be reflected on the spatial level in the early Israelite pattern of multiple holy places. The two levels are most clearly developed in Genesis 10, 'The Table of Nations'. The text includes two types of genealogy – segmentary and linear. The segmentary genealogies reflect micro-structure and the linear macro-structure.

In the biblical text and the culture it reflects, there is a clear emphasis on macro-structure. This emphasis is found on the spatial level with the centralisation of the cult and sacred space in the Temple in Jerusalem. The macro-level emphasises the unity, the oneness of Israel, and therefore the cult as opposed to the unity of the nations. It is likely that macro-structure is highlighted to support the ever stronger preference of endogamy. This may have been threatened in the cultural and historical context which saw the redaction of the biblical text. Later rabbinic texts and the community which emerged in the diaspora focus on micro-structure. No longer is there a single focus of sacred space or, on the human level, a single group or hierarchy with a monopoly in sacredness or cult. As in the segmentary opposition model, the system accentuates the smallest unit, i.e., the family.

THE SYNAGOGUE AS SACRED SPACE

The synagogue also fits within this model of micro-structure.[11] Each synagogue, symbolically based on ten men (or ten people in the Progressive community), is the smallest community unit and is the communal equivalent of the family in the structural pattern. It is likely that the cultural transformation reflected in the structural transformation is a change in internal and external relations. Prior to the diaspora, endogamy needed to be enforced internally, and therefore the structure reflected this need by emphasising macro-structure. In the diaspora period the community was isolated, and endogamy was enforced externally. In this situation an emphasis on macro-structure was not needed and thus micro-structure could come to the fore.[12]

The home is not alone in being perceived as being contiguous with the Temple. The synagogue also has elements of such continuity. The clearest tie of this sort is in the concept of *avodat halev*, 'service of the heart'. One major rabbinic innovation with the destruction of the Temple was the transformation of the means of communication with God. Prior to the destruction, the primary means was through the sacrificial cult, the *avodah*. By the time of the Second Temple period all such sacrifices were conducted by the priests in the Temple in Jerusalem. With the destruction of the Temple came a spiritual crisis due to the closing of this channel. The rabbis resolved this crisis through declaring that service of the heart was equivalent to service in the Temple. Although service of the heart, or prayer, was associated with the home, it was primarily associated with the synagogue. Thus, the synagogue in this respect was seen as being contiguous with, and replacing, the Temple as the space where one could communicate with the divine.

The internal structures of the synagogue retain many of the elements of sacred space which were developed on the ideological level. These elements are most apparent in the traditional form of the synagogue. Thus, the first part of this discussion will focus on the traditional synagogue with reference, when appropriate, to the differences in non-traditional patterns.

The synagogue has a section in which men pray and a second section for women. The women's section is often a gallery or a section separated from the main part of the synagogue by a partition. The primary focus of the synagogue is the Ark, which is placed on the eastern wall. Most of the service, however, is conducted from the *bimah* (the raised reading desk) which is often in the centre of the synagogue. The men's seats are placed along the north, south and west walls facing the *bimah*.

Like the Temple in Jerusalem, the synagogue is divided into spaces in which only specific segments of the community are allowed. There is, however, a difference for this type of division between the Temple and the synagogue. In the Temple the division of spaces was based on relative purity, while in the synagogue women are excluded from the men's section due to the fear that their voices may be seductive and draw men's minds away from prayer. This division in space is one of the primary differences between traditional and non-traditional synagogues. Non-traditional synagogues will usually have men and women sitting together.

The synagogue also has a hierarchy of sacred spaces. The building itself has an element of sacredness. This is reflected in many ways, e.g., laws concerning the disposal of a building which had been a synagogue, and the fact that a synagogue does not need a *mezuzah*.[13] Within the building, the sanctuary, the room where the services are conducted, is relatively more sacred. This is followed by the *bimah*, the reading desk, and culminates in the Ark, where the scrolls of the Law are kept. This pattern of sacred spaces is, however, not as exclusive as that in the Temple. With the exception of women (discussed above) all the sacred spaces are open to all male members of the community.

The synagogue also includes several other reflections of ideological sacred space. The significance of 'up' has been maintained. This significance is found in several areas. The *bimah* is always on a raised platform. Thus, the most important elements of the service are led from a symbolic mountain or positive liminal space. The positive and sacred aspect of 'up' is also found in the word used to describe the action of being called to the Torah: *aliyah*, i.e., a 'going up'.[14] (Interestingly, this same word is used by modern Zionists to describe going to live in the State of Israel.) The Ark is also built in a raised position in, or on, the wall.

We have already alluded to the transformation of the significance of directions of the compass. In the biblical text west was positive while east was negative. In most diaspora communities this relationship has, at least in part, been inverted.[15] In most synagogues the orientation of prayer and the Ark are towards the east. The eastward alignment is linked to the connection between the synagogue and the Temple, and the ideological priority given to the Temple as a locus for communion with God. Although the rabbis recognised that prayer was possible anywhere, they still recognised in the Temple a more concentrated presence of God. Synagogues face towards Jerusalem and the Temple. Some non-traditional synagogues have intentionally moved away from this directional orientation. This transformation is linked to a significant ideological change. Non-traditional Jews, especially Liberal and American

Reform Jews in the early part of the twentieth century, rejected two key elements. One was the importance of the Temple and a desire to return (in the Messianic Age) to the sacrificial cult practised there; and the other, the notion that Jews were a nation with national aspirations, tied to a specific national homeland. Thus, the rejection of the eastward orientation reflected the rejection of both the Temple and the Zionist dream of a national homeland.[16]

Sacred time and sacred space

Before we examine the use of sacred space among Orthodox and Progressive Jews, one other aspect of sacred space needs to be mentioned. To a degree, sacred space in rabbinic Judaism has been transformed to sacred time. Thus *Shabbat*, a time rather than a place, has become the locus of much of what once was the essence of sacred space. *Shabbat* is understood as being a taste of the World to Come, and it thus replaces the Temple as the focus of messianic hope. By celebrating and keeping *Shabbat*, one carries sacred space to wherever one is. This is reflected in a statement by A.J. Heschel (1951): 'The Shabbat is a palace in time'. This statement reflects the close connection between the concept of sacred space and sacred time in Jewish thought. *Shabbat* and other festivals are therefore the most extreme examples of dynamic sacred space.

A case study: comparison of Orthodox and Progressive use of sacred space

It is with a comparison of the use of sacred space between the Orthodox and the Progressive Jewish communities that many significant aspects of modern Jewish sacred space and place are clarified.[17] The key difference between the two approaches is the issue of the democratisation of sacred space. While in the Orthodox community there is general access to sacred space for the male members of the community, in the Progressive community, which gives equality to men and women, there also appears to be an emphasis on the priestly function of its rabbis, and thereby reducing general access to sacred space.[18]

In order to contextualise this comparison a summary of the key aspects of a *Shabbat* morning service is necessary. The service begins with a preparatory section. This section is recited individually in an Orthodox synagogue. In a Progressive synagogue this section is shortened and recited by the leader and the community together. The first key prayer is a communal call to worship, which is followed by a statement of belief and obligation. The service then continues with a prayer section. In an Orthodox community this is first recited silently by the congregation and then led aloud by the leader. In most Progressive synagogues it is only read aloud. The service continues with the reading of the Torah which is the central focus of the service. During this segment a section of the Torah is read. In an Orthodox service seven men will be called to recite blessings before and after the Torah reading. In a Progressive service sometimes only one person is called. The service ends with concluding prayers and a memorial prayer.

One of the primary distinctions between the two forms of service is the use of individual as opposed to communal reading of prayers. As we have shown, the Progressive service includes little or no individual reading. The congregants read as a group when indicated in the prayerbook and listen to the leader when it is indicated that he/she should read. In an Orthodox service much of the reading is done individually at one's own pace. This distinction is linked to the enhanced priestly function of the rabbi which is discussed below.

There is also a clear difference in atmosphere between an Orthodox service and a Progressive service. Orthodox services are much less decorous. People talk throughout the service and greet each other. In many ways the service feels more informal. This type of atmosphere is in keeping with the general pattern of micro-structure which is focused on individual access to sacred space. The Orthodox community is, in general, more comfortable with its sacred space than is the Progressive community. The Progressive service is much more decorous. Rubrics in the prayerbook are often taken seriously, and individuals are apparently more respectful. This pattern of behaviour is associated with a strengthened priestly function and a more exclusive use of sacred space.

The respective architectural plan of Progressive and Orthodox synagogues is the first area which reveals the different approaches to sacred space. The Orthodox community places the *bimah* in the centre of the sanctuary and therefore in the centre of the community. The community is thus made part of all that occurs on the *bimah*. The architectural plan of a Progressive synagogue usually contains a significant difference. The *bimah* is placed in front of the congregation, almost as a stage. The Ark is on the wall facing the congregation at the back of the *bimah*. There is no women's section as men and women sit together. The service and the actions on the *bimah* are therefore separated from the congregation. The Progressive synagogue plan is similar to that of Christian churches and thus supports the priestly aspect of the rabbinical role.

The use of the *bimah* is equally significant. In the Orthodox synagogue the leader of the service faces in the same direction as the congregation and thus is not distinguished from the congregation; in the Progressive synagogue the leader usually faces the congregation. Thus in some sense, he/she is leading rather than praying with the congregation.

The choice of person to lead the service (and to read the Torah) also reveals a similar trend to that revealed by the respective architectural plans. In Orthodox synagogues where there is a rabbi, the rabbi will not necessarily be expected to lead the service. Often knowledgeable laypeople will lead significant parts of the service. Equally, many men other than the rabbi will read from the Torah scroll. In Progressive synagogues, however, the rabbi will be expected to lead the majority of the services and usually read from the Torah scroll. It is possible that this distinction, at least in part, stems from the fact that very often the rabbi is the only person (or one of the few people) in a Progressive synagogue with the skills needed. Whatever the reason, this distinction in roles further enhances the separation of the Progressive rabbi from the congregation and thereby the priestly aspect of the Progressive rabbi's role.

Several other rituals associated with the Torah are relevant to this discussion. In a traditional service (on *Shabbat*) seven men are called up to the Torah (to do a blessing before and after the reading of the scroll). Several other men also participate in taking the scroll to and from the Ark. Thus, a large number of individuals participate in this part of the service. In a Progressive service the number of blessings is often limited to one, and occasionally only the rabbi recites the blessing. In some Progressive synagogues only two or three people participate in this part of the service.[19] The respective atmosphere of the synagogue during the reading of the Torah is also indicative of this general pattern. On the one hand, in an Orthodox synagogue there is an audible connection between the congregation and reader; everyone is reading with him. Should he make a mistake members of the congregation will correct him. On the other hand, in a Progressive synagogue there is a profound silence. No one would dream of interrupting or correcting.

The procession of the scroll is also significant. In an Orthodox service the Torah scroll is processed around the synagogue twice during the service. As it passes, men touch it with their prayer shawls. This ritual both emphasises that the Torah is part of – i.e., not separated from – the community and that each individual has a personal connection with it and therefore with sacred space. The Torah is treated with respect but also familiarity. Within many Progressive synagogues the Torah processions were removed as being undignified and perhaps even verging on idolatry. In these communities the Torah has a strong aspect of respect but very little familiarity in the community.

These few examples reveal a general pattern. In Progressive synagogues we find a strengthening of sacred space. The *bimah* and the Torah are increasingly becoming the preserve of an almost priestly caste – the rabbis – who are almost qualitatively distinguished from the congregation. In the Orthodox community, although sacred space is maintained, it is less exclusive. This trend in Progressive Judaism is probably tied to the cultural shift mentioned above. On the synagogue level, the Progressive community is using a macro-model which emphasises the exclusive aspect of sacred space. Due to the Progressive community's higher level of assimilation and participation in the wider culture, there is a corresponding quicker movement to a structural model which emphasises group endogamy. In the Orthodox community, due to its separation from the wider community, we find a slower movement towards the macro-model. Many aspects of their synagogue ritual still reflect the micro-model's emphasis on the individual within a pattern of segmentary opposition. Thus, at the level of sacred space, Orthodox communities appear to be more egalitarian than Progressive communities.[20]

The Hasidic community and the Rebbe as dynamic sacred space

A similar phenomenon is found in developments within the ultra-Orthodox Hasidic community. The Hasidic community emerged at the same time as the Jewish community was being allowed to enter into closer connection with the wider European society. Thus, in many respects it is responding to the same pressures as the Progressive community. The Hasidic community moved in the opposite direction, emphasising traditional practice rather than modernisation. We do, however, find a similar cultural transformation moving towards macro-structure. Although the Hasidic community has emphasised the importance of the individual, it has simultaneously recreated the priestly function and a new form of sacred space. This priestly function is concentrated in the person of the *Tzaddik* or Rebbe. The *Tzaddik* is understood as being the direct conduit between the individual Hasid and God. Sacred space is concentrated in and around the person of the Rebbe.

This transformation and concentration of sacred space is exemplified among the Habad Hasidim. Their preferred place of residence, even above the State of Israel, is in Crown Heights in New York City – the area in which the Rebbe lives. The focus on the Rebbe and Crown Heights is further emphasised by the fact that the Habad Hasidim have built a house for the Rebbe in Israel which is identical to his home in New York. The focus is reversed; Israel is tied to New York and the Rebbe rather than New York being tied to Israel. The home in Israel was built in preparation for the coming of the Messiah, which is the only time when the Rebbe would go to Israel. Thus, the Hasidim, like the Progressive community, in the face of a more open community which no longer externally supports the rule of endogamy, emphasise the distinction between the Jewish people and the nations by accentuating the priestly function and the macro-model of sacred space.

The State of Israel as secular sacred space

We find an interesting related phenomenon in the development of the State of Israel and secular Zionism. This phenomenon is also closely tied to the transition from micro- to macro-structure. Whereas in the earlier form of macro-structure the land of Israel was spiritual sacred space, in modern Jewish thought (especially in western communities influenced by Zionism) the land has become secular sacred space. Although it retains many of the attributes of the spiritual form, it exhibits them in a secular way. This transformation is most apparent in the mission statement of the World Zionist Organization. This statement lists the following goals of Zionism and the State of Israel:

> The unity of the Jewish people and the centrality of Israel in Jewish life;
> The ingathering of the Jewish people in its historic homeland . . . through aliya from all countries;
> The strengthening of the State of Israel which is based on the prophetic vision of justice and peace;
> The preservation of the identity of the Jewish people through the fostering of Jewish education and of Jewish spiritual and cultural values.
>
> (Hirsch 1993: 14)

Notice that the spiritual aspect of the land is left to the end. The statement emphasises the centrality of the land in relation to the national and therefore secular existence of the people. In effect the text is a secular form of macro-structure. Israel (the land of) is the embodiment of the unity of the Jewish people in structural opposition to other peoples and cultures.[21]

Commandments and sacred space

There is one element which joins all *loci* of sacred space, both ideological and functional. Each space, be it the Temple and the Holy Land on the ideological level, or the home and the synagogue on the functional level, is the focus of *mitzvot*, i.e., commandments. Although there are commandments which have no spatial focus, each one of these locations has a large number of commandments which must be performed there. Thus, from this perspective, sacred space becomes such through the performance of God's word. The difference between the two levels, however, is maintained. The commandments associated with ideological space can be performed (for the most part) only with the existence of the Temple and thus will come into force only with the messianic age. The commandments associated with the home and the synagogue are in force both in the diaspora and in the Holy Land.

Conclusions

In this chapter we address several aspects of the Jewish understanding of sacred place. The first dichotomy addressed was the distinction between ideological and functional sacred space. Ideological space is primarily concerned with the nature of geography and an abstract understanding of space. It is seen that two interrelated models structured the understanding of space. The initial model is based on a pattern of concentric circles with the smaller circles being progressively more sacred. This model ultimately relied on the external distinction between Israel and the nations. The second model is based on the social structure of segmentary opposition. This aspect of the structure worked from the smallest level to ever larger levels, culminating with the borders of Israel. It is shown that the models applied to both geography and social structure. These two respective models within ideological space were identified as macro- and micro-structural patterns. The two models work together to create a structural pattern which, although it is based on a recurring structure, is significantly also a closed structure. The pattern of decreasing holiness concludes with the borders of the Holy Land. Land and space outside these borders, on the ideological level, are, by definition, profane.

We examined two aspects of functional sacred space: the home and the synagogue. Both of these spaces are distinguished from ideological space through being essentially dynamic. They are not based on specific locations. Rather, they are based on the presence of a community or as *loci* of commandments. It was suggested, however, that the home and synagogue have key structures based on ideological space. Both of these spaces, for example, were understood as being contiguous with the Temple in Jerusalem. The influence of the ideological level was also apparent in the structural plan of the synagogue, which is based on a hierarchical pattern similar to that found in macro-structure. Other related elements included the use of raised areas and direction as symbols emphasising the sanctity of certain areas within the synagogue. This sanctity arises due to either the sacredness of the space (or objects kept in the space), e.g., the Ark, or the importance of the rituals conducted from that space, i.e., the *bimah*. Direction was also used to make a symbolic association between the synagogue and the Temple in Jerusalem.

One of the underlying themes of the discussion is the relationship between macro- and micro-structure. Macro-structure is based on the distinction between Israel and the nations. It is tied to the need to maintain the preference for endogamy. On a geographical level the structure makes clear distinctions between sacred and profane spaces, echoing the distinction which it makes between people, i.e., Israel and the nations. Micro-structure is based on the logical extension of Israelite endogamy and social structure culminating in a pattern similar to segmentary opposition. This structure focuses on the smallest geographic space. It is suggested that, although both macro- and micro-structural patterns are always present, the relative weight given to either pattern will depend on broader cultural situations and contexts. Thus, macro-structure, which emphasises and justifies the preference for endogamy, is itself emphasised when that preference is endangered.

In the chapter it is shown that one period of cultural transformation, which is reflected in a change in the respective weight of macro- and micro-structure, is the move from a centralised community based in the land of Israel to a diaspora community.[22] In the Holy Land, during the Persian period (fourth century BCE and beyond), the preference for endogamy needed to be maintained internally in the face of a culturally mixed society. Thus, there appears to be a progressive centralisation and unification of sacred space based on the macro-model. During the diaspora, due to anti-Semitism and the ghettoisation of the Jewish community, endogamy was in effect enforced externally, and thus the micro-model – based on the logic of endogamy and social structure – became the dominant pattern. One of the key aspects of this initial realignment was the democratisation of sacred space.

It is suggested that the Jewish community's becoming more connected with the modern western multi-ethnic community and more assimilated, will be associated with a realignment of structural weight. This realignment is seen in both the Progressive and Hasidic communities. Both have re-emphasised aspects of the priestly element of Jewish culture and the associated aspect of exclusive sacred space. It is suggested that the modern State of Israel also plays a part in this structural realignment. In a sense it has become secular sacred space, emphasising the Jewish people's nationhood in structural opposition (within the macro-model) to other people's nationhood.

NOTES

1. It is clear that during the biblical period, just as today, there must have been a functional level which worked in relationship with the ideological level. The biblical text preserves and is the basis of the ideological level. It also includes hints of the biblical functional level. The ideological level should not be understood as merely pertaining to the biblical period; it interrelated with the modern functional level as well as playing a significant role, in its own right, in modern Jewish thought.
2. The term Progressive is used here to include all non-traditional forms of Judaism. Thus, it includes a wide range of practice and belief. The cases examined come from several different Progressive communities.
3. The Mishnah is a rabbinic text which was edited in the second century CE. It is significant that the text under discussion was edited (and probably written) at least one hundred years after the destruction of the Temple in Jerusalem.
4. This text comes directly after a text listing the degrees of impurity. Thus it suggests that in this aspect of the ideological model impurity is the structural opposite of sacredness. The significance of this opposition is seen below in the discussion of the reasons given for women being refused access to sacred objects in some Progressive synagogues.
5. The key elements of the structure can be illustrated by the set of equations: (Israel:Jerusalem :: Jerusalem:Temple :: Temple:Holy of Holies) :: World:Israel :: Profane:Sacred. ':' is used here to mean 'is to', which indicates that the two elements are in some type of relationship. In the equation here they are in opposition. '::' is used here to mean 'as', this indicates that the two elements in the second half of the equation are related in a similar way to the first two elements.
6. We use the name Abraham here in order not to cause confusion. The biblical text actually uses the name Abram.
7. It is possible that in recent years east has regained some of its negative connotations. During the Holocaust, going east was analogous to being sent to the concentration camps. Equally going west during the last one hundred years was associated with going to the new world and therefore qualitatively positive.
8. It should be noted, however, that the rabbis maintained both the static and dynamic understanding of God's presence. *Sifre Zuta*, for example, states, 'The land of Canaan (i.e., Israel) is fit to contain the House of the Shekhina (i.e., the Temple) but Transjordan is not fit for the House of the Shekhina' (*Sifre Zuta*, Naso, v.2, p. 228). For a complete discussion of this aspect of Sacred Place see: Ephraim E. Urbach (1979) *The Sages*, Cambridge, Mass., Harvard University Press, pp. 37–46.

9. *Shekhinot* is the plural form of *Shekhinah*.
10. It is likely that the dynamic nature of the *Shekhinah* developed in relation to the needs of the diaspora community. A similar development occurred in the prophetic texts which described God as going into exile with his people during the Babylonian exile.
11. A comprehensive discussion of the synagogue as sacred space is found in Samuel Heilman's *Synagogue Life*. There are, however, several significant problems in his exposition. Many of the problems are due to a fundamental misunderstanding of the nature of holiness in respect to Jewish ritual objects. Thus, he attributes holiness to the candle used in the ceremonies opening and closing the *Shabbat*. He bases this understanding on the fact that the light of these candles may be used only for the light of the celebration and not for any other purpose. The candles, however, are only sacred by virtue of their being used for the performance of a commandment, not for any particular virtue of their own. Almost any object can gain such contextual holiness through being associated with the performance of a commandment. This problem is also seen in his discussion of profane objects, e.g., a light-switch or the *tefillin*, neither of which may be used on *Shabbat*. He states that touching them on *Shabbat* is taboo (Heilman 1976: 49). Like the candles, the objects themselves are neutral; they gain contextual 'tabooness' because one is forbidden to use them on *Shabbat*. It is not because they are profane in and of themselves, but rather because their use is considered to be work (which is forbidden on *Shabbat*). Many aspects of functional holiness are contextually rather than essentially holy. The only objects which are essentially holy are those which have the name of God written in them, e.g., prayerbooks and Torahs. One distinguishing feature of intrinsically holy objects is that they must be buried and may not be thrown away.
12. In modern Judaism the situation has again changed. With the emergence of the Jewish community from the ghetto, the external community no longer enforces endogamy. It is likely that as structure develops there will be a gradual emphasis on macro-structure and centralised institutions.
13. A *mezuzah* is a box containing verses from the Torah which is placed on the door-post of all Jewish buildings with the exception of synagogues. A synagogue does not require a *mezuzah* because it (the building) serves as its own *mezuzah*.
14. In a traditional *Shabbat* (Saturday) morning service seven men are called to recite a blessing before reading a section of the Torah portion. The Torah is divided into weekly portions which are read in the synagogue during the *Shabbat* morning service.

15. The symbolic power of the direction west is occasionally reflected in rabbinic texts. One such text, based albeit on an attempt to distinguish between the orientation of Jewish prayer and that of Christian prayer (also towards Jerusalem), suggests that prayer should be toward the west because 'the *Shekhinah* is in the west' (Urbach 1979: 62). Interestingly, many early synagogues were built with a westward rather than an eastward orientation (Urbach 1979: 62–3).
16. For the most part, all Jews have accepted the importance of a homeland. This, in part, is tied to the Holocaust and the insecurity which it created. It is also tied to the movement back towards macro-structure. Nationalism emphasises unity in opposition to other nations.
17. Although most of this discussion refers to ritual patterns among the British Liberal and the American Reform community, many of the conclusions and observations are applicable to the Progressive community as a whole.
18. By priestly function we mean the interrelationship of several factors: a distinction between the rabbi and congregation in terms of participation in ritual; a view of the rabbi as being in some way spiritually distinct from the congregation (ranging from a spirituality professional to being a conduit of communication with the divine); and, giving the rabbi a monopoly of access to sacred space. This priestly function is in structural opposition to the more traditional role of rabbi as teacher and judge of Jewish law. It should be noted that in almost no Progressive community have rabbis taken on all elements of the priestly function. Rather, these elements must be understood as extreme forms at the ends of polar axes.

    Two conscious examples of this emphasis on the priestly function are: the use of the word 'Temple' for the synagogue; and, the inclusion of the 'Priestly Benediction'. In the American Reform movement synagogues are called temples. Although this de-emphasises the centrality of the Temple in Jerusalem, it also introduces a conscious association of the synagogue with the Temple and thereby with a specific kind of priestly sacred space. At the conclusion of the service in most Progressive synagogues the rabbi recites the 'Priestly Benediction'. Very often the rabbi will raise his hand in imitation of the priests in the Temple. This makes a direct association of the role of the rabbi with that of the priests as being a conduit of blessing for the congregation.
19. There is one area in which the Orthodox include a priestly element not found among Progressive communities. The Orthodox reserve the first two Torah blessings: one is reserved for a *Cohen*, a descendant of the Priest and the second for a *Levi*, a descendant of the Temple functionaries. In a sense, these two groups open the sacred (the Torah) to make it available for the rest of the community. This, however, is

not relevant to the priestly function of the rabbi or the general access to sacred space because both the *Cohen* and *Levi* are now part of the general community.

20. It is possible that this trend is also reflected in respect to women. We have already mentioned that women are excluded from the men's section in the Orthodox community due to their sexual attraction. In some Progressive synagogues, which limit the role of women (and granted most give full equality), we find a very different reason given. People will say that women are not allowed to read from the Torah because they might make it impure if they are menstruating. (In Jewish law, however, it clearly states that a Torah can never be made impure.) Thus the reason given is symbolically associated with macro-structure which used purity as the primary category for access into sacred space.
21. There is an interesting concomitant transformation in modern Jewish thought. Earlier in this century the model used for Jewish cultural creativity was bi-polar – with the diaspora (or America) and Israel as the two poles. This reflected a transition from the earlier micro-model which was more multi-faceted. In more recent years there has been a progressive shift to viewing Israel as the primary centre for the development of Jewish cultural creativity, thus moving to a stronger version of the macro-model. This transformation is reflected in a paper published by World Union For Progressive Judaism in which the authors suggest that acceptance of the bi-polar model is 'a depreciation of Zionism as the vital preservative and creative force of Jewish life' (Hirsch 1993: 14).
22. It is possible that the Persian period reflects an earlier realignment. In some biblical texts we find a multiplicity of sacred spaces. Other texts emphasise the pre-eminence and exclusiveness of Jerusalem as a sacred space. If a strong form of the preference for endogamy was primarily an innovation of Ezra and his followers after the return from exile, then it is likely that the weight given to macro-structure in the biblical text reflects that specific cultural transformation. The texts emphasising micro-structure may reflect earlier cultural patterns.

FURTHER READING

Altmann, A., Lewy, H. and Heinemann, I. (eds) (1981) *Three Jewish Philosophers*, New York, Atheneum.

Cohen, A. and Mendes-Flohr, P. (eds) (1987) *Contemporary Jewish Religious Thought*, New York, Free Press.

Douglas, M. (1966) *Purity and Danger*, London, Routledge & Kegan Paul.

Heilman, S. (1976) *Synagogue Life*, Chicago, University of Chicago Press.

Heschel, A.J. (1951) *The Sabbath*, New York, Farrar Straus Giroux.
Hirsch, R. (1993) *The Israel-Diaspora Connection*, Geneva, World Union For Progressive Judaism.
Urbach, E.E. (1979) *The Sages*, Cambridge, Mass., Harvard University Press.

6. Sikhism

Beryl Dhanjal

In the Panjābi language and tradition, the nearest concepts to 'sacred' are probably 'pure'; 'relating to *dharam*' (that which is right); and 'relating to the *paraṃparā*' (the succession of teachers which is found in eastern traditions). Purity is a value of greater importance in Hinduism, though it is a value which also exists for Sikhs. Gurdwaras are described as *pavitar asthān*, a 'pure place', and this is often translated into English as 'holy'.

Institutions

The original Sikh meeting houses were called *dharamsālā*s – places where the *dharam* is done. There are no descriptions of such buildings. The one mentioned in the India Office Manuscript, B 40 mentions the *dharamsālā* being situated 'below the Raja's palace'. *Dharamsālā*s which are in use nowadays are very simple buildings, like hostels, with plain rooms for people to stay. Later meeting houses came to be called *gurdwara*s, which means doorway to the Gurū, or the Gurū's grace. The change probably came about because of the concepts of the Gurū Granth and *Gurū Panth*. If the authority of the Gurū was lodged in the book or in the assembly, then the places where these were housed were places of the Gurū. There are gurdwaras at sites associated with the Gurūs, at their birthplaces, and the places where they stayed, lived, paused for breath, and places where they died, were martyred, and were cremated.

Sacred place or sacred space?

Maybe it would be more helpful to talk of space in general, rather than one confined area. All space is sacred because all there is, everything that exists, is an expression of the True Timeless One, *Akāl Purakh*. It is by his creation that we can know him. As much as we can know and understand is right in front of us, it is the *Nām* made manifest. He is immanent, he pervades the universe. He reveals himself through his creation.

The Sikh Gurūs, and especially Guru Nanak, revelled in the wonders of nature and God's creation. Guru Nanak noticed blossoms on the bough, and even little ants, bees and worms, and all the creatures. He saw God through the wonder of the creation and through God's *hukam*, his order – a concept similar to the English word 'order' in that it covers God's design – the rule by which we have to live, but also the pattern which is behind everything, the rules, laws of nature. The Sikh Gurūs relished and enjoyed what they saw of his creation, and they obviously enjoyed describing it. But we all see it. What matters more is how people respond to it. In this regard, the space that really matters is the internal space. Guru Tegh Bahadar said:

> O Sir, why goest thou to search in the forest?
> God though ever apart dwelleth everywhere, and is contained *even* in thee.
> As in flowers there is odour and in a mirror reflection,
> So God dwelleth continually in thy heart; search for him there, O brother.
>
> (Macauliffe, vol. IV, 1909: 402)

Internal space

From the outset, because internal space was more important than any geographical location, Guru Nanak was no great respecter of the notion of sacred places. He rejected the notion of going to a *tīrath*, a place of pilgrimage. Some pious Hindus went to sixty-eight of them. For Nanak, listening to the Word was the equivalent of visiting all sixty-eight and bathing in each of them. In *Japjī Sāhib* (*pauṛi* 6) he says:

> I would bathe at the place of pilgrimage, if that would please God, but without his blessing nothing is gained. Throughout all creation nothing can be achieved except by means of his grace.

A few lines later:

> By listening to the word, one finds truth, contentment, spiritual perception. Listening to the word secures all that pilgrimage can achieve, the merit earned by bathing at all sixty-eight sacred sites.
>
> (*Japjī*, *pauṛi* 10)

No wanderings to sacred places can wash off the dirt of misery. Guru Nanak even uses humour about the idea of pilgrimage, pointing out that white herons live in places of pilgrimage where they rend and devour living things in the holy water. They ought not to be called white, for their hearts are black! A saint who bathes at a place of pilgrimage is still a saint afterwards, and a thief is still a thief – so what is the use?

The true pilgrimage is the company of the holy; the Gurū is the *tīrath* – the pilgrimage which is within.

> Pilgrimages, austerities, charity and alms earn no more merit than a sesame seed (which is very small indeed). Hear, believe, nurture love in your heart, for thus one is cleansed by the waters within.
>
> (*Japjī*, *pauṛi* 21)

The importance of interior religion cannot be overstated. In the face of such emphasis, sacred places and pilgrimages are insignificant. This idea did not change. Bhai Gurdas wrote:

> If bathing at places of pilgrimage brings liberation, frogs must certainly be saved. If growing long hair sets one free, the banyan tree with dangling tresses is saved. If going about naked serves a purpose, then the deer in the forest must be pious. And the ass which rolls in the dirt must too, if smearing ashes on the body can gain deliverance. The cows in the field are saved if silence gains salvation. Only the Guru can give us salvation. Only the Guru can set man free.
>
> (Bhai Gurdas, 36:14)

Although place matters little, since God pervades everywhere (Gurū Granth Sāhib, 1345), *simaraṇ*, remembering God, still remains essential. People must gather for *simaraṇ* and for *sevā*, service. As the Gurū Granth Sāhib is made up of poetry and is sung, communal worship is preferred. Sikhs believe that the custom of coming together for worship began in the days of Guru Nanak and that, subsequently, the notion of *laṅgar* was added by Guru Amar Das, and that the installation of the scripture, which became the Gurū Granth, created a fixed centre to Sikh life and activity. The *saṅgat*, the *Gurū Panth*, the congregation of people, also became central. It is among the congregation that the Name of God is treasured and repeated (Gurū Granth Sāhib, 72). It is also described as the 'school of the True Guru. There we learn to love God and appreciate his greatness' (Gurū Granth Sāhib, 1316).

Singing God's praise is essential. It is a means to liberation. 'Sing his praise. Hear it sung and love him with all your heart. Then you will gain joy in your heart and throw away all your pain' (*Japjī*, *pauṛi* 5).

Gurū Granth and Gurū Panth

In Sikhism, the place which is special is the place where the Gurū Granth Sāhib is installed and where the community is functioning – coming for *darśan*, reading the *gurbāṇī*, cooking and sharing food – getting on with life. What makes the place special is the presence of the Gurū. The Gurū is in the Granth, the book, and in the *panth*, the assembly. It does not matter where these elements are placed: any building will do – a home, a school, a hired hall, disused garages, cinemas – one place is as good as any other. It does not even have to be a building: sometimes a tent or an awning is used. Architectural splendour is welcome, but not essential. The people and the activity matter more than the place. Guru Arjan said, 'Very beautiful is that hut in which God's praises are sung, While the mansion in which God is forgotten is of no avail' (Macauliffe, vol. III, 1909: 23). This attitude means that Sikhs abroad have managed to cope until the community was established enough to build a satisfactory gurdwara.

Historic sites

The background to the development of Sikhism is the Panjab, a province of Northwestern India. The Panjab was an area in which the majority of the people were Muslims, and Hindus were the next most numerous community. Sikhs were always very much a minority. Although Sikhs have migrated abroad, few non-Panjābis have ever converted to Sikhism, making it a localised religion.

Panjab was divided in 1947 and the major part of it went to Pakistan. Muslim refugees travelled west to Pakistan and many Sikhs and Hindus left these areas and moved east toward India. The bulk of the Sikhs were squashed into a few districts in the Indian Panjab, and cut off from the areas where many of the Sikh Gurūs lived and where some of the major shrines were situated.

Fortunately, pilgrimage was not an important aspect of life. While Pakistan allows people to visit the sites, this involves travel and formalities. There are *granthī*s at important sites associated with the Gurūs, and caretakers at other sites. Many of the buildings were unable to function any more: they might be called historic gurdwaras, lifeless shells, with neither Gurū Granth nor *Gurū Panth* to make them live.

Responsibility for Sikh and Hindu sites fell to the Department of Archaeology in Pakistan. This must be a unique situation. It is unusual for the early sites of a religion to be largely inaccessible to devotees. Perhaps because of their inaccessibility, the actual places assume great importance and sentimental value to many people, especially sites associated with stories from the *janam sakhī*s. However, the Governments do make arrangements for Sikhs to travel from India to Nankana Sahib in Pakistan for the celebration of festivals, in the same way as the Governments have always allowed Muslim pilgrims from Pakistan to travel to the shrine of Khwaja Muin-ud-din Chishti at Ajmer Sharif in India for the festival there.

HISTORIC SITES ASSOCIATED WITH GURU NANAK

Guru Nanak was born and spent his childhood in a village called Talwandi Rai Bhoi, about forty miles from the city of Lahore. The place is now called Nankana Sahib in deference to the Gurū.

There is a large complex of buildings at the site known as the birthplace, the *janam asthān*. Many of those usually pictured are buildings of the modern period which were erected as hostels and other facilities to house and minister to the needs of pilgrims. Nearby, there are historic shrines which tradition associates with events in the life of the Gurū. There is a shrine at the place where the Gurū used money his father had given him to invest in business to buy food for holy men. Nanak justified this by saying that it was a profitable investment for the life to come, making it a truer bargain than any business deal. There is a shrine at the site where the buffaloes that Nanak was sent to look after invaded a field and ate the crop, but which was remarkably restored when the assessors went to survey the damage.

The site of the birthplace is said to have been marked by Guru Arjan during a visit. There is another gurdwara to mark Guru Arjan's visit and that of Guru Hargovind, who stayed in the same place. The existing buildings, however, are much later. In 1818–19 Maharaja Ranjit Singh ordered the building of the gurdwara at the birthplace, and several other local gurdwaras.

Another popular site in Pakistan is especially associated with Guru Nanak. This is Panja Sahib, which is at Hasan Abdal in Attock District. The story is one of the most popular of all. The *janam sakhīs* relate that Guru Nanak and Mardana were in the area when Mardana became thirsty. Guru Nanak told him to go up the hill and ask a Muslim holy man called Vali Kandhari, who lived at the top, for water. Vali Kandhari refused to give him any. Three times Mardana laboured up and down the hill, each time to be refused. Then Guru Nanak struck the ground with his staff and water spurted forth. Finding that he had no water in his well, Vali Kandhari flung a huge rock at Guru Nanak and Mardana, but the Gurū stopped it with his palm, and the imprint of his hand can be seen on the rock to this day.

The area was annexed during the reign of Ranjit Singh, and a shrine and a tank were constructed at the site. Later, another building, which apparently had beautiful frescoes, was erected but in 1928 the Gurdwara Prabandhak Committee took over the management of the site and had a new temple built, enlarged the tank, paved the area, and created a quadrangle with large buildings to house pilgrims. There is a spacious hall and a *laṅgar*. The area is encased in white marble with steps leading down into the pool and only the handprint is showing.

This story is very popular and the handprint is something tangible, and such a pleasing and personal mark of the Gurū's presence. Perhaps it is a story which shows the powers of the Gurū, and powers are valued by followers. The Panjābi writer, Kartar Singh Duggal, used it as the background to *Karamāt* (Miracle), a short story about a child doubting that miracles could happen, and then being in the area when, during the independence struggles, the local population stopped a train full of Indian prisoners by lying down on the railway line. This incident really did happen and some of those people were killed by the speeding train. If mere humans could stop a speeding express train, why, any miracle could happen.

The Sikh Gurūs did not all stay in one place and are not associated with one area. Guru Nanak's birthplace and the place where he spent his old age mark the ends of a life spent travelling. There are other gurdwaras which mark incidents in his life.

SITES ASSOCIATED WITH OTHER GURŪS

Guru Nanak's successor, Guru Angad, lived at Khadur and instructed Guru Amar Das to live in Goindwal, and it was here that Guru Amar Das had a significant piece of construction work done. He had a *baolī* prepared. A *baolī* is a well or a tank. This one has eighty-four *pauṛi*s (steps) leading to it. The number eighty-four echoes the traditional Hindu belief in eighty-four *lakh*s of lives. There is a popular belief that if a person bathes and says Guru Nanak's *Japjī Sāhib* on every step, then he or she would achieve liberation and would not come back again to this life. But the devout claim that liberation would be achieved by the contemplation on the Name achieved by these repetitions of the *Japjī*, and not by the bathing.

It is odd that the Gurū should have instituted a pilgrimage site when Guru Nanak had been so opposed to them, but some writers have pointed out that times were changing and that by the time of the third Gurū, there were few people left who remembered Guru Nanak, and the needs of the new group had to be considered. By instituting such places, the Gurū was adapting the old ways and teaching new ones. People were not to go on mindless pilgrimages to the old centres; this new pilgrimage was specifically Sikh. He also instituted meeting days, gatherings and festivals.

Amritsar

Guru Amar Das also started the construction of the pool at Amritsar. The site on which Amritsar is built is one which is surrounded by legends. People associate it with earlier religions. There was a pool of *amrit*, nectar, which was a sacred place from antiquity. Some say that it was visited by the Buddha and some say that the Hindu deity, Rām, and his sons fought there. Rām was killed and was revived by water from the pool. It is also associated with an incident involving a girl called Rajani, from a village called Patti. She was married to a man who was suffering from a horrible disease. She used to care for him. One day she had left him near the pool, and as he waited for her he noticed that the large black Indian crows which hopped into the water emerged pure white. He dragged his poor body into the water and was miraculously healed. There is a modern gurdwara to commemorate Rajani.

The Sikh Gurūs were keen on establishing new towns and centres. Amritsar was founded in 1577. The name *Amritsar* means pool (*sar*) of nectar (*amrit*). It was to impart immortality to the devotees who bathed in it. The pool was constructed during the reigns of the third and fourth Gurūs and was brick-lined during Guru Arjan's time. It was Guru Arjan who had the idea of building a temple in the middle of the tank. Early accounts say that Guru Arjan himself laid the foundation stone, though a second tradition has grown up recently that Mir Mohammad (1550–1635), known as Mian Mir, a Muslim holy man of Lahore, was asked to do the honours. The original foundation stone was apparently laid crooked and a mason straightened it. This was seen as an omen and it was said that, had it been left crooked, the temple would have stood forever. As it was, it would have to be rebuilt. And indeed, this has been necessary. The temple was demolished several times and rebuilt. The last time it was reconstructed was in 1764. The pool, temple, bridge – everything needed rebuilding. The basic structure was in place by 1776, though decoration, especially the gilding, was added later by Maharaja Ranjit Singh. The temple was originally called *Harmandir*, meaning simply 'the temple of Hari' (God). People called it *Harmandir Sāhib* to show respect. It was covered with gold by Maharaja Ranjit Singh and thereafter became popularly known as the Golden Temple.

Guru Arjan had the temple built on a lower level than its surroundings, and it is said that this meant that even the lowest had to go still lower to gain admittance. Most Indian temples are built high on plinths. Where most buildings have one door, this building was open on all four sides, and this is said to symbolise the four *varṇa*s – the *brahman*, *kṣatriya*, *vaiśya* and *śūdra*. The pattern of entrances on all four sides has been followed in many other historic gurdwaras.

The Sikh Gurūs and many other Panjābi poets have praised Amritsar, the temple and the pool. The poets say that bathing in the tank washes away sin and brings liberation. On the construction of Ramsar, a pool in Amritsar, Guru Arjan wrote:

> Ever bathe in Ramsar [God's tank]; Stir it up and drink the great nectareous juice. God's name is holy water; He who batheth in it shall have his desires fulfilled. Where God is spoken of in the company of the saints, The sins of millions of births are erased.
>
> (Macauliffe, vol. III, 1909: 60)

Ramsar was the name of the tank and it also means the association of saints, the congregation.

The Gurū Granth Sāhib was installed inside *Harmandir Sāhib* in 1604.

Obviously the city became a pilgrimage place, a cult centre. As time went by, individuals, groups, communities and various bodies of people built residences there. Amritsar is the only city which has *katra*s, nowadays meaning a residential area with a market. Originally *katra*s were walled fortresses owned by individual families. Ranjit Singh gave the city a single wall, and in modern times the city has developed outside its original limits. The plan of many Indian towns shows the centrality of religion, for the religious institutions are in the middle and residential districts and bazaars closely surround the temples. Outside of this traditional centre there may be airy suburbs and industrial estates.

Guru Arjan had another tank excavated about ten miles south of Amritsar, at a place now called Taran Taran (Pool of Salvation). Taran Taran rapidly became associated with healing, and is particularly known as a centre for people with leprosy. Guru Arjan built several other towns which flourished. Apart from contributions and gifts from devotees, the taxes, the *octroi* (taxes on goods entering the city), and the build-up of trade meant that the Gurūs became rich and powerful. The Gurū began to be addressed as *Sacca*

Padśah (True Emperor). This had all happened fairly quickly. Nanak had died in 1539 and by the early 1600s the Gurūs were sufficiently rich and powerful to be noticed by the Mughul emperor. Sikh tradition claims that the emperor, Akbar, was friendly toward Sikh Gurūs. However, when Akbar died his successor, Jahangir, was not so tolerant. Akbar inspired affection and accomplished things by making friends and influencing people. By contrast, Jahangir was a manager, an administrator. His memoirs are those of a man running an enormous enterprise and trying to make a success of keeping it in hand. Jahangir says in his memoirs that the Gurū 'was noised about as a religious and worldly leader'.

Jahangir's attention was focused on the issue of the Sikh Gurūs by the problems he had because of his son's rebellion. The rebellious son, Khusrau, had fled and had met Guru Arjan, who had made a mark on Khusrau's forehead in saffron. Jahangir also mentions that he had had it in mind to 'put an end to this false traffic'. Certainly, Guru Arjan came to an untimely end. At the traditional site where he disappeared in Lahore there is a historic shrine, *Dehra Sāhib*, just outside the walls of Lahore Fort. It has the gilded dome so characteristic of a Ranjit Singh building.

Akāl Takht

The seventh Gurū, Hargovind, erected a new building in Amritsar. This is known as the *Akāl Takht* or the *Akāl Bunga*, the throne of the timeless one. It contrasts with the *Harmandir*. When it was suggested to Guru Arjan that the *Harmandir* be raised on high, he had it built low so that people have to go downstairs to get in. The *Akāl Takht* is on a platform; it was a centre for holding court, administration and earthly rule.

Harmandir Sāhib is, and always has been, a building totally devoted to religious activity. The only activity inside is the reading of the Gurū Granth Sāhib. The other activities have always taken place at the *Akāl Bunga*. The Gurū, when he was alive, stayed in the *Akāl Bunga*. He held court there, dispensed justice and watched fighting and military activities. The Gurū practised swordsmanship and raised an armed unit of bodyguards. He had eight hundred horses, three hundred troopers and sixty men with firearms always in his service. He encouraged hunting. It is also said that, apart from the hymns at the *Harmandir*, *vār*s, heroic ballads, were recited by musicians at the *Akāl Bunga*. The purpose was to encourage a spirit of heroism. This militarism may strike modern readers as somewhat at odds with the usual image of an Indian holy man, but in India it was not unusual for holy men to bear arms. Many of them had armed and militant retinues, and there are still armed *sādhu*s today. There are Sikh warriors called *nihaṅg*s who still go about with swords and spears, like eighteenth-century warriors.

*Hukamnāmā*s, orders, were issued from the *Akāl Takht*. Meetings were held, and decisions taken. It is claimed, although there seems little evidence to support such claims, that the eighteenth-century warrior groups kept an administration system involving files called *misl*s at the *Akāl Bunga*. These files recorded their areas of rule, which is why the Sikh eighteenth-century groups were called *misl*s.

It is said that *pāhul* (initiation ceremonies) took place there too. Ratan Singh Bhangu says in *Pracin Panth Prakāś* that the warriors held the *Akāl Takht* in high esteem and that they used to frequent the place. He records some ceremonial practices, some rituals relating to the warrior tradition of India. After these had been performed, the warrior would take a bath in the tank, would then be dressed up like a bridegroom, and go fully armed to the *Akāl Takht*. Drums and military music accompanied the proceedings.

Throughout subsequent history, meetings have been held at the *Akāl Takht* and *morcā*s (literally battlefronts, demonstrations) launched from thence. Like *Harmandir* itself, the actual building has been destroyed and rebuilt several times. The building normally shown in pictures dates from Ranjit Singh's times. It was damaged during Operation Bluestar (a military operation during which the complex was entered by the army) in 1984. It has since been largely reconstructed, and work is still underway.

Forts and other buildings

Some Sikhs were militarised during the Gurū period, and, throughout the eighteenth century, defensive works and the building of forts became an important activity. An early fort was Lohgarh (the castle of steel), which dates from 1610 CE. Guru Hargovind also built a city called Kiratpur (the abode of praise) on land given him by a Rāja. The seventh Gurū, Har Rai, retreated to the foothills of the Himalayas. He was away from the main centres of Sikh activity. He seems to have been a man of peace. People mattered more than things to him. He is quoted as saying, 'You can repair or rebuild a temple or a mosque but not a broken heart'.

His successor, Har Krishan, died at the age of eight, so he had no opportunity to build. He died in Delhi and the site is commemorated. A popular gurdwara called *Bangla Sāhib* (the place of the residence) has been erected. Many Sikhs go there to do *sevā* by offering water to visitors. The water comes from a special spring associated with the Gurū.

The ninth Gurū, Tegh Bahadar, was also a man of retiring habits, a poet and contemplative teacher, not a fighter. He was discovered in a village called Bakala, for the dying child had said *Baba Bakale* (the Gurū is in Bakala) and Tegh Bahadar, his grand-uncle, was living in Bakala. Rivals gave Tegh Bahadar a hard time. The doors of the *Harmandir* in Amritsar were slammed in his face. The relatives made Kiratpur unendurable. He went into the wilderness where he bought a hillock and built himself a village which he named Anandpur (the City of bliss, joy). He hoped to find peace in Anandpur, but he was hounded out of Panjab and travelled to Delhi, Agra, Banaras, and Gaya, and eventually arrived at Patna in Bihar. Here his wife gave birth to a son. The Gurū was in Dhaka at the time of the birth. He went to Assam before returning and then, after some years in eastern India, he went back to Panjab. Sites where events happened on these travels are marked by shrines. He was executed in Delhi. The details of the execution are unclear. The site where he was executed is marked by Gurdwara Sis Ganj, the place of the head. The head was cremated in Anandpur and there is another Sis Ganj there. The Gurū's body was cremated at the site where Gurdwara Rikab Ganj stands in Delhi. These gurdwaras are very popular. Guru Govind Singh says:

> He suffered martyrdom for the sake of his faith.
> He lost his head but revealed not his secret
> He disdained to perform miracles or juggler's tricks,
> For such men fill God with shame.
> He burst the bonds of mortal clay
> And went to the abode of God.
> No one has ever performed an act as noble as his.
>
> (*Bachitar Nāṭak*, 5:15)

Once Guru Govind Singh regained control of Anandpur, which was where the *Khālsā* was formed and which was the *Khālsā* centre, the area was fortified by the Gurū. He bought land and built a chain of forts which lie along the foothills between the Satluj and Jamuna. The sites associated with the Gurūs have a special place in the heart of the community. The gurdwaras are always mentioned in *Ardās*, the prayer.

Temporal authority

Traditionally, decisions affecting the social and political life of the community were taken in gurdwaras through a consensus of the *saṅgat*. Such decisions were binding. Nowadays, some gurdwaras have been designated as seats of temporal authority, *takht*s (literally, thrones). These are the *Akāl Takht* at Amritsar, Patna Sahib in Bihar where Guru Govind Singh was born, Keshgarh at Anandpur Sahib, Nander in Maharashtra where Guru Govind Singh died, and in 1976 Damdama Sahib, where Guru Govind Singh dictated the Gurū Granth Sāhib from memory, was declared a *takht* by the Shiromani Gurdwara Prabandhak Committee. The shrines associated with Guru Govind Singh were built on the orders of Maharaja Ranjit Singh.

The *takht*s are spread around India. Important decisions were always taken from the *Akāl Takht*. The other *takht*s are perhaps more concerned with supervising correct practices and ensuring adherence to orthodoxy. Their role has frequently been political.

The eighteenth century

The eighteenth century was a period of chaos; Amritsar was out of bounds much of the time, the temple was desecrated, wrecked, and the pool filled in. In 1763, the Sikhs gained some control of the area and began rebuilding. There had been huts around the temple and pool from early times. During the eighteenth century, the *sardār*s (chieftains) began to build *bunga*s (rest houses, dwellings) as places for soldiers to stay for the purpose of defence. Eventually there were *bunga*s belonging to individual *sardār*s, to rich and influential communities, and to religious orders, *udāsī*s, *nirmalā*s, *sevā panthi*s and *akālīs*. The *bungas* were built between 1765–1833 and many became seats of learning, where scholars and poets were in residence. The scholars included Rattan Singh Bhangu who wrote *Pracin Panth Prakās*. Other scholars included exponents of vedantic learning, poetry, theology, Sanskrit and sanskritic learning. Guru Govind Singh himself had despatched five Sikh scholars to Kashi, now called Varanasi, the centre of Indian learning, where they had stayed for some time (seven or possibly ten years). They are considered the founders of the *nirmalā* order. The arts of music and calligraphy were practised. There were craftsmen. There were doctors. The *bungas* were a sort of university. Madanjit Kaur (1983: 184) observes that *bungas* have now all but vanished. They were knocked down in order to extend the *parakrama* (path) around the pool. She says, 'No attempt was made to preserve them in one or the other form. It appears the Gurdwara Prabandhak Committee could not visualise this eventuality'.

Many shrines were erected around the complex at Amritsar by the *sardārs*. Some mark sites where the Gurūs sat while the work was in progress. There is one site called *Atsath Tīrath*, and bathing there is said to be as effective as bathing in all of the sixty-eight pilgrimage sites of India. Some lofty and impressive buildings of the eighteenth century are still standing. One is Baba Atal, a tower with nine storeys, each of which commemorates a year in the life of Atal Rai, the son of Guru Hargovind. The little boy raised a dead play-fellow to life. Miracle-working is considered against Sikh tradition. So when the Gurū reprimanded his son, the boy lay down and did not regain consciousness, giving his life to make up for the mistake.

Ranjit Singh's era

Although Ranjit Singh was a Sikh and ruled in the name of the *Khālsā*, government was run not from Amritsar but from Lahore. Lahore was the capital of the *subā*, the province, and holding the city gave legitimacy to Ranjit Singh's rule. The centre at Amritsar was embellished and expanded and the religious side was financed and encouraged. It is interesting to note that Amritsar was apparently above mere politics. Lahore remained the site of Ranjit Singh's *darbār* and administration.

The Maharaja certainly visited and worshipped at Amritsar and performed acts of service to *Harmandir Sāhib*. He had gold inlay and white marble provided for the walls, and he paid for decorations. It has been said that everything that could be done with white marble and gold was done. Ranjit Singh presented golden doors with floral designs and illustrations showing episodes from the lives of the Gurūs. He gave canopies, jewels, lands and riches. The ultimate administration of the temple was in the hands of the Maharaja. He decided disputes and sorted out who should have what from the income. He took on the *Akālīs*, the *nihaṅgs*, the warriors whose kind can still be seen with their swords and spears. The other Sikh chiefs also gave wealth to *Harmandir Sāhib*, but the actual control remained with the court at Lahore.

GENEROSITY TOWARDS ALL RELIGIOUS INSTITUTIONS

Ranjit Singh's generosity was enormous. He also paid for the gilding of another Golden Temple, the one at Varanasi, dedicated to Śiva as Lord of the Universe. Ranjit Singh and other *sardārs* also gave land revenues to religious persons and their institutions as charity. They gave *dharmath* (grants). Such a large number of individuals gave grants of village revenues to the *Harmandir Sāhib*, from such a wide geographical area, that there had to be a special staff of accountants to cope with the arrangements and collect the revenue. Indu Banga (1978: 148ff.) describes something of the complexity of the grants and the system, and also comments on how Maharaja Ranjit Singh's instructions regarding the management of the *Harmandir* indicate the nature of his control.

The largest group of recipients of grants were *Bedis* and *Sodhis*, descendants of the Gurūs' families who were revered by the Sikhs. Khushwant Singh (1963) observes, 'Until recent years several members of the Sodhi caste claiming descent from the Sodhi Guru were in the habit of styling themselves Gurus and accepting worship and offerings from credulous peasants'.

The munificence of Sikh *sardārs* towards religious institutions of all sorts is truly amazing. They gave grants to the *maths* of *jogīs*, the religious centres maintained by *jogīs*. Jogī Tillā, the premier *math*, which is rather a long and difficult journey from anywhere, perched up on the summit of a mountain in the Salt Range, was generously provided for. The buildings must have been splendid, and even now traces of fine paintings can be seen on the walls. There were grants to the famous Jwalamukhi Temple of the Goddess in Kangra. There were grants to *Vaiṣṇava Bairāgī* establishments, and *madad-i-ma'āsh* grants to Muslim establishments. The *sardār*s supported all manner of religious institutions, practitioners, craftsmen, painters, poets and singers – endless lists of generosity. They were splendidly catholic in their tastes. They were generous with their gifts but their extraordinary generosity of spirit is one of their most endearing qualities. They were not passively tolerant, but actively encouraged all kinds of religious activity.

Many of the Sikh sites in Panjab are associated with holy men. Some are sites where special events took place, or where trees which gave shade and shelter to holy persons grow, or are *samādh*s, where they were cremated. Many of the old shrines were not particularly *khālsā* oriented. Some were the *darbār*s of members of the Gurūs' families. Some shrines are places associated with saintly people. Some were admirable examples of inter-faith practice. Gurdwara Jogan Shah in Peshawar is a thriving and busy gurdwara. Jogan Shah was a person equally respected by Muslims, Hindus and Sikhs, and on his death the gurdwara was founded.

The sites which are more especially *khālsā* oriented often mark the scene of some dispute in the struggles of the *Akālī*s to gain control of the shrines during the 1920s. These sites are memorials to people who were killed during the clashes.

Architecture

There are few studies of Sikh architecture. *Harmandir Sāhib* is recognised and admired, but few other Sikh buildings attract attention. Many of the old buildings have disappeared long since and been replaced by more modern ones. There are no descriptions of the actual buildings of the earliest *dharamsālā*s. According to the *janam sakhī*s, when Guru Nanak defeated someone in argument, that person fell at his feet and opened a *dharamsālā*. But no one described such a structure.

There was a major period of building during Ranjit Singh's reign. He had commemorative gurdwaras and other works erected across India, Pakistan and Bangladesh. Ranjit Singh's architectural style has sometimes been called late Mughul. The craftsmen and artists who had been employed in the mughul *karkhanas* (studios) left their jobs when the empire began to crumble and sought their fortunes in smaller, regional courts. It should be remembered that Indian artists and craftsmen were supported in the studios kept by the princes and the aristocracy. *Rājas* and *Nawābs* supported vast numbers of people and kept them in employment, practising their special skills and using their talents. The influence of post-Mughul art can be clearly traced in Panjabi painting. Artists went to work for the rich states in the Panjab hills, like Guler and Kangra, where schools of art developed. Many artists, building on these traditions, were employed by Ranjit Singh too. Perhaps Ranjit Singh is a little overshadowed by Mughul magnificence. Their buildings were quite extraordinary, and many were still in good condition and available for use by the rulers, like Ranjit Singh and the British, who came after them.

Traditional gurdwaras often take *Harmandir Sāhib* as a model. Thus many older gurdwaras were two-storeyed, with the first floor having a gallery, looking down on to the ground floor. The upper floor is supported by pillars and the outer walls. The Gurū Granth Sāhib occupies the central position, demarcated by the pillars. There is a canopy above the holy book. The congregation sit around the outside. There were doorways on all sides. Windows, supported on brackets, bulge out from the upper floor.

Traditional buildings always have domes. A traditional Sikh dome has a characteristic shape. It is ribbed or fluted and has what is called an inverted lotus symbol at the top. The domes have a wide base and reach their maximum circumference less than half way up, which gives them a characteristic shape. They have a *kalas* on top, a short cylindrical construction which has some concentric circles and a little canopy at the top. Some pendants hang from the rim of the canopy.

Many gurdwaras have a *deorhī*, an ornamental gateway through which people approach and get their first glimpse of the sanctuary. Some *deorhīs* accommodate the gurdwara's treasury.

In the days when people liked to view Sikhism as syncretism, drawing elements from both Islam and Hinduism, it was accepted that the architecture revealed this. The buildings have domes and arches, which were an Islamic introduction into India. Sikh buildings like *Harmandir Sāhib*, however, have more domes than do the classic Mughul buildings. *Harmandir Sāhib* has one main dome, surrounded by many smaller domes, and tiny ones line the parapet.

Some of the decoration is of a Hindu form, so what emerges is perhaps a synthesis of the older styles into something new – a style of its own. It was something new, but it emerged from its time and place. The craftsmen came from various backgrounds.

Ranjit Singh's buildings were highly decorated. The gold was certainly an astonishing feature. When Emily Eden, the sister of the Governor General, visited in December 1838, she admired the frieze, the height of a man, decorated with birds and flowers. Ranjit Singh thought that she was insufficiently impressed and took her hand and made her feel the metal. It is actually covered with sheets of copper which are gilded. The white and gold building, reflected in the pool, is a striking sight. It stands surrounded with water and is reached by a causeway. *Harmandir Sāhib* is decorated using various techniques.

Gurdwaras were decorated with frescoes, mirror work, plaster decorations, filigree, and other striking techniques. They often showed Indian mythological themes. There are also walls decorated with verses from the Gurū Granth Sāhib, similar to the Muslim practice of using finely calligraphed religious verses as a decoration. Sometimes buildings even as recent as those of Ranjit Singh's time have been replaced. Priceless frescoes and plasterwork have been destroyed and, in the process, historical evidence has been destroyed too. Art has been replaced by marble, gloss paint and concrete. After Ranjit Singh died there was too much unrest for costly and time-consuming building works to be undertaken.

In old books on architecture, such as Latif (1892), no distinction is drawn between Sikh and Hindu buildings. *Śivāla*s and *thākurdwarā*s, *samādh*s (Śaiva and Vaiṣṇava temples, cremation sites) and other buildings bear eloquent witness to the wealth and generosity of officials and courtiers at the court of Ranjit Singh. Latif gives a description of the *dharamsālā* existing in the 1890s, the *dharamsālā* of Bawa Khuda Singh. Khuda Singh was originally called Jaswant but, we are told, he changed his name on becoming a *fakīr*, and called himself Khuda Singh, Khuda being an Islamic word for God. His *dharamsālā* was built of masonry. There was a gateway to the north leading to a large courtyard lined with brick houses. There was a large hall for assemblies and the Granth was kept there. There were meetings every third day for the singing of *bhajan*s before large assemblies. Offerings were made to the holy book, and bread was distributed to *fakīr*s (hermits, beggars, *sādhu*s – poor or holy people).

Latif also describes in detail the *thākurdwarās* existing in Lahore, which housed Sri Kṛṣṇa as well as the Gurū Granth Sāhib. This sort of arrangement was not uncommon. Within living memory there were institutions with both deities and Gurū Granth Sāhibs. The post-Singh Sabha/*Akālī* reformist view is that such things are heresy and that those in charge of the institutions should be censured. One major initiative by the Singh Sabha was the removal of the deities and the removal of the traditional practitioners from their positions. Many of the old buildings have been destroyed and with them, priceless works of art.

The shrines were divided among the peoples of Panjab in 1925. The Sikh Gurdwaras Act specified and provided a schedule laying down which buildings were Hindu, which were Muslim and which were Sikh. The Gurdwara Act of 1925 placed the management of Sikh shrines in the hands of the Shiromani Gurdwara Prabandhak Committee. There had never been uniformity in Sikh practice and in 1931 the Committee decided that a code should be prepared to regulate individual and corporate life. On 3 February 1945, Sikh Rahit Maryādā was approved. It is a code with strong *Akālī* and Singh Sabha influence. Many individuals do not necessarily agree with, or practise their religion according to, the *Rahit*.

Pools

Perhaps the focus of Sikhism has changed. Many of the older books on the Sikhs place greater emphasis on the pools – e.g., the pool of *amrit* (Amritsar) – rather than the buildings. The focus seems to have been *isnān*, bathing – the third element of the often-quoted summary of desirable Sikh practice – *Nām dān isnān* (the Name, charity and bathing). Cunningham and early writers barely mention the temple; the pool seems to have been the focus of the site.

After a general introduction in which he mentions *Harmandir* and Ranjit Singh's generosity, in the entry on Amritsar in the *Mahān Koś* (1930), Kahan Singh of Nabha first lists the pools – Santokhsar, Kaulsar, Bibeksar and Ramsar. These come before the *Akāl Takht* and the other buildings. Perhaps the embellishment of the buildings in Ranjit Singh's times changed the importance of the elements in the sites. The possession of the buildings became a focus for the *Akālī* movement this century, and, because of the bitterness of the disputes and the cruelty involved, the buildings probably now hold more importance than they ever did before.

New building

Sikh buildings are given contributions by devotees. Therefore, nowadays most pieces of marble are inscribed with the name of the person who contributed that particular slab of stone. In fact, even the individual blades of fans and other fitments are often similarly inscribed with the name of the donor. It seems to be becoming important to people to have their name, or the names of their dead kin inscribed on something in a sacred place.

There has been a major period of construction this century. Many of the buildings which can be seen today were erected fairly recently. There are new gurdwaras on many sites. They commemorate sites of importance in the lives of the Gurūs and subsequent history. One interesting modern development is Gurdwara Hemkunt, which is situated in the Himalayas. In *Bachitar Nāṭak*, Guru Govind Singh relates that before taking birth, he was busy performing penance at this place in the hills, where seven peaks are visible. He was practising austerity and worshipping the god of death. His parents performed high spiritual efforts, pleasing the Almighty who commanded the Gurū to go into the world. The site was discovered by Pandit Tara Singh Narottam, and in 1936 a hut was built at the site. Subsequently, a Gurū Granth Sāhib was installed and a gurdwara erected.

As people have become richer, they have erected new buildings and rebuilt old ones. Before the troubles, Panjab was quite a prosperous state. It was better developed than parts of Europe and there was disposable wealth. Houses stopped being made of mud and became *pacca*, made of bricks – and sometimes, very fancy brickwork. People were also minded to improve the gurdwaras.

Modern gurdwaras are also erected by new sectarian groups. Gurdwaras erected by independent groups are not subject to the control of the Gurdwara Prabandhak Committee and they do not participate in *Akālī* politics. Their practices may also vary from the Rahit Maryādā practices. In many ways these small groups reflect the traditional pattern of religion – a man and his disciples – which is always trying to emerge. Perhaps running a religion by committee does tend to create arenas for group disagreements. The politicisation of some areas of Sikhism has not given universal satisfaction.

NEW BUILDING OVERSEAS

With the migration of Sikhs abroad, there has been an enormous growth in the building of gurdwaras all over the world. It takes several years for any community to organise well enough to take on the expense and responsibility of building or adapting old buildings. Sikhs, like Hindus and Muslims, have taken over a great variety of old buildings. Some gurdwaras have been purpose-built. Some groups favour modern building styles and others prefer to have traditional domes and decorative styles. The form gurdwaras take in Europe and North America depends on taste and planning regulations.

Modern gurdwaras

The layout of gurdwaras varies according to geographical location, the community, taste, and other factors, but there are some features which are common to most gurdwaras. However, it should be recalled that there are differences of opinion, and some sectarian groups do not necessarily follow the pattern.

There is almost always a flagpole outside the building. The pole is wrapped in orange coloured cloth and a pennant waves on high. It shows that the building is a gurdwara.

Ideally, a Sikh should go daily to the gurdwara, to join the *Gurū Panth* before the Gurū Granth Sāhib. The Gurū Granth Sāhib can be read at home, but then a person would miss the benefit of joining the congregation.

Gurdwaras are open to all. All communities and castes are welcome and all are equal, though shoes, tobacco, liquor and other intoxicants are prohibited. There is always a place where visitors can leave their shoes. In small gurdwaras, there may be just a room or compartmented shelves for this purpose. In large gurdwaras, there may be a properly organised system and Sikhs may do *sevā* by receiving and storing people's shoes away. Sometimes people who have done wrong may perform penance by cleaning the shoes.

Visitors also cover their heads to show respect. Most gurdwaras have a collection of suitable scarves kept in a basket near the door for loan to anyone who has not come prepared. If the visitors are not Sikhs, and are clearly strangers, Sikhs will invariably come forth and receive the persons, and escort them around, explaining about the gurdwara and Sikhism.

It is the presence of the Gurū Granth Sāhib which makes it necessary to cover one's head and remove one's shoes. One is similarly required to remove one's shoes and cover one's head on visiting a bookshop in Amritsar. A shop is not sacred, but the books are.

On entering the gurdwara, there is often a board on which is written the *wāq*, the 'orders for the day', meaning the verse which has presented itself when the Gurū Granth Sāhib was first opened in the morning.

The prayer hall is an important room. In India, public areas are usually floored with marble, but areas where the congregation sit are often carpeted and the carpets are covered with white sheeting, so that it can be kept clean. In Britain, the prayer room has a carpet. The congregation sit on the floor with the women on one side of the room and the men on the other side. There is an aisle up the middle of the room by which those who arrive can approach the Gurū Granth Sāhib, make contributions and bow. The fact that men sit on one side and women on the other is not a religious requirement. It is customary. When women are holding *Īstrī Sabhā*, the women's meeting, they sit on both sides.

The prayer hall is arranged like the traditional court of an Indian king. The meeting is called *darbār* or *dīvān* (royal court). The Gurū Granth Sāhib is installed upon a special throne called a *mañjī*, a cot. It is covered with rich, decorative cloths called *rumālā*s. There is a canopy above the Gurū Granth Sāhib, and there are often attractive rugs and fresh flowers placed in front of the *mañjī*. In modern gurdwaras, the *mañjī* is usually located at the front, facing the congregation. The reader sits behind the Gurū Granth Sāhib.

Swords, *chakra*s, and arrows are also placed in front of the *mañjī*. The sword is used to touch the *kaṛāh praśād* before it is distributed. Some gurdwaras also have a *nāgāra*, a large drum, which is beaten at the conclusion of worship, to invite attendance at the *laṅgar*. The drumming at *Harmandir Sāhib* is very dramatic indeed, especially at night, when the Gurū Granth Sāhib is put to rest.

Gurdwaras also have a separate room where the Gurū Granth Sāhib is kept at night. After the final prayer, the *rumālā* and the side cloths around the Gurū Granth Sāhib are removed. Then the book is closed and wrapped in two white cloths. There are three small cushions which are normally underneath the Gurū Granth Sāhib. These are placed on top and the Gurū Granth Sāhib is then placed on top of the *granthī*'s head and taken to its room. In the morning, it is brought out again. When it is moved, everyone stands up to show respect. If there are extra copies of the Gurū Granth Sāhib, they are kept, similarly wrapped up, in the same room. At *Harmandir Sāhib*, the Gurū Granth Sāhib is brought out in a palanquin made of gold and silver and the Sikhs throw rose petals as the procession emerges.

In many gurdwaras, there are no pictures in the hall where the Gurū Granth Sāhib is installed. Bhai Gurdas said that the true picture of the Gurū is in the Gurū Granth Sāhib. However, some gurdwaras are decorated with assorted pictures of the Gurūs and incidents in Sikh history.

There will probably be a place to the side of the Gurū Granth Sāhib allocated to the musicians, who sit and sing. On the opposite side there is usually a small table on which rests the bowl of *kaṛāh praśād*, covered with a clean, white cloth.

Visitors bow down before the holy volume and touch their forehead to the ground. They make some offering. This may be money or may be food, milk, fruit or sweets. These are used in the Gurū's kitchen. Every gurdwara has a *laṅgar*, a kitchen, and an eating area. In India, the historic gurdwaras have huge kitchens. The *rotīs*, unleavened Indian bread, are cooked on huge, platform-like stoves. The vegetables are cooked in vats and stirred with large wooden paddles. At a popular gurdwara, food is available at all times and to all comers, so there is always activity in the kitchens. In India, people sit in lines on the floor to eat. Sikhs perform *sevā* by cooking and serving food. Of course, all this activity produces a lot of washing up. Gurdwaras have special rooms for this, separate from the kitchen, so that the dirty dishes can be returned to the washing up area without going through the kitchen.

In overseas communities, kitchens may also be busy. There may be tables provided for serving the food and some gurdwaras provide tables for people to eat at. Some gurdwaras provide chairs for diners to sit down and eat in comfort, but at others, diners stand at the tables. In some gurdwaras, Sikhs do *sevā* by attending to and waiting on those who are eating and offering more food or tea. In some overseas communities, diners sit in lines on the floor as they do in India. Arrangements are a matter for the local community, and presumably the accommodation available and the climate have a bearing on the provision. The congregations are practical people.

In Asia, gurdwaras provide rest rooms, bathrooms and toilet facilities. Travellers can stay free of charge for a day or more. Facilities are available at some gurdwaras elsewhere. Communities try to meet local needs. In the daytime, the dining areas of some British gurdwaras are used by old people as a place to come and gather. It is more or less an informal day centre. Gurdwaras are not just places of worship; they are social institutions as well.

Gurdwaras are run by management committees elected by the members. Office bearers are volunteers. Community gurdwaras (as opposed to historic gurdwaras) are independent and not subject to any outside authority. The community is therefore free to make its own decisions.

Although gurdwaras have different names, such as the Singh Sabha, Ramgaṛhīā Sabhā or Sikh Temple, there are no differences of doctrine or belief. Anyone is free to attend any *dīvān*. The names show which of the cultural or sectarian groups within Sikhism established the gurdwara and provide the management committee. If there are several gurdwaras in an area, they will probably arrange to hold *dīvān* on different days so that people can make maximum use of the facilities. Gurdwaras are open from dawn to dusk and people are welcome to come in at any time.

FURTHER READING

Babraa, Davinder Kaur (1981) *Visiting a Sikh Temple*, London, Lutterworth.

Banga, Indu (1978) *Agrarian System of the Sikhs*, New Delhi, South Asia Books.

Dhanjal, B. (1994) *Amritsar*, London, Evans Brothers.

Kaur, Madanjit (1983) *The Golden Temple, Past and Present*, Amritsar, Guru Nanak Dev University Press.

Khan, Mohammad Waliullah Khan (1962) *Sikh Shrines in West Pakistan*, Karachi, Department of Archaeology, Ministry of Education and Information, Government of Pakistan.

Khushwant Singh (1963–66) *A History of the Sikhs*, vols I and II, London and Bombay, Oxford University Press.
Latif, Syad Muhammad (1892) *Lahore: Architectural Remains*, Lahore, Sandhu Printers (reprinted 1981).
Loehlin, C.H. (1958) *The Sikhs and Their Scriptures*, Lucknow, Lucknow Publishing House and ISPCK Delhi.
Macauliffe, M.A. (1909) *The Sikh Religion*, Oxford, Clarendon Press (reprinted 1985, Delhi, S. Chand).
Randhir, G.S. (1990) *Sikh Shrines in India*, New Delhi, Government of India, Ministry of Information and Broadcasting.

7. Chinese Religions

Xinzhong Yao

The Chinese had long viewed their homeland as the centre of the world, both geographically and politically, and so named it *Chungguo*, the Middle Kingdom. The whole of China was taken as a holy land, surrounded by barbarians and seas. Within this land, nowhere was not sacred. In the period of the Warring States (403–221 BCE), the founder of the *yin–yang* school, Tsou Yen (*c.* 350–270 BCE), in his theory extended and upgraded this idea's religious significance. According to Tsou Yen, China was one of the eighty-one continents in the world. This continent was also the most sacred land and, therefore, was called *Chih Hsien Shen Chou* – the Divine Continent of the Red Region. From that time, the idea that China was a sacred land exerted a great influence on Chinese literature, philosophy and religion.

In a more specific sense, the Chinese concept of sacred space comes from their peculiar world-view. The world, or cosmos, is conveniently said to be composed of three most important existences: heaven, earth and humans. The theory of cosmic parallel between heaven and earth, and the superiority of the former to the latter, prepares the way for the recognition of sacred space. The places that present the most similar geographical features to heaven, or are conceived to be nearest to heaven, would be the most sacred. Consequent on this belief, there come, in order, the sacred mountains, rivers, cities and regions.

Furthermore, human beings are not isolated from heaven and earth, and all three are in a close and mutually affecting relationship. Heaven is above and earth is below, with human beings standing in between. First of all, human beings are viewed as the creatures of heaven and earth. In some sense, heaven is taken as the male force and earth as the female force, and these two fundamental powers produced the human beings as well as ten thousand things as 'brothers and sisters' of humans. Human beings originally came from heaven and earth, therefore it is believed to be an ideal for human beings to return to their origin and live in a place in complete accordance with the principles of heaven and earth. This is exactly what Lao Tzu means by saying, 'Humans follow the earth, earth follows heaven . . .' (*Tao Te Ching*, Chapter 25). Thus the exploration of the relationship between human beings and heaven and earth becomes a central topic and an essential pursuit of Chinese philosophy and religion. Taoism distinguishes the cultural from the natural, and regards the former as the destroyer and exploiter of the latter. A place is sacred not because of its utilitarian benefit for the people but because of its possible function of incarnating *Tao*, and the more uncivilised a place is, the more valuable and sacred. Confucians integrate the natural and divine – *Tao* of Heaven – and the cultural and secular – *tao* of humans – and believe that the only way to carry out *Tao* of Heaven is to follow *tao* of humans, that is, to perform human duties to heaven, to state and to family. Therefore, the sacred place is not in the natural world but in social centres.

To live a harmonious life with heaven and earth does not mean only to imitate and repeat their routines. Human beings are also viewed as essentially connected with heaven and earth. Without humans, the harmony of the cosmos could not have come into being, or it would have been meaningless even if this harmony did exist. Confucians firmly believe that only by the effort of human beings, especially by the heroic activities of sages, would the principles of heaven and earth become realised, just as Tung Chung-shu (179–104? BCE) expressed it,

> Heaven, Earth and man are the three origins of all things. Heaven gives them birth, Earth nourishes them and man perfects them.
>
> (Fung, vol. II, 1953: 32)

In this process, places in which originally there was little or no significance became the places that were imbued with great appeal to the people, such as the birthplaces of sages and the worksites of heroes, which thereafter were believed to be sacred places.

Sacred places are expected to perform certain religious functions, that is, some of them, either by their natural features or by the features attached by human beings, can easily undertake the job of mediators between human beings and the spiritual world. By this mediatorship, humans should be able to avoid or lessen coming disasters, to invite blessings from gods or spirits and to obtain a harmonious relationship between the human world and the spiritual world. In order to strengthen this kind of mediatorship, special buildings were set up, either as parts of the original sacred places or as new sites for sacrifices, and rituals were conducted within them. These buildings gradually became centres of religious worship and places that linked human beings with God or gods. The religious buildings that were used for the purpose of sacrifices, offerings and worship are normally differentiated into two categories: outdoor altars and indoor temples. The outdoor altars are dedicated to sacrifices or worship of heavenly and earthly spirits, the most powerful among them being *Shang Ti* (Lord on High) or *T'ien* (Heaven). The indoor temples originally were used only for the worship of the ancestral spirits, but they were later extended to all other human deities or even supernatural spirits.

Sacred space in China was thus present in two kinds of phenomena: natural places that were believed to function as the most efficient 'bridge' between humans and the spirits, and social places that were created to imitate or pay homage to the gods or deities of the spiritual world. The mountains, rivers and land belong to the first phenomena, and altars, temples and cities belong to the second. Among these sacred places, the Altar of Heaven, the Temple of Ancestors and the sacred mountains are the most representative examples that have been recognised as great cultural heritages of China.

Altar of Heaven

In the capital of imperial China, there were four places that were of greatest significance for the state religion: the Altar of Heaven, the Altar of Earth, the Temple of Ancestors, and the Altars of Land and Grain. Their locations were arranged strictly according to the description of the ancient capitals of the Chou dynasty (1122–221 BCE) in the *Book of Rituals*: the Temple of Ancestors is located in the east side of the imperial city while the Altars of Land and Grain lie on the west side. The Altar of Earth is found in the northern suburb and the Altar of Heaven is situated in the southern suburb of the forbidden city.

T'ien (Heaven), in the religious sense, had been regarded as the Lord of Heaven or the place where this God and other deities live, therefore the Altar of Heaven (*T'ien Tan*) became the most splendid building among all kinds of religious buildings, and one of the most ancient sites of the religious activities. It is said that the Altar of Heaven was built in the southern suburb of the capital at the beginning of the Chou dynasty. In the *Book of History* we can read that, having set up the eastern capital, the Duke of Chou raised an altar in the southern suburb, where the great sacrifice to *Shang Ti*, Lord on High, was held. Since then, until the beginning of this century, though the dynasties were replaced one after another, and the capitals were moved from one city to another or were destroyed and then rebuilt on the same ground, the Altar of Heaven was a necessary part of the imperial capital and the most important place for every royal house. Any dynasty had to obtain the blessings of peace and permission to rule from *T'ien* or *Shang Ti* by making proper sacrifices in the Altar of Heaven. Without this blessing and permission, the dynasty was doomed and the world would descend into chaos. For this reason, worship of Heaven in the appropriate place and at the proper time was believed to have been a necessary condition of the harmonious life not only for dynastic rulers and the upper classes, but also for the common people.

The holiness of the Altar of Heaven can still be seen from its structures and symbols that remain intact in today's Beijing. From north to south, three parts constitute the main buildings of this huge complex. The Hall of Annual Prayer, a triple-eaved temple built on a three-tiered platform, was where the emperor went to pray for peace and for good harvests. Between the Hall in the north and the Altar in the south, there is in the centre a smaller round, single-eaved building, called the House of the Imperial Firmament, which functioned as the repository of the spirit tablets of *Shang Ti* and the imperial ancestors. The third and main building is the three-tiered altar that is round and opens to the sky. The worship held in this altar was perhaps the most august religious activity in ancient China. Its ceremony included nine steps accompanied by the playing of different music, the performing of various dances and the reading of prayer documents. The emphasis of the whole ceremony was put on presenting the offerings and making obeisance to *Shang Ti* or *T'ien*. The offerings were special cooked meats, wines, food, silks, jades, incense and so forth. The only qualified worshipper for this great sacrifice (*ji*) was the emperor. The emperor, being the son of Heaven, ruled the whole country on behalf of *Shang Ti* and therefore he could sit on his throne to accept homages from his subjects. However, during this great sacrifice and a few others such as worship of his ancestors, the emperor had to prostrate himself before the tablets of *Shang Ti* and of the ancestral spirits, to pay his homage to them.

In order to understand the religious significance and other symbols that are revealed by the structure and building of the Altar of Heaven, we have to discuss them in connection with the Altar of Earth, with the *yin–yang* principles that represented respectively heaven and earth, and with the theory of Five Elements. Heaven and earth are inseparable and the Altar of Heaven and the Altar of Earth are in complete correlation. While the Altar of Earth is located in the northern side of the capital, the Altar of Heaven is located in the southern side. In the Altar of Earth, the great sacrifice to the Sovereign Earth, the spirits of mountains, rivers, seas and other earthly spirits was performed at the summer solstice. In contrast, in the Altar of Heaven, the great sacrifice is dedicated to the Sovereign Heaven, together with other heavenly spirits – the sun and moon, the stars and planets, winds, rains and thunder at the winter solstice. Colours were carefully used to distinguish the surfaces of the Altar of Earth from those of the Altar of Heaven. According to the theory of Five Elements, earth is yellow, while heaven is green-blue. Therefore, in the Altar of Earth, not only the surfaces of the buildings and of the walls, but also the ritual objects such as the jades and the vessels, should all be yellow, and in the Altar of Heaven the tilted roofs of the halls, the altar tents in which the spirit tablets were enshrined at the time of the great sacrifice were green-blue, symbolising the blue sky, the living place of the heavenly spirits. At the end of the ceremonies held in the Altar of Earth, the offerings were buried in the ground so that they could go down to the living quarters of the earthly spirits, while for the heavenly spirits, the offerings were burned, symbolising that these offerings would ascend to heaven along with the flames and smoke.

Besides these minor contrasts, there are two major correlations that have more symbolic meaning. The first is the forms of these altars. Just as the square is the symbol of earth and the main feature of the Altar of Earth, roundness is the symbol of heaven and the main feature of the Altar of Heaven. The Altar of Heaven symbolises the sphere of the heavenly and the infinite, because it is open, non-framed and circular, while the Altar of Earth represents another principle of which the square is its best representation. Therefore, the Altar of Earth symbolises the realm of the earthly and the finite that is measurable by its edges, is predictable by its flatness and is understandable by its simplicity. The roundness and openness of heaven would arouse certain feelings of fear, awesomeness and respect, which should be the basic attitude of the son to the father and of the subject to the sovereign, while the square and the thickness of earth could give rise to attachment, trust and affection, which were the fundamental emotions towards the mother and towards the goddess. Though there is a clear distinction between the roundness of the Altar of Heaven and the square of the Altar of Earth, we can also see some evidence of their conjunction in their buildings, and this conjunction reveals that the earthly principle and the heavenly principle are inseparable.

The second major correlation is the numbers that were used to build these altars. The numbers used in the structure of the Altar of Earth and the Altar of Heaven are in accordance with the binary principles of *yin* and *yang*. The *yin* numbers, also called the earthly numbers, are the even series, especially 4, 6 and 8 and their multiples, while the *yang* numbers, also called the heavenly numbers, are the odd series, especially 3, 5 and 9 and their multiples. Among the *yang* numbers, the number 9 has special religious and cosmic meaning. Nine is the highest *yang* number within ten and therefore symbolises heaven itself, or its representative on the earth, the emperor. According to the provisions for religious buildings, the *yin* number should be used without exception for all the buildings of the Altar of Earth, and the *yang* numbers for the whole complex of the Altar of Heaven. For example, the Altar of Heaven is on three levels, and the centre of the highest level is a single round stone, which is increased by nine stones at each circle (Meyer 1991: 92). In contrast to the Altar of Heaven, the centre of the Altar of Earth is made of four square stones, which are extended to twelve and then to twenty as its second and third circles. By using these mythical numbers, the places were bestowed with more sacred implications.

Temple of Ancestors

Next to the worship of *T'ien* or *Shang Ti*, the greatest significance was attached to the worship of the ancestral spirits. In traditional China, every household had its place for the veneration of the ancestors; some held this worship in the best quarters of their houses and some held it in special halls or temples. Among these halls and temples, the imperial Temple of Ancestors in the capital – *Tai Miao* – is the most splendid and sacred building.

There is no evidence to show what kind of building the first *Tai Miao* was, or when it appeared in the capital. It is also not clear whether there is any relation between *Tai Miao* and another sacrificial building, *Ming Tang*, which has been regarded as the oldest worship building in China. Some scholars believe that *Tai Miao* was originally a part of *Ming Tang*, and that the ancestral spirits were worshipped as correlates of *T'ien* or *Shang Ti*. Others, however, insist that the main purpose of *Ming Tang* was the worship of the ancestral spirits, and *Ming Tang*, as a centre of religious worship, gave way to *Tai Miao* in the late Chou dynasty or in the early Han dynasty. What we do know is that, from the beginning of recorded history, the temple for worship of the ancestral spirits was the centre of the state, where not only the sacrifices to the ancestral spirits were performed, but also the various divinations were made, and the enthronement of a new king, the imperial marriage and the engagement of war were announced. In the early period of imperial China, it was in this temple that the kings held their audience with feudal lords and officials, issued orders concerning both civil and military matters, heard news of victory in battle, and dispensed rewards to meritorious officials (Bilsky 1975: 66). All these ceremonies in the Temple of Ancestors, and all the practices of combining government activities with the sacrificial offering were used to perform a symbolical function, to convey a belief that the kingship was sacred, not only blessed by *Shang Ti*, but also protected by the ancestral spirits who were believed to have a great influence on *Shang Ti*'s mind.

Tai Miao of the last period of ancient China became a religious complex, which was built on the plan recorded in the *Book of Rituals*. It usually included one main hall where the sacrifices were held, two side halls that were used to store the lineage records, and a rear hall where the tablets of the ancestral spirits were put when they were not receiving the sacrifices. About this place, there were two significant symbols that added sacredness to the building: one was its double function of providing a place for the ancestral spirits to receive sacrifices and a place for the descendants to worship their ancestors; the other was that the building, the hall and the tablets were all arranged on a north–south axis.

According to the rituals, in the Temple of Ancestors of the royal house there could be seven tablets at most, in that of the great officials, five, for the other officials, three and for the common people, only one – that of their father – though this rule was not always followed, and various numbers of ancestral tablets could be seen in various temples of ancestors and even in families' shrines of ancestors. Among the seven tablets, the first, that of the founder of the dynasty or the first ancestor of the clan, was placed in the middle, and was irremovable. The six others were arranged in alternate rows on the east side and the west side. When the two rows of three were complete, a place had to be found for a tablet of the latest deceased, so the tablet at the head of his row was taken out of the temple, and was kept in a storehouse (Legge 1968, vol. XXVII: 223–5). The sacrifices to these seven tablets and to those ancestors whose tablets were kept in a storehouse should be conducted carefully and regularly, and the temple was thus taken as the sacred place in which the continuation of the family or the dynasty was blessed.

Apart from these symbols of the family line, the Temple of Ancestors was endowed with a more mystical meaning by its emphasis on the north–south axiality. When Jeffrey Meyer talks about the structure of the ancient capitals in China, he says that 'The north–south axiality . . . sets the Chinese apart from other classical civilisations where north–south and east–west axiality were equally important' (Meyer 1991: 40). Not only temples of ancestors, but also all the religious buildings such as the altars of Heaven and Earth, the altars of Land and Grain, and the non-religious buildings such as the royal palace, and the houses of the common people, all followed this axiality: back to the north and open to the south. In order fully to search for its reasons, we perhaps have to explore the deepest psychology, cosmology and philosophy of the Chinese. As far as the Temple of Ancestors is concerned, the main considerations are of astrology and of *fengshui* – Chinese geomancy.

The main characteristic of Chinese astrology is its emphasis on microcosmic–macrocosmic thinking. The centre of the universe was not in the geographical middle, but in the northern part of the sky, in the area of the polar constellations, where the Purple Palace of *Shang Ti*, or the Jade Emperor in the popular religion, was located. His location being in the north, the highest God must rule the universe with his face to the south. The position of the pole star is connected with the ways of the government by Confucius when he says that 'the rule of virtue can be compared to the Pole Star which commands the homage of the multitude of stars without leaving its place' (*The Analects*, in Lao 1979: 63). Joseph Needham explains the reason for this connection: 'the celestial pole corresponded to the position of the emperor on earth, around whom the vast system of the bureaucratic state naturally and spontaneously revolved' (Needham 1957, vol. 3: 230). Facing south and backing north became a symbol of sovereignty and superiority. Because the ancestors were conceived as the source of the descendants, they must have a higher position than their descendants. Therefore, their tablets must face south, their living place also must be oriented towards the south. The sacrifices have to be offered from the southern direction as a symbol of obedience.

Another consideration for the axiality of the Temple of Ancestors is that of *fengshui* geomancy and the *yin–yang* theories. According to one of the *fengshui* theories, the north is the *yin* that was believed to be harmful for humans, the south is the *yang* that was believed to be healthful. With the wall backing to the north, the temple was used to ward off the cold and damp *yin* force, and with the door opening to the south, the temple would invite more bright and warm *yang* force. The same principle was also used for the tablets and the worshippers. Besides the reason that the north was the noble position, and that facing the north was therefore a symbol of making obeisance, there are two other explanations from the *yin–yang* consideration. One is that with the tablets' 'back' being toward the north, the ancestors would not be hurt by too much *yin* force, and, therefore, would keep in good spirits and give blessings to their descendants. The other explanation is that the ancestors, being in the north, would keep the harmful force from invading their worshippers and thus continue their duties for the family or clan.

Sacred mountains

Mountains, with their mysterious features, have a great appeal to religious feelings of the Chinese and therefore are believed to be special places for religious activities. The worship of mountains and on sacred mountains was an ancient practice in China. In the *Book of History*, a passage describes the imperial tour of inspection, made by the sage king Shun (2255–2206 BCE). During the course of the tour, Shun visited the four quarters of his domain. In each section he offered a sacrifice on the top of a sacred mountain, announcing to heaven his arrival and sacrificing to the hills and streams. From then on, sacrifices and pilgrimage to the mountains never ceased in traditional China. The mountains that were believed to be sacred places in four quarters were gradually identified with the four well-known peaks: Mount Tai in the east, Mount Hua in the west, Mount Heng in the south and another Mount Heng in the north. These four mountains, together with the Mount Hsung in the middle comprised the famous five sacred mountains in China.

Why are these mountains believed to be sacred? The most primitive reason for this was perhaps a belief that mountains, especially those great mountains, were pillars separating heaven from earth. According to Chinese cosmology, the round heaven covered the square earth. From this understanding, the obvious fear arose that heaven would fall down without being supported. Therefore, the mountains were naturally believed to have performed this function. In the myth of the 'reparation of heaven', Goddess Nu Wa, having repaired the broken sky, killed a huge turtle and cut its four feet and made them four pillars in the four quarters, and the world again enjoyed the peaceful and harmonious life. The pillars were believed to be what were later also regarded as the sacred mountains.

Heaven was believed to be a place where *Shang Ti* and other heavenly gods lived. For human beings, the only way to gain access to this spiritual world was to make sacrifices to them. Experientially, the top of mountains was the highest point that the ancient Chinese could have reached. The clouds surrounding the peaks of these mountains, the mist shading their tops, often gave rise to more imagination about the symbolism and the special function of those mountains in the sacrificial rituals. Obviously, the offerings made on the top of the sacred mountains were believed to be more acceptable to the gods of heaven. Of these five sacred mountains, the Eastern Peak, Mount Tai, was the most favourite place where the ancient emperors made sacrifices to heaven. This kind of sacrifice was believed to be a common practice of the ancient sage kings and a main reason for the ancient golden ages. However, *T'ien* or *Shang Ti* would not receive the offering from those kings or emperors who lacked virtues and humanity. It is said that the first emperor of Chin (*r.* 255–210 BCE), being a tyrant, was frustrated by a storm of wind and rain when he tried to offer his sacrifice to heaven and could not reach the top of Mount Tai.

According to the animism of the ancient Chinese, the spirits of mountains were more powerful than other spirits in controlling such natural phenomena as the wind, the clouds and rain. Thus, these deities could be asked to provide good weather for farming and to be protectors of the common people. As early as in the Shang dynasty (1765–1123 BCE), special sacrifices were used for the worship of these spirits of mountains. By the time of the Han dynasty, because of the prevalence of Buddhism and Taoism, these spirits had been credited with more power in deciding human affairs. The temples for worshipping them not only appeared on the top of mountains, but also were built at their foot and even in the city. Pilgrimages to mountains, visiting their temples and making offerings to the deities are always a colourful part of Chinese religious life.

Along with the struggle conducted between Buddhism and Taoism in their preaching, efforts were also made to set up their own centres on the famous mountains. Mountains were now given special names and titles, and were connected with this or that Taoist immortal or Buddhist *bodhisattva*. Generally speaking, Taoism had an obvious victory over Buddhism on traditionally sacred mountains (though Buddhism did have certain influence on them), while Buddhism set up new centres for itself and formed 'four holy mountains' of its own. One way for Buddhists to create sacred mountains was to connect them with specific manifestations of the Buddha's enlightenment. On Mount Wu-tai in the north, there was Mañjusrī (Wen-shu in Chinese) who was an idealised incarnation of Transcendent Wisdom, and in the temple dedicated to him Wen-shu was presented in a statue riding a lion. On Mount Pu-tuo in the east, there was *Avalokiteśvara* (Kuan Yin in Chinese), the Goddess of Mercy, sitting in or standing on a lotus. On Mount Omei in the west, there was Samantabhadra (Pu Hsian in Chinese), who was the incarnation of Universal Goodness and who always rode on a white elephant. On Mount Chiu-hua in the south, there was Ksitigarbha (Ti Tsang in Chinese), who was Head of Hell and once promised Sakyamuni that he would not become Buddha until he saved all between the *nirvāṇa* of Sakyamuni and the Birth of Maitreya. As abodes of these Buddhist gods or goddesses, the famous mountains became centres of Chinese Buddhism. Temples that were dedicated to these gods or goddesses were set up and *bodhisattva*s not only enjoyed the offerings and sacrifices but also gave their blessings and protection to their worshippers.

Sacred space in China is by no means confined to those traditional places which we have discussed above. The attractiveness of the sacred place always changes as time changes and thus different ages often see different places which are shining their sacred light. In this century, the Communist revolution brought a new concept of the sacredness and many secular places were regarded as sacred. These places, which were called the 'revolutionary sacred places', ranged from the original regions of the Communist revolution, the sites of the important meetings, to the birthplaces of the Communist leaders. Today, even this concept is not new any longer and it, like many of its predecessors, is passing away. However, underlying these traditional and modern concepts of sacred places, the religious spirit of the Chinese people will perhaps remain. This spirit is what this chapter has tried to reveal through its discussion of traditional sacred places: the correlation between the spiritual world and the human world, and the transformation from the secular to the sacred.

FURTHER READING

Ahern, Emily M. (1973) *The Cult of the Dead in a Chinese Village*, Stanford, Stanford University Press.

Bilsky, Lester James (1975) 'The State Religion of Ancient China', in Lou Tsu-K'uang in collaboration with Wolfram Eberhard (eds), *Asian*

Folklore and Social Life Monographs, (vols 70 and 71), Taipei, Chinese Association For Folklore.
De Korne, John C. (1926) *Chinese Altars to the Unknown God*, Grand Rapids, Mich., Smitter Book Company.
Feng, Gia-fu and English, Jane (trans.) (1972) *Lao Tsu: Tao Te Ching*, London, Wildwood House.
Fung, Yu-lan (trans. Derk Bodde) (1953) *A History of Chinese Philosophy* (2 vols), Princeton, Princeton University Press.
Goodrich, Anne Swann (1964) *The Peking Temple of the Eastern Peak*, Nagoya, Japan, Monumenta Serica.
Lao, D.C. (1979) *Confucius: The Analects (Lun Yü)*, London, Penguin.
Legge, James (trans.) (1968) *The Liki*, in F. Max Müller (ed.), *The Sacred Book of the East*, vols XXVII and XXVIII, Delhi, Motilal Banarsidass.
Meyer, Jeffrey F. (1991) *The Dragon of Tiananmen: Beijing as a Sacred City*, Columbia, South Carolina, University of South Carolina Press.
Mullikin, Mary Augusta and Hotchkis, Anna M. (1973) *The Nine Sacred Mountains of China*, Hong Kong, Vetch and Lee Limited.
Naquin, Susan and Yu, Chun-fang (eds) (1992) *Pilgrims and Sacred Sites in China*, Berkeley, University of California Press.
Needham, Joseph (1957) *Science and Civilization in China*, vols 2 and 3, *History of Scientific Theories*, Cambridge, Cambridge University Press.
Shryock, John (1931) *The Temples of Anking and Their Cults – A Study of Modern Chinese Religion*, Paris, Librairie Orientaliste Paul.
Steinhardt, Nancy Shatzman (1987) 'Taoist Temple Compounds', 'Confucian Temple Compounds', in M. Eliade (ed.), *Encyclopedia of Religion*, vol. 14, pp. 380–3, New York, Macmillan.
Watters, T. (1917) *A Guide to the Tablets in a Temple of Confucius*, Shanghai, American Presbyterian Mission Press.

8. Japanese Religions

Ian Reader

Introduction

Concepts and expressions of sacred space and place in Japanese religions are multiple and multi-layered; the notion of what is regarded as sacred in spatial, locational and geographic terms straddles a multiplicity of meanings and exists at numerous levels. In its most general terms there is a strongly conceived notion that the entire Japanese landscape is sacred; this concept is given its most overt expression in the indigenous religion of Shinto, but is also found in Japanese Buddhism, particularly in its interaction with folk religion. Besides the general concept that the whole landscape itself is sacred, either in actuality or potentially, there is further widespread recognition that some parts of it are more specifically marked out as holy and as settings in which the spiritual realms are manifest or encountered. This may be for reasons of natural setting – prominent geographic features such as waterfalls and mountains, which have, as will be discussed later, long had a deep religious significance, have tended to be venerated as *loci* of spiritual power – or due to the occurrence of some special event or manifestation, such as a miracle or apparition, that is considered to demonstrate that the place is a particularly important centre of religious power. Often, also, specific places are transformed into sacred space through the religious actions of holy figures such as ascetics and religious charismatics who recognise some special quality in a place, or who, through engaging in austerities there, imbue it with their power. This is a theme that is equally true also for the sacred centres and headquarters of many of Japan's new religious movements, which often regard places associated with their charismatic founders as holy.

Sacralising the landscape: Shinto and Buddhist perspectives

The view that the entire geographical setting of Japan and the Japanese landscape are themselves sacred, is affirmed through early sacred texts such as the *Kojiki* (completed in the early eighth century) that express deep-seated Japanese myths of origin, and is expressed in the world-view of Shinto as an indigenous religion relating to the myths and origins of the Japanese people and to their relationship to the indigenous deities (*kami*) of Japan (see 'Japanese Religions' in *Sacred Writings* and *Myth and History* in this series). In this mythological view, the islands of Japan were created by the *kami* who then gave birth to further *kami* who peopled the land and gave life to the landscape and every form of life within it, including the Japanese people who, in terms of the myth, descended from the *kami*. The underlying theme of this myth, from the perspective of a study of sacred space, is that it implies that all places and locations are inherently or potentially sacred, and that *kami* may be located and hence encountered in any and every place. There is an implicit hierarchy here which ranges from powerful deities who are national protectors (for example the Sun Goddess Amaterasu, whose main shrine, at Ise, is regarded as the most important in Japan and is the centre of a national cult) to local deities whose *locus* of power and influence may extend little beyond the immediate vicinity of the tree or rock in which they are believed to reside.

At the broadest levels, this identification of the Japanese landscape, people and deities has underlined Japanese notions of national unity and identity, and has affirmed an underlying assumption that Japan is somehow special and unique. In its most benign form this concept may do little more than help affirm a sense of national pride and belonging, but in the past it has also helped fuel, and been used to legitimate, more pernicious strands of nationalism such as those seen during the ascendancy of nationalistic Shinto during the period of Japanese military expansionism from the 1930s until 1945.

Because Shinto is concerned with relations between humanity and the natural world, perceptions concerning the presence of the *kami* and of the sacred have largely been focused on the world of natural phenomena. Thus trees and rocks, especially ones with strange and odd shapes that seem to signify a sense of the other, may be considered the abode of a *kami*, and be suitably adorned with signs and symbols marking them out as sacred. Examples of such signifiers of the sacred may range from a simple rope twisted around the object, to mark off the boundary within which the *kami* is said to reside, to a more defined building, such as a small shrine, constructed at the spot. The Shinto view that all places are locations of the *kami* also means that any action that alters the nature of the land, whether through farming or building, should be accompanied by ritual activities to appease or humour the deity of the locality. Thus, the building of a house or office block involves rites to appease the local protective deities, and usually a small shrine, at which they can be venerated as guardians of the site, will be constructed within the precincts of the building. One of the most prevalent actions Shinto priests in contemporary Japan are called upon to perform is the ground-breaking ritual (*jichinsai*) in which the local *kami* are pacified before building commences.

The Shinto concept of sacred space which means that everywhere is the potential dwelling place of the holy was reinforced from early on in Japan by Buddhist and Taoist influences. Buddhist concepts of inherent and realisable enlightenment meant that any place was potentially sacred, a place and space in which enlightenment and buddhahood could be attained and manifested. These perceptions were, in Japan, further heightened by the influence of Taoism and the mountain religious cults which developed through the fusion of indigenous cults with Taoism and Buddhism; these perceived the world, and especially the wild and liminal world of nature and of the mountains, as the setting for encounters between the human and the sacred, the *locus* where enlightenment, transcendence of the mundane human world, and entry into the world of the *buddha*s and deities, were to be encountered (for further discussion, see Grapard 1982).

Sacred settings and natural phenomena: waterfalls and mountains

On the broadest levels, then, anywhere and everywhere in Japan may be holy, a potential setting for enlightenment *and* an abode of the *kami*. The landscape itself therefore serves as a transcendent realm, the meeting point and the link between the human and the divine, between the physical and spiritual worlds. As a result, places that appeared to stand somewhat apart from the normal geographic settings of the everyday world, and that thus symbolised the indistinct boundaries between physical and spiritual realms, were seen as being endowed with special sacred properties. Extraordinary geographical locations such as mountains, caves and waterfalls, which seemed imbued with the awesome powers of the world of nature, were seen as places where the dividing line between the physical and spiritual worlds was markedly thin. Although appearing to be part of the mundane world, such places were felt to be more closely aligned to the spiritual and sacred realms, and consequently they were especially sought out as settings for ascetic and religious practice. If anywhere and everywhere may be, as has been previously suggested, a potentially sacred place, in reality some places were clearly more potentially sacred than others. It was such places that evolved as centres of asceticism and that acquired reputations as especially sacred locales and as sites of pilgrimage.

Waterfalls, caves and mountains have been especially sought out for such purposes, often acquiring a reputation for sanctity because of a deity believed to reside there, or because of the feats of ascetics who practised there. Great waterfalls such as the Nachi falls, Japan's highest waterfall, located in the Kumano region in the Kii peninsula, were often venerated as shrines in their own right. Before the Nachi falls one finds all the signs and markers signifying a Shinto shrine, such as the *torii* or Shinto gateway that marks out the boundaries of the sacred space; the central focus of the shrine is the waterfall itself, which stands in place, as it were, of a main hall of worship. The waterfall *is* the shrine. Similar patterns are found at many holy mountains in Japan as well, with a *torii* marking out the approach to the sacred territory but with no special building constructed as the main centre of the shrine, for the mountain itself is the shrine.

Mountains, which are among the most prominent geographical features of the Japanese archipelago, have long occupied a prominent position in Japanese religious cosmology as sacred centres and as the focus of pilgrimages and religious veneration. Until modern times mountains were regarded almost wholly as religious sites, and many of them continue to retain a religious significance alongside more contemporary tourist themes. Mountains were often considered the homes of powerful deities, especially those connected with the provision of water and hence of the production of crops, and were regarded as the abode of the souls of the dead. This belief, found throughout Japan in pre-modern times, is still widely found today, as at places such as Osorezan (the name means 'fearful mountain') in northern Japan, whose desolate volcanic landscape of barren rocks and sulphurous fumes seems to confirm to the onlooker its folk religious reputation as a place where the souls of the recently departed congregate. Each year, in summer, there is a large religious festival at the mountain. During the festival *itako* (blind female shamanic mediums who claim to be able to contact the dead) gather together, and many thousands of Japanese people, some simply curious, others earnestly hoping to make contact with a deceased family member or friend, visit them (see Reader 1991: 130–2).

Many mountains became the centres of pilgrimage cults. Groups of ascetics and devotees usually ascended them dressed in white (the colour of purity and death). Among the most prominent of these have been Mount Fuji, Mount Ontake and the Yoshino–Kumano range south of the ancient capital of Nara. Such ascents were conceived of as metaphorical ascents through the world of enlightenment, with each stage in the pilgrimage representing a stage in the progress through the realms of existence conceived of by Buddhism. Mountains were divided ritually into ten stages (to represent the ten realms of existence of Buddhism), with each stage marked off by a religious ritual at a specially designated site. Physical and spiritual ascent thus occurred simultaneously, and thus the mountains served not just as sacred spaces but also as ritual maps on the path to enlightenment.

Mountains were also viewed as graphic representations on earth of paradises and hells. Tateyama, a mountain in central Japan, was the centre of a cult until the middle of the last century, in which the mountainside represented hell on earth. Pilgrims to the mountain passed through a series of religious sites, representing symbolic hells, at which they performed austerities and penances to atone for their sins, and to enable them to go directly to the Pure Land at death (Seidel 1992–3). Other examples of the superimposition of spiritual landscapes on to the physical realms of the mountains included the belief that such spiritual realms as Fudaraku (the Buddhist Pure Land presided over by the *bodhisattva* Kannon) were located in the Yoshino–Kumano mountains, and that pilgrimages there were thus journeys to paradise.

The processes of modernisation and mass tourism in particular have influenced contemporary views of the physical world.

Mountains such as Fuji and waterfalls such as Nachi have become places to visit in order to gaze at their natural beauty, rather than to venerate for their spiritual meaning. However, despite these processes, such natural settings continue to contain religious meaning and significance for many people. Religious ascents and mountain pilgrimages still occur on large numbers of Japanese mountains; Fuji and Ontake both still are host to particularly flourishing cults and attract groups of religious pilgrims each year. The imprint of such religious ascents can also be seen in the ways that the paths ascending mountains such as Fuji continue to be marked off into ten stages, at each of which there is a rest-station serving refreshments to the hiker. Tourists, as they ascend Fuji, can now take a bus up to the fifth station before walking up to the tenth station at the top, and in doing so can find some sense of continuity with the ascetic ascents of the past, especially when, as sometimes occurs, they happen to encounter members of a *Fujiko*, or Fuji pilgrimage association, dressed in white on a religious ascent.

Ascetics, religious practitioners and the sacralisation of place

The religious ascetics who climbed mountains and performed austerities at waterfalls and in caves, contributed greatly to the development of a sacred geography in Japan, and to the formation of holy sites linked to their endeavours. Of the numerous examples of the relationship between geographical locations, sanctity and ascetic figures in Japan, two will be given here.

The legendary ascetic founder of the Shugendo mountain cult, En no Gyoja (literally, En the Ascetic), is said to have performed pilgrimages and austerities in the Yoshino–Kumano mountain range in the late seventh century. Through these he was able to visualise Buddha and acquire magical powers which enabled him to vanquish demons and perform miracles. While the whole Yoshino–Kumano area is generally regarded as an especially sacred region (representing, as has been noted above, Kannon's paradise), for Shugendo practitioners its sanctity is enhanced because of its relationship with En's practice. Generations of ascetics and pilgrims of the Shugendo order, which continues to flourish in present-day Japan, have made the pilgrimage through these mountains, following in En's legendary footsteps.[1]

The second example concerns Kukai, the great Japanese Buddhist monk and religious teacher, who became the centre of a major cult of worship in Japan under his posthumous name Kobo Daishi, under which guise his already prodigious life became embellished with legendary achievements and miraculous deeds. Kukai spent some time performing austerities on his native island of Shikoku in the latter part of the eighth century at sites frequented by ascetics of the time, such as the cave by the sea at Muroto in the south of Shikoku (where according to the legend the *bodhisattva* Kokuzo is said to have entered his body during meditation) and at Mount Tairyu in central Shikoku. Later, when Kobo Daishi posthumously became the focus of a cult of veneration, practitioners, mostly from the sect he had founded, went to Shikoku to perform austerities at the places where he had been. Consequently, Muroto and Tairyu, already holy places in their own right, became even more sanctified because of their association with Kobo Daishi (Kukai), and eventually became integral parts of a major pilgrimage route that circles the entire island of Shikoku, taking in eighty-eight temples and centred on devotion to Kobo Daishi. (For a more general discussion of Kobo Daishi, the Shikoku pilgrimage and its symbolism, see Reader 1993.)

Temples, shrines and concrete representations of the sacred

Japan's landscape, which has been overwritten with symbols of the sacred in terms of natural geographical features that are adorned with sacred regalia and symbols, has been further transformed by human-made works that represent the presence of the sacred and spiritual within the mundane. There are large numbers of Shinto shrines and Buddhist temples throughout Japan, built in every conceivable setting from steep mountainsides to the centres of major cities. The underlying meaning of any such institution, whether Shinto shrine or Buddhist temple, is that, in theory at least, it has been built in a location already designated as sacred, and as a place where the spiritual filters through into the physical world. In the Japanese perception, space does not become sacred because it has been sanctified by the construction of a religious edifice; rather, space and place become sacred because of events that occur at them, and temples and shrines, as signs of the sanctity of place and the manifestation of sacred space, have been built there because of an event and in recognition of the location's sanctity. Shrines and temples usually have founding stories (*engi*) which narrate an event, usually legendary and miraculous and often involving the manifestation of a deity or *buddha*, through which the setting has come to be seen as sacred, and stimulating the construction of a place of worship.

An example of a typical *engi* is found at Enkyoji, a popular pilgrimage temple atop Mount Shosha outside the town of Himeji in western Japan. Its founder was a tenth-century ascetic named Shoku who saw, during his travels, a purple cloud[2] floating ahead of him; he followed the cloud which led him to Mount Shosha, where it stopped. Shoku took this as a sign that the place was sacred, and built a hermitage there. While practising austerities there he had a vision in which he saw the *bodhisattva* Kannon in a tree; he carved a statue of Kannon from the tree and worshipped it. Eventually a temple was built on the spot, dedicated to Kannon, with Shoku's statue as its main image of worship. Later tales of miracles, of people who prayed to Kannon and were cured of disease or who received some benefit or other, came to be woven into a wider framework of legendary stories that further affirmed the sanctity of the place.

Although *engi* are clearly literary constructions aimed at creating an aura of power and sacrality and promoting a particular site (see 'Japanese Religions' in *Myth and History* in this series), they serve to underline a basic perception that space is inherently and potentially sacred, and that what is built upon it is a recognition of this inherent power. In the case of Enkyoji, the sacred nature of the site is provided by the oracle that directed Shoku there, by his own spiritual power which is distilled into the location, and above all, by the 'fact' that this place is one where Kannon is present and thus may be manifest and encountered – a 'fact' underlined by subsequent miracle tales.

Often the setting and architectural structures of shrines and temples serve further to underline their occupation of sacred space. Many are built in locations that suggest the presence of the sacred, with the building itself symbolically suggesting that it stands between this and other worlds; a good example of this is the temple Iwayaji, one of the temples on the Shikoku pilgrimage route, which is built into a wall of rock on a mountainside in such a way that (as its builders intended) it appears suspended between worlds. The setting of religious buildings is enhanced by a symbolic separation from the mundane; both shrines and temples are marked out by a gateway that acts to delineate the sacred space within. The Shinto shrine has a *torii*, a vermilion gateway straddling the approach to the shrine, which demarcates the sacred space enclosed within, while inside the *torii* there is a path leading up to the main hall of worship and altar, where the *kami* is enshrined. Just inside the *torii* there is a fountain where one may wash one's hands and mouth in an act of purity before approaching the *kami*. The gateway of the Buddhist temple is known as a *sanmon*, in the sides of which stand the statues of two ferocious guardians known as *nio*, who symbolically ward off evil.[3]

The replication of sacred space: temples and miniature pilgrimages

Mention has already been made of mountain pilgrimages such as those to Fuji or Yoshino–Kumano. There are many other pilgrimages in Japan, most commonly those that incorporate a number of important temples which, although all marked out as sacred through their *engi* and location, are made even more so by being part of the wider framework of sacred space created by such pilgrimages. The most prominent examples of these are the thirty-three stage Saikoku pilgrimage in western Japan (the aforementioned temple Enkyoji is one of the sites on this) and the eighty-eight temple route around the island of Shikoku. Such circuits can extend the notion of sacred space to a whole region; pilgrims in visiting the Shikoku temples make a circuit of the island which, because of the pilgrimage and because of its close relationship with Kobo Daishi, is transformed into a wider sacred space in its own right.

One of the most important features of Japanese attitudes to sacred space and place, and one that is especially related to pilgrimages, is the understanding that the sacred is a transferable and moveable entity. Just because a particular location is sacred, does not mean that it alone has a prerogative on the sanctity that accompanies its location or its association with a spiritual entity such as a *buddha* or *kami*. Rather, sacrality of location can be transferred by replication, a process that is best seen in the practice from around the sixteenth century onwards, of constructing small-scale localised models of pilgrimage routes (most commonly of the Saikoku and Shikoku routes, each of which is several hundred miles long and, prior to the development of mass transportation took several weeks to do) throughout Japan. These routes were developed originally in order to allow people who were unable to travel to these areas, to perform the pilgrimage in their own region. Some of these small-scale routes may be done in a few days (as with the popular eighty-eight temple route on the island of Shodoshima, which is one-sixth the length of the Shikoku model it copies), while others are so small they can be done in a few minutes. Although such routes developed in response to a popular need at a time when widespread travel was not possible, many remain important and popular today. Indeed, many of them have developed their own legends and miracles – many of these also borrowed from the larger pilgrimages they copied – that underline their sacred nature. The point behind them all is that they represent a replication of sacred space and the perception that the sacred can be copied and moved in accordance with popular needs (for fuller discussion of these pilgrimages see Reader 1988).

The house as sacred space

It is not just temples, shrines and other such official religious edifices that serve as centres of religious action, or as symbols of sacred space. The Japanese house itself, which has traditionally operated as a setting for religious rituals, expresses a further sense of sacred space. Even though modern developments, including urbanisation, have altered the shape and size of houses, consideration is still given to the notion that the house is not simply a functional unit for living in, but represents a potentially sacred location. Usually a diviner is consulted and geomantic considerations are taken into account when building a house, which will be laid out facing the direction which, according to Taoist and folk conceptions, is the most propitious. As has been mentioned earlier, rites to propitiate the local *kami* who guard over the space where the house is built, are also carried out.

Various deities have traditionally been venerated and enshrined within the household, especially those concerned with the practical functions of the house, in particular the gods of the kitchen and toilet, and while such folk practices may have declined somewhat in contemporary society, they are still widely observed. It is not uncommon to find a talisman or a small shrine in the kitchen or toilet areas of modern homes. Within the house, too, the *kamidana* (Shinto god shelf) and the *butsudan*, or family Buddhist altar, have long been important. The former enshrines protective deities and is often the repository of amulets from major shrines, representing the presence within the home of important Shinto deities, whereas the latter memorialises the household's ancestors, who are believed to guard over the fortunes of their descendants, and contains mortuary tablets (*ihai*) that symbolise the ancestors' presence in the household. They remain so in modern Japan, where it is estimated that around seventy-five per cent of households have one or other of these altars; around forty-five per cent have both.[4] The Buddhist altar, which in effect is a small temple within the home, serves as a place of encounter between the living and their ancestors, and is the setting for various religious rites; many families will summon a Buddhist priest to perform memorial services for the ancestors before the *butsudan* on a periodic basis. Thus, the house itself, which is implicitly linked to concepts of sacred space because it is located in the Japanese landscape, is also a sacred place enshrining its protective deities along with the spirits of the ancestors of the family.

Sacred centres in the new religions

Thus far, the examples of sacred centres and space that have been discussed have been involved with the general life-style of the Japanese, with folk religion and with Shinto and Buddhism. Besides these there are many other sacred places that are sacrosanct to specific sects and religious organisations. This is especially the case among the Japanese new religions, each of which has its own specific sacred centre, very often associated with its founder. In general terms it may be suggested that the processes whereby such places become recognised and marked out as sacred spaces are very similar to the processes we have already discussed, and in order to illustrate this, two examples relating to the new religions and their holy centres will be given.

The first involves one of the oldest, largest and most established of the new religions, Tenrikyo, and its headquarters in the town of Tenri, not far from the city of Osaka in western Japan. The town of Tenri is itself a holy place for believers, for it consists almost entirely of buildings and institutions associated with the religion. It was at this place that, according to Tenrikyo belief, God the Parent created human beings, and where they first emerged on the earth; it was also here that in 1838 God the Parent spoke to people on earth, through the mediumship of Nakayama Miki, the nineteenth-century peasant woman founder of the religion, who lived there.

The location of these events has become a sacred centre for the religion, and a huge temple complex has been built around the *jiba*, the place where humankind was, according to the religion, created, where the Nakayama family later lived, and where Nakayama Miki first became possessed (and chosen as his vehicle) by God the Parent. The whole complex is known to believers as *oyasato* ('parental home') and visitors to the centre are greeted with the words *okaerinasai* ('welcome home') to denote Tenrikyo's view that in visiting the place one is returning to the sacred source of origin.

Nakayama's preaching of the words revealed to her, supported by various miraculous deeds of prophecy and healing she was said to have performed there, caused a religious movement to grow and eventually to mushroom into a huge organisation with branches across the world and several million members. She became not just the prophetess of the deity, but a powerful figure of worship in her own right, adding to Tenri's sacredness through her presence both in life and afterwards. When she passed on in 1887 she did not, according to Tenrikyo, die, but continued to remain spiritually at Tenri, presiding over the spiritual growth of the religion and its believers. Offerings are made daily to her at her home in the sacred complex, and members pay as much homage to her as they do to God the Parent.

Again, as with temples and shrines, it is the occurrence of a special event (or in this case, of two events, the creation of humankind and the revelation of the deity) that confers sanctity on the site. Though the buildings (which are constructed in a manner that utilises both Shinto and Buddhist architectural styles) that occupy the site serve to recognise and to confirm this sanctity, the place was sacred prior to any building; the space is sacred not because of the concrete manifestations of religious architecture that glorify it, but because of the events that are said to have occurred there.

A second, very contemporary, case that exhibits many of the mechanisms and themes already discussed, is provided by Agonshu, one of the 'new' religions of Japan that have risen to prominence since the early 1980s. Its charismatic founder, Kiriyama Seiyu, acquired some land on the hillside at Yamashina, on the outskirts of Kyoto, on which to build a new sacred centre for the religion. Kiriyama had had a vision at this place which convinced him it was a sacred spot, and soon after the land was offered to him and he purchased it. According to Agonshu, the offer of the land to them, and the acquisition of the money to purchase it (at a time when the religious group had no money to speak of) were miraculous events that affirmed to them not just the sanctity of the place, but the fact that it was predestined to belong to them. The sanctity of the site has been further affirmed, in the religion's eyes, by the appearance of numerous *buddha*s and deities during rituals performed there. Each year on 11 February, Kiriyama conducts a vast fire ceremony at the site, during which numerous deities and *buddha* figures come to him in apparition to offer their protection for the site and to signify their approval for his actions.

When Kiriyama visited India in the early 1980s he claimed to have received a transmission from the Buddha at Sahet Mahet (the site of the first ever Buddhist monastery) in which he was told to build a 'new Sahet Mahet' at Yamashina; this vision affirmed a fundamental point of Agonshu's doctrine and self-perception, which was that it was destined to revive the traditions of Buddhism for the modern age. The construction of a new Buddhist temple and the creation of this new sacred place (the 'new Sahet Mahet') at Yamashina has been a central part of this process. Agonshu preaches a message of world salvation and renewal, and claims that, from this sacred centre, it will spread a message of renewal to save the entire world from impending doom.

Visitors to the Yamashina temple site are greeted, just as are visitors to Tenri, with the words *okaerinasai*, welcome back, to denote their symbolic return. Whereas in the case of Tenrikyo this return is to the sacred centre from which humankind emerged, for Agonshu it is to the symbolic centre of religious awareness, to the sacred space of buddhahood, and to a place graced by the presence and protection of *buddha*s, that is destined to be a centre of rebirth and religious revival in the modern age. As a sacred centre it is thus seen not just as a magnet drawing in people wishing to imbibe its powers, but also as a force radiating power outward to the world at large.

In the new religions, then, one can find very similar patterns in the perception and determination of sacred spaces as are found in Japanese religions in general. Signs, visions, encounters and miraculous events, such as the descent of God the Parent to Nakayama Miki in Tenrikyo or the manifestations of *buddha*s and messages given to Kiriyama Seiyu in Agonshu, mark out a place as holy. This is further enforced by the connection between site and founder figure; the sanctity of Tenri is reinforced because Nakayama Miki lived there and because, in Tenrikyo belief, she remains spiritually present there, while Yamashina is further sanctified for Agonshu because of the stories and events that link its founder to the site. There is, as it were, a part of the founder in the site, and this interplay of holy person, charisma and place replicates the patterns and nature of the sanctification of geographic locations seen in the earlier discussion of other sacred sites and pilgrimage centres.

Although the sacred nature of the place is specific, in the first instance, to the particular new religion concerned, it is, because of the claims of universality posited by those religions, implicitly sacred for all humanity. The new religion's understanding of sacred space has a universalist dimension, in which that space and place become sanctified both in reality and potentially (as a centre from which humanity may be saved) for all humankind. Moreover, when they 'return' to the sacred centre, the followers of the religion are themselves spiritually recharged and fired up to spread the message of their religion to the wider world. In such ways, too, the sacred centre acts as a means through which the spiritual world is encountered and its presence further emphasised within the physical world.

Conclusion

The multiple and pervasive nature of sacred space and place in Japan in conceptual and locational terms forms a very potent and vital element within the Japanese religious world, extending from the more clearly numinous aspects of mountain peaks to apparently more mundane places such as the family home with its religious symbols. This pervasive nature demonstrates the ubiquitous nature of sacred space in Japanese religious terms, in which anywhere and everywhere is potentially sacred, and where many places are, due to factors such as natural location, legend and association with holy figures, explicitly so.

Japanese religious culture is focused very much on the encounter and interaction in this world between the human and the spiritual realms, between humans, deities and *buddhas*. Human beings, who in myth descend from the deities, interact with them through the physical realm, which in turn symbolically takes on the aura of the sacred and spiritual. In this interaction, which is at the heart of all Japanese religion, whether in Shinto, Buddhism or the new religions, the landscape itself plays a vital role as the meeting place between the physical and spiritual. As such, concepts and notions of sacred space and place are central to the whole of Japanese religion and play a vital part in its dynamics.

NOTES

1. Anyone wishing to pursue the matter of the Yoshino–Kumano pilgrimage, its relationship to En, and its symbolic and geographical meanings, should look at Paul Swanson's (1981) essay on the subject.
2. Floating clouds are a popular theme in Japanese folk tales and *engi*: the colour of purple is significant because it is a colour associated with the imperial family and imperial regalia.
3. Fuller details about the nature, construction and formation of shrines and temples can be found in Reader 1991: 134–67, from which this information has been taken.
4. These details are from Reader 1991: 7. For a further discussion of the *kamidana* and *butsudan*, see Reader 1991, especially pp. 63–4 and 90–6.

FURTHER READING

Grapard, A. (1982) 'Flying Mountains and Walkers of Emptiness: Toward a Definition of Sacred Space in Japanese Religions', *History of Religions*, 21/2: 195–221.

Reader, I. (1988) 'Miniaturization and Proliferation: A Study of Small-Scale Pilgrimages in Japan', *Studies in Central and East Asia Religions*, 1/1: 50–66.

—— (1991) *Religion in Contemporary Japan*, Basingstoke, Macmillan.

—— (1993) 'Dead to the World: Pilgrims in Shikoku', in Ian Reader and Tony Walter (eds), *Pilgrimage in Popular Culture*, Basingstoke, Macmillan.

Seidel, A. (1992–3) 'Mountains and Hells: Religious Geography in Japanese Mandara Paintings', *Studies in Central and East Asian Religions*, 5/6: 122–3.

Swanson, P. (1981) 'Shugendô and the Yoshino–Kumano Pilgrimage: an Example of Mountain Pilgrimage', *Monumenta Nipponica*, 36/1: 55–79.

Index